Skiing Zen

Searching for
the Spirituality
of Sport

Rick Phipps

Skiing Zen: Searching for the Spirituality of Sport

Published by Iceni Books®
610 East Delano Street, Suite 104
Tucson, Arizona 85705 U.S.A.
www.icenibooks.com

International Standard Book Number: 1-58736-450-6
Library of Congress Control Number: 2005938695

To John Lennon for his courage and vision

To Yuichiro Miura for his kindness and
masterful example

To my mother, Lee Phipps, for her wisdom,
guidance, and faith

To my sons, Aidan and Dylan, for the joy
they bring as my new dreams incarnate

author's note

This is essentially a true story. A few of the characters in Tokyo are composite and I have manipulated certain scenes and sequences for storytelling convenience.

introduction

I saw the car a split second before it hit me. I noticed the sunlight glinting off the windshield and heard the curiously high shriek of the screeching brakes but, most of all, even as I flew through the air toward a headfirst landing on the sidewalk, I was transfixed by the utter slowness of the moment before impact. I was ten years old.

None so dramatic, but I had several more brushes with clarity as a boy. They came cloaked in mystery, with an altered sense of time and a powerful sense of omniscience. These episodes continued through my teens, coming occasionally in hardship but most often in the heat of athletic competition. This was intoxicating awareness, at once addictive and intriguing. By my early twenties I was compelled not only to seek such moments, but to understand them also, and this led me, in large part, to undertake a solo journey around the world.

Much will be said in these pages about that trip and the youthful experiences I've alluded to, but suffice to say now that the end of that search marked the beginning of this story, of this attempt to describe and explain these moments of clarity. Specifically, it began on the side of a mountain where, in the midst of a long sweeping turn at breakneck speed, in the midst of a moment so delicious I could taste the wind and sense every miraculous molecule of my being, I had three utterly distinct thoughts crystallize in my mind: *Write a book. Describe this moment. Call it* Skiing Zen.

I cannot overstate the effect of these three thoughts; even words like epiphany or thunderbolt are insufficient. I quit my job the next day and, within two weeks, moved to the Canadian mountain town,

Banff. My friends and family were surprised; few realized how unsettled I had been since my return. My travels had affected me so profoundly that I often found myself overcome with emotion, unable to express what I was thinking or feeling. I had seen too much, learned too much, to be again the young man they had known.

In Banff, I soon found a place to live and a job waiting tables. I bought a season's pass and skied most days but also spent a lot of time reading and writing. It is comical, in retrospect, to see how I gradually came to grips with the realization that a moment's inspiration does not a book make. It would take work, and lots of it, and I wasn't even sure where to begin.

After a few months it occurred to me to get my ski instructor's certificate. I did this soon after, near the end of the ski season, and then took the next logical step by applying for the summer writing program at the prestigious Banff School of Fine Arts. In lieu of a portfolio I submitted an essay linking epiphanistic vignettes with sweeping spiritual conclusions. From my rejection letter, I learned that the ideas were valid and my writing was good but my approach was naïve.

What I had was an idea, or rather, an aggregation of intuitive realizations that were frustratingly difficult to convey. I also had a title, *Skiing Zen*, and the certainty that somehow I would turn all this into a book. Actually, I did have one other guiding principle, that is, I didn't want a treatise, filled with theories, or a compilation of comparative philosophy. I wanted a story with characters and dialogue that would serve as the vehicle to carry the ideas. It was this conviction, combined with the inherent aspects of my pre-visualized title, which pointed me in mid-August to the next logical conclusion: Write about a ski adventure in Japan.

A few months later, armed with karmic conviction, a round trip ticket, and about $600, I arrived in Japan. It started badly but by late March I was skiing with that nation's most famous skier, a descendant of Samurai, on the former site of the Olympic Games. All considered, it was a wonderful but difficult winter, full of weird challenges and serendipitous results. For some, this story will read as a ski adventure; others will think of it a young man's spiritual quest. As for me, who took this strange gamble and experienced the tumultuous result, this book has always been intended as a vehicle for ideas. I repeat this earnest truth because it is an important, perhaps critical, part of the story.

It should be noted that these events occurred years ago, before Japan was an economic powerhouse, before visualization and spirituality were commonly spoken of in terms of sports, and before shaped skis revolutionized skiing technique. I have gained considerable perspective with the passage of time; in fact, much of what I realized that winter in Japan took me the long years since to describe, clarify, and refine. In this I owe a considerable debt of gratitude to the audiences I have addressed and to the many friends who have read and commented on preceding drafts. Without their feedback I could never have taken this story through the evolutionary process it required.

As I now know well, the conveyance of spiritual knowledge has inherent challenges in both the medium and the message. To begin with, each reader has a unique blend of experience and education, of emotion and empathy, but I can't tailor my words as I would if we were speaking face-to-face. I cannot hear your questions and gauge your mindset; I can't listen to your personal anecdotes or hear in the dialogue how my ideas are influencing yours as they pass though the filter of your perception. I've had many such exchanges over the years, either with teams I was coaching or with groups in workshops, but unfortunately this intimate communication is impossible in the one-way medium of writing.

This is awkwardly self-conscious, I realize, but let me take this one step further. Beyond your personal differences, your respective accumulations of experience and knowledge, each of you will be slightly different, *even from yourself,* each time you sit down to read this story. Think of it. What is your emotional state, right now? How much might it vary in the two to twenty times you pick up this book in the coming days as you come home tired or energetic, elated or despondent? Since this story, at its core, speaks of intuitive, spiritual moments, you will relate to it best with that elusive combination of a calm heart and an open mind.

This leads us to the last challenge and the main reason why spiritual wisdom is elusive and difficult to convey. All writers, except poets, employ a logical structure with sentences, paragraphs, and chapters to organize their ideas. Readers generally read the same way, that is, in a linear manner using their rational intelligence to connect the images and concepts. The trouble with this method, applied to spiritual matters, is that the tools are inappropriate for the job. Analytic processes will neither reveal nor resolve intuitive dilemmas. We can talk about, or around, the epiphanistic moment but, as spiritual leaders have said for centuries, you must experience it for yourself to truly understand.

One of the best things about sports as a spiritual path is that so many athletes have already had a breakthrough experience, what I now call a "moment of clarity." Instead of studying philosophy for years, or heading off to hear gurus, or sitting cross-legged in ashrams, you need only search through your memories for those moments where you felt mysteriously, wondrously, powerfully alive—connected to all things.

The problem is that we come to the sublime through sports but afterwards have no context to understand it and few friends with whom we can share such intimate insight. These moments are too powerful and personal to explain, even if we could find the words. So what happens? We store these epiphanies along with our other memories and try forever after to ignore their haunting, almost radioactive, resonance. This is painful. We can't forget this clarity but we can't understand it either.

Hopefully, this book will change that to some degree and lead you to other books, experiences, and like-minded people who can help you comprehend and integrate this intuitive knowledge. As you read this book, however, or embark on any path of spiritual inquiry, remember the inherent challenge: Since your rational mind can overshadow your intuition, words and thoughts are poor navigators in this realm. Searching for epiphany through analysis is like using a straight-edged ruler to draw a circle.

You must act instead on faith. Challenge yourself in passionate pursuits. Gain experience resolutely. Develop your trained abilities and, as you do, let your intellect and intuition find their proper balance. Most importantly, when the crystalline moment does approach, and time slows down and all becomes deliciously vivid around you, resist the temptation to retain or analyze your awareness. Just let it happen. Go with it, flow with it. Bathe in it joyfully. Without trying, you will understand it best.

one

After a ninety-minute train ride from Tokyo and a mile walk from town, we found the monastery deep in a sprawling grove of tall trees. The Torii gate appeared first, tall and starkly red, looking like the mathematical symbol: π. Beyond it we entered a garden bordered on three sides by dark wooden buildings, each covered by a thick straw roof. Our guide, a young monk in street clothes named Nobu, explained the rules quietly. Talking was discouraged. Each action or task was to be performed as swiftly as possible. After every morsel at mealtime was consumed, each bowl was to be wiped with our final bite of pickle, then rinsed with our last bit of water poured from one to the next. Sitting meditation sessions, or Zazen, would be one hour, three times a day, and we would also chant sutras for one hour. The rest of our time would be spent polishing floors or sweeping the garden. At the conclusion of the weekend retreat, he said, we could each ask one question of the Roshi, or Master.

His briefing finished, Nobu excused himself. I left the three other foreigners, an Australian, a New Zealand woman, and a Scotsman, and wandered into the center garden. It was sparse yet beautiful, well tended yet natural. The main hall, with a wooden walkway fringing it and the exterior wall panels slid open, seemed like an extension of the garden. Beneath the heavy thatched roof, I saw several empty rooms with plain white walls and uncluttered floors. On one end was the altar room with its wooden mantle and simple ornamentation. At the other was an eating area, with long tables in a horseshoe arrangement. The mood of the monastery was tranquil, but ancient energies glowed like the embers of a well-banked fire.

An elderly Japanese woman, dressed in kimono and wooden sandals, shuffled past me to the water well. I watched while she delicately rinsed her hands using a bamboo dipper, then tilted it backward to cleanse the handle where she had touched it. She stepped to the shrine and tossed a few coins into the grate of a huge collection box. Looking upward, she clapped her hands, made an earnest prayer in a gently rocking motion, and then clapped her hands twice again. Finally, she pulled heartily on a braided rope that hung before the shrine, using all her slight weight to ring the attached bell, then turned and left quietly.

Nobu reappeared wearing a monk's robe, a striking contrast from his street clothes, and soon gave us rags and the task of wiping the wood floors. They were perfectly clean already, as attested by the persistent whiteness of my cloth, but we did as we were told. While the others scooted along in a half crouch, I moved as best I could on my scarred knees. The pain bothered me at first, but as I settled into the task, I paid more attention to the grain of the wood, the deep hues and vibrant luster. Polishing the wood seemed to give it warmth, a residual glow of human attention. I had this same feeling later when I swept the garden with a long bamboo rake. Even though leaves fell behind me as I worked, adorning the brown dirt with their random colors, the grounds felt tended now. I felt more comfortable too, as if I were blending my energy with the monastery.

At lunch we saw three other monks, including the Roshi, each with long robes and scalp shaved bald, but there was little time for scrutiny. We rushed to our places, sat on our shins and feet as bidden, and served ourselves from the rice, vegetables, and soup passed round. We ate in silence but my knees and ankles screamed in agony. To me, the traditional way of sitting, called Seiza, with the lower legs and feet directly below the thighs, was either an acquired skill, a stoic act, or collective masochism. Judging from the expressions of the other foreigners, I had company in my misery. Had they also undergone knee surgery? After cleaning our bowls carefully, we rose at the master's signal and walked—hobbled would be more accurate—to the cupboard where we stored them until our next meal.

Summoned for afternoon meditation by a resonating gong, we walked in single file around the garden, then down a shaded hallway and into a darkened chamber. We moved carefully, as if the ground were sacred. I felt nervous now, with dryness in my mouth and a pounding in my chest.

A wide platform, two feet off the floor, ringed the square room. It was divided into small cubicles, each with a single black pillow. Walking one by one around the room, we peeled off and sat cross-legged facing the white wall. Still no one spoke. I kept my face forward, as directed earlier, but watched the others out of the corner of my eye. What were they thinking?

A small bell, high pitched and pure in sound, signaled the start of meditation. I struggled to quiet the thousand thoughts in my mind but images flashed incessantly on the wide screen of my consciousness: the Roshi sitting placidly, the color of the leaves on the dark soil, the grain of the wood as I polished it. Doubts swirled through also, like breezes in a drafty house.

What am I doing here?

Can my knees really last an hour?

What do I hope to gain in one weekend?

I chided myself. A spiritual education could take years, perhaps a lifetime, but I couldn't sit still through lunch. Gradually though, as my breath deepened, I grew aware of the rustling branches outside and the slow footsteps of the attendant monk. Calm settled over me like a warm blanket until I saw nothing, finally, but retinal glow. I felt myself floating, a yellow warmth rising up my spine and bubbling down through my body like a fountain of energy. When the bell sounded to end the session, its rich tone echoed through the stillness of my being.

Afterwards we chanted sutras, using phonetic sheets to drone on in an ancient foreign language. My mind wandered back to a similarly dreamlike, but far more bizarre, experience in the Himalayas, at the Tibetan monastery of Tangboche near Everest. Sustained chanting had been coming from the monastery since the death of a monk earlier in the day. With the head lama's permission, I had been up earlier to observe, so after dinner I went again.

It was a beautifully clear sky, with a full moon pouring down and reflecting blue-white off the towering peaks nearby. In the moonlight, I saw a pair of dogs rush toward me as I climbed the monastery path, growling more fiercely with each step. When I placed my foot on the entrance threshold, the larger animal lunged forward and sank his teeth deep into my calf. I jumped, whirled, and ran, the dogs nipping at my heels.

Paranoia and adrenaline surged through me—bitten by a dog at a full moon reincarnation ritual in the Himalayas! Worse yet, the hikers in the lodge cited the high incidence of rabies in Nepal and offered grisly descriptions. I could abort the trip, they said, walk three days back to the nearest medical facility and hope they had vaccine, or make a fateful judgment call that it was merely an overzealous watchdog.

At dawn after a restless night's sleep, with the distant sutras still echoing into the Himalayan silence, I decided to press on to Everest. Over the next few days, as each labored step drew me further amidst those extraordinary mountains at the roof of the world, I wondered if God's most sublime landscape would be the last thing I would ever see.

Nobu returned when darkness fell over the monastery and we walked with him for evening meditation. It was deathly quiet as we slipped in and took our places facing the wall. Already this seemed familiar, but this time I had greater trouble quelling my thoughts. Don Juan[1] called this: *"stopping the internal dialogue,"* the relatively constant

---

1   Don Juan was a Mexican shaman who taught author Carlos Constaneda the mystical ways of Yaqui warriors, as described in *Tales of Power* (Simon & Schuster, 1974) and other books.

mental conversation one holds with oneself that supports our respective notions and prejudices. Only when this happened, he said, was a warrior capable of *"seeing,"* that is, perceiving the world correctly. The terminology was different, but these notions seemed similar to the Buddhist notion of direct learning, of discerning the *"is-ness"* of things.

Typically, I was thinking about thinking. This was the trickiest type of meditation, like balancing a pin on a pin. I discovered in my youth that I could slow my thoughts down, reduce them to a crawl through my mind, but my analytical side had grown much stronger while traveling. Seeing so many cultures, each outwardly different yet essentially similar, while at the same time exploring my inner terrain, I was often thinking on unfamiliar planes. It was fascinating, almost addictive, but it also had, at times, the confusing quality of a house of mirrors.

But in sitting meditation the objective was not to analyze or compare but instead to let those swirling thoughts come to rest. For awhile I focused consciously on my posture and breathing and tried to let everything else slip away, but then realized that even this well-meaning effort was a distraction. It was only later, near the end of the session when I essentially forgot what I was doing, that I slipped briefly into a clear state.

After meditating, we gathered around a small fire near the kitchen. Nobu prodded the logs with a short iron poker while the others talked about Buddhism. For an hour or more, while terms like *samsara* and *nirvana* were bandied about, I thought of the old woman who had come that afternoon to pray at the shrine. I had been close enough to see the earnestness on her face, the simple humility of her actions. *What was she thinking,* I wondered. *What was she imagining?*

The thought of her caused me to flash back over memories in Asia, Europe, and the Middle East, where I'd seen Jews bobbing fervently before the Wailing Wall in Jerusalem, Tibetan Buddhists whirling their prayer wheels in the Himalayas, Malaysian Muslims prostrating themselves to Mecca, Balinese women offering food to the gods at a Hindu temple, and widows kneeling solemnly at a Vatican mass. *What did they think, feel, say, or imagine?*

Their prayers, meditations, and rituals seemed so similar in essence, as did their places of worship. Mosques, synagogues, temples, cathedrals—all were refuges of orderly calm amid the tumult of life, all used harmonies, fragrances, and rituals to instill feelings of serenity, all provided or reinforced a subtle resonance of spirituality. The more I saw, in fact, of such places and the solemnity they evoked, the more obvious it seemed that no one belief system could have a monopoly on the truth.

Instead of proclaiming or defending our differences, shouldn't we search instead for commonalties in our beliefs, for shared and synthesized wisdoms, for mutual understanding and personal peace?

Finally, after an hour or so, the others went off to bed. Only Brian, the Australian, remained with me, staring into the glowing embers. The silence was comfortable. Brian's friendliness at our hostel in Tokyo was the reason I had heard about this monastery retreat. Although hardly noticeable now, bundled as we were against the chill of the evening, he was tall, and angular. He had a long neck and a rusty orange beard that made his tanned face look enormous, an impression aided by thick, frosted eyebrows and abundant red hair. His jade eyes, set deep within a myriad of tiny squint wrinkles, were laced with ashy flecks.

Brian turned to me. "You're a quiet one. I'll say that."

He startled me from my thoughts. "I suppose so," I said, unable to disagree or offer any clever comeback. This happened increasingly often now, as if I were mute. After being decidedly vocal for years in my various roles as captain, coach, or president of various groups and teams, I had withdrawn gradually from active discourse. I rationalized that it was not simply quietness; it was carefulness, speaking only when I had something worthwhile to say. This seemed natural, even proper, in Asia, where people respect silence and feel no compulsion to be talking always, but too often it inspired self-consciousness among westerners. At such times, I found myself guessing people's thoughts and worrying about their opinions, and that was old behavior I wished to avoid.

But Brian wasn't reading thoughts or judging anyone. He was just chatting casually. As easily as he probed me earlier, he now changed the subject. Leaning forward, his green eyes sparkling mischievously, he asked, "So, what will you ask the Roshi tomorrow?"

His question caught me off guard. I hadn't yet thought about it. Several seconds passed until finally, I said, "About sports."

"Sports? What's that got to do with Zen?"

"Depends how you look at it."

"Wait a second. You've got a pile of gear back at the hostel. Are you some kind of athlete?"

"Ski instructor."

"Really? Lookin' to ski here in Japan?"

"Hope so."

"Got anything arranged?"

I shook my head.

"Working papers?"

"No."

"Speak Japanese?"

"Not much."

"Any connections?"

"No."

Brian laughed. "You're either a man of faith or you got lots of money."

"No money, I'm afraid."

"So it's faith then. Good on ya." He smiled and sat back in the sunlight as if pleased with this notion, then asked, "What gave you this idea anyway?"

"Hard to explain." This was certainly true; I couldn't understand it myself.

"Ah, give it a go," Brian said.

"It was sort of an inspiration."

"I reckon it would be, to get you over here." Brian clearly wasn't letting it go. He just sat there, waiting patiently, poking the fire with a long wooden stick.

"Well, it happened suddenly but the background is kind of important. I'd just come home from a long trip."

"Oh yeah? Where'd you go?"

"Fiji over to New Zealand by sailboat, then up to Australia and through Asia."

"That's a lot of miles."

"Yeah, well, I did it over about a year so that wasn't really the hard part. It was coming home that messed me up. I had changed physically, mentally—every way possible, really—but everyone expected me to be the same. It was frustrating. I had seen too much, learned too much, to be again the person they had known, but I just couldn't explain how I felt. Not with my friends, not even with my family."

Brian nodded, arching his eyebrows.

"Anyway, two things were strangely clear. The first was that I needed a new direction, a new goal, a new dream, call it whatever you like. My other distinct urge was to go skiing. Repeatedly during my trip, in the strangest places like hot beaches or jungles or deserts, I'd seen myself up on some mountain, sliding downward, feeling the sun and enjoying the sheer pleasure of adjusting to the snow and the terrain and the speed. This vision had been tantalizing me for months.

"So, as soon as I could after returning, I took off for the mountains. The first day was like a blur; I was up and down, up and down, over and over again, skiing like a madman. It was like a drug and I couldn't get enough. Then it happened."

"What's that? What happened?"

"It was midafternoon. I was alone on the mountain, swooping downward with long, clean turns. Each one was effortless, delicate, a perfect transfer of weight and control from ski to ski. I was lost in the motion, rhythmic, caressing. I could taste the sun and the wind and feel every inch, every crystal of snow beneath me."

"Sounds like sex to me."

"Yeah, well, at this level it is remarkably similar. Both are exquisitely sensuous. Anyway, I was skiing fast, really fast, but I started having these incredibly lucid thoughts and surreal memories of other times when I felt this bizarre clarity, this frozen moment when time expands and everything is forgotten and you become what you do . . . when you're detached, peaceful, effortless . . . when you feel so utterly alive.

"Suddenly, I saw my new challenge. I was cutting hard across the mountain, aware only of the inner edge of my downhill ski, when everything stopped and I heard my quietest voice guiding me, compelling me: Write a book. Describe this moment. Call it *Skiing Zen*."

"I'll tell you, mate," Brian said. "I can't ski a lick or a stroke or whatever skiers do but, since you mention it, I reckon I've had a few Zen type moments on my surfboard. I remember a time in Bali, out at a place called Ulu Watu. It's a beautiful beach with palm trees and old women that gave massages for a dollar, with lots of Aussies with their boards and motorbikes and pretty Balinese girlfriends, and great waves breakin' over coral that'd cut you up if you fell."

I nodded, having been there and seen horrendous wounds on the brash young surfers.

"One day," Brian continued, "I was out there, feeling a little spaced 'cause I'd done mushrooms the day before, and these beautiful waves were coming in about seven feet or so. I don't know why, but I started getting wave after wave. Great waves too, the kind you dream about. I'm not the greatest surfer but I'm not the worst either. Anyway, I was droppin' in perfectly, cutting back, ridin' em out . . . It was incredible.

"Towards the end of the day I had one of those moments: I was up there, in control, feeling the sun and the water and wind . . . I don't know, I can't describe it, but it was like . . ."

He looked down for a moment, and then continued. "I remember coming into shore feeling all peaceful like, noticing how soft the sand was and how green the trees were. It felt like I was stoned again. Then I saw an old peasant beside his rice paddy, squatting on his heels the way they do. All these Aussies were roaring by on their bleedin' motorcycles, each with a Balinese girl on the back that could have been this guy's granddaughter. At that instant, the old man turned his head toward me, just enough that I could see into his eyes."

Brian stopped and looked down again, then went on in a softening voice. "It lasted forever, that moment."

I could picture it perfectly. I'd seen many such scenes myself, in Bali and throughout the rapidly changing countries of Asia. In Brian's moment of clarity, the old man's world was laid bare. On the one side were the rice paddies, perfect rows of silent green, the mainstay of his society since time began; on the other was the future, noisy and irreverent. The old way was dying with him, yet somehow he was peaceful.

There was a long silence before Brian went on. "Talkin' about that stuff is hard, don't you think?"

I nodded and shrugged. Brian had summarized the dilemma perfectly. I had enjoyed the finest moments of my life during football, hockey, scuba diving, mountain climbing, and skiing, yet could scarcely convey to others the vividness of these experiences and the utter aliveness I felt. Talking with others such as Brian, I was also increasingly aware that this frustration was common; sports evoke intense clarity that all can feel but few can describe or understand.

We both sat back and fell into a private reverie, watching the embers glow and the sparks rise in the echoing stillness of the night.

After a short, cold sleep on a thin mattress, I awoke with the others to meditate in the pre-dawn darkness. I was stiff and it was hard to stay focused with pain radiating from my knees and lower back. The discomfort of meditating made the floor polishing and the raking later seem blissful by comparison. Finally, after the afternoon meditation and another session of chanting, we each had our chance to question the Roshi.

Brian went first, followed in turn by the others. I waited near the kitchen, on the sunny walkway overlooking the garden. The fresh air was laden with cooking aromas and the thatched eaves overhead glowed in the late afternoon light. Nearby, small birds with ivory breasts and brown spotted wings flitted back and forth on the naked branches, calling cheerfully to each other.

As the moments shrank before my turn, I was still wondering what to ask of the Master. It was comical in a way, too much like the cartoons about religious seekers climbing the mountain and crawling to the foot of the Master to ask their one cherished question. Seen in a harsher light, my paid-weekend query was trivial, insulting to the myriad of lifelong spiritual disciplines.

Settle down.

Don't overthink this.

Focus on the question.

What is it that I want to know?

I saw Nobu approaching. I rose to my feet, bowed slightly, then followed him on the walkway around the garden. My thoughts were swirling still.

What is it that I came to learn, or confirm?

Nobu led me into the main hall and showed me where to kneel. The Master sat cross-legged with his back to the altar, watching impassively as I lowered into a deep bow. When I rose finally and prepared to speak, he closed his eyes and tilted his bald head, as if to listen more intently.

The moment was upon me. Without preconception I began to speak slowly, allowing each word to surface spontaneously. My voice sounded distant, as if not my own.

"I play many kinds of sports," I said.

As the words hung there in space, a moment's panic slipped in. *Is this crazy? What am I doing?* But the Master sat impassively as Nobu translated my brief statement.

I drew a breath and started again. "Sometimes, there are moments when . . ."

I paused, searching for the right words. "There are moments when time seems to slow down, when everything is clear and effortless. I know what is about to happen and just what to do. Sometimes it doesn't even seem like it's me playing. I feel detached, empty—like I'm watching myself play."

Nobu translated slowly then turned back to me.

"But it's more than just sports. In these moments I feel something bigger, as if I am connected to everything at once somehow. I feel transcendent, religious, spiritual—whatever you might call it."

The old man nodded slowly.

"But these moments are elusive," I said. "If I stop to think about them, they slip away. The harder I try to grasp or analyze them, the faster they leave."

As Nobu relayed my words, the Master tilted his head the other way. Apparently, it was time for my question. I took a long breath.

"If sports require concentration and faith and years of discipline, and one comes through them to such moments of clarity, are not sports a type of . . . spiritual path?"

The translation seemed to take forever. Nobu paused twice in mid-sentence, searching for the correct words. The old man listened solemnly, his head bowed slightly forward. As Nobu finished, the master opened his eyes and fused his gaze on me. A deep calm filled me as he spoke, slowly and clearly, in perfect English, "Of course."

I expected something more, an explanation perhaps, but the Master sat silently. A long moment elapsed. I want to speak again, to ask another question, but Nobu rose with a rustle of robes. The interview was over.

Stunned, I bowed a final time, touching my forehead to the *tatami* mat, then stood to follow. I walked on the smooth wooden floors around the garden, returning to my sunny spot near the kitchen. I sat back against a broad wooden pillar, the Master's reply echoing in my ears. "Of course."

I felt silly. I had confirmed what I felt sure to be true, but ended up without the answer I really needed. My trouble was that I couldn't figure out the question.

Across the garden, Nobu re-emerged from the altar room and walked again toward me. "Make I speak with you?" he asked.

"Of course," I said. "Please sit down."

The monk gave a half bow, then deftly tucked his robes behind his knees and sat. We watched the garden quietly until finally Nobu spoke. "Have you enjoyed your time here, Rick-san?"

I paused before answering. Certain aspects had been difficult—meditating in the cold darkness, sitting too long in *seiza*—but I knew that experience easily garnered is soon forgotten.

"Yes," I replied finally. "Very much."

A light breeze swept over the garden as he spoke again. "The Master was interested by your question."

My pulse quickened.

"It's important, Rick-san, at certain times especially, to have guidance. He feels that you are ready for a Master."

I watched a branch sway in the breeze. My breath seemed loud.

"He also mentioned that we once had a foreigner stay here with satisfactory results. There is room if you wish to gather your things and return with me next weekend."

I could only stammer, "Thank you for telling me."

"You're welcome, Rick-san. Think about it this week." He returned my bow and added before slipping away, "You know we're leaving for Tokyo in ten minutes?"

I nodded. Nobu bowed again and left, walking quietly around the garden. As he passed from shadow to light in the late afternoon sun, the orange of his robe and the woven gold of the *tatami* harmonized perfectly with the leaves of the garden. I looked around with new eyes. *Could I really live here? Is this where my search will end?*

two

The sun hung low as we left the monastery, casting golden light across the countryside that warmed our backs and sent long ambling shadows out ahead of us. As we walked into town, past the fish shops and produce stalls on the main street, the sunlight glistened off the fish, moist on beds of ice, and gave the neatly stacked vegetables an appealing glow. Merchants attested loudly to the freshness of their wares while pensioners and young mothers filled their small baskets carefully. I loved the fragrance and bustle of the open-air Asian markets, especially after shopping all my life in air-conditioned, sanitized, freeze-dried shopping centers. More was occurring around me than mere shopping. In Japan, as in many countries around the world, the market is a social hub, an arena of social ritual, as important still as it was in centuries past.

Beyond the traditional came the modern. Familiar signs—McDonalds, Kentucky Fried Chicken, Dunkin' Donuts—hung vertically amidst a jumble of others near the train station. Rows of vending machines lined the street, with small groups of teenagers trying too hard to look cool. The cramped, right-angled architecture, the jarring music that escaped from swinging doors, the bleak bustle of workers and patrons—it all looked garish after the dignified simplicity of the monastery. This typified my early impressions of Japan: tradition despite transition, spaciousness beside congestion, tranquility amidst turmoil.

The 5:25 train arrived, punctual to the minute, and we luckily found seats. The cars would fill as we neared Tokyo and returning weekenders jammed in. Brian sat across from me, while Nobu and the others took seats across the aisle. Gathering speed, we passed line after line of compact cars and light trucks, waiting patiently at railway crossings. As the town gave way to the perfectly furrowed fields, I wondered how many times in the past two years I had sat this way, staring out at time and the world rushing past. How many trains? Cities? Farmers' fields? I didn't know anymore. The images blurred in the kaleidoscope of memory.

I imagined again the parched plains of India, with women in saris and children in rags walking gracefully beneath balanced jugs of water; the throngs in black on their bicycles in China, pedaling past antiquated buildings and lush green fields; the French towns and vineyards growing and shrinking at twice the normal rate as the bullet train streaked south. From just such a swaying witness chair, I had seen the moisture-laden jungles of Malaysia and Thailand, the parched expanses of Australia, the rustic English countryside, each vision framed by flashing black telephone poles.

As quickly as it came, the vision faded. I looked over at Brian, staring out at silhouettes of Shinto shrines and high voltage towers on the horizon. His tall frame lifted his flaming red hair above the seat, high enough to cause stares and muted discussions throughout the car. He smiled amiably if he noticed, but after two weeks in Japan, he was growing oblivious to reactions on his size and appearance. At our hostel in Tokyo, he treated the shocked Japanese guests with unfailing cheerfulness.

I thought again of Brian's surfing story. It had a familiar ring. Many athletes, if you can get them talking, tell a similar tale of transformative experiences involving sport. Like my childhood neighbor, Norm, a young genius who built a laser when he was twelve and ended up, just twenty years later, with his own small department at MIT. I hardly knew him as a boy, since he was a quiet loner that shuffled home reading a book each day, and was as surprised as everyone else when he tried out for the football team in Grade 10. But Norm had guts, and he hung in all season in a short sleeve jersey even though his arms were purple with cold and both elbows seemed to drip blood constantly. He never played a single down that year and no one expected him back, but the next fall he not only came out, but won a starting position and played damn well. We were all so impressed that we invented an award for Most Improved Player and gave it to him. The telling moment came years later when I visited Norm in Boston at MIT and heard him describe what those years on the team, and that trophy, meant to him. Here was a guy inventing cyber-universes before anyone had even heard of such a thing, and lecturing at Los Alamos while still in his twenties, and he had tears in his eyes telling me about a six inch trophy in high school.

Brian was watching me, a slight smile creasing his face. "You're a million miles away."

"Your surfing story started me thinking."

That stopped him cold. Finally he replied, "So incredible yet I could never say why."

The train lurched and the lights flickered. Brian spoke again. "It was like that when I came home from traveling. Worse really. I was away from Aus three times and each time I came home I got totally frustrated. Couldn't talk to my friends. Could hardly leave the house."

"Same with me. My friends and family wondered why I was so quiet, but they worried even more if I spoke up."

Brian's nod was sympathetic. "Thought you were a little off, did they?"

"I can't blame them. Before traveling, if I'd met a stranger talking about cultural imperialism, social commonalties, and decaying spirituality, I'd have called him eccentric, at best."

"But you weren't a stranger."

"In a sense I was. They were all looking for the old me—the outgoing, hard-partying jock."

"Doesn't sound so bad."

"Don't get me wrong. I had fun in those days before I traveled. But I always knew there was more to learn and to do."

"Which took you to Asia."

I nodded. "And once I had seen and learned a bit about the world, especially India and Nepal, I just couldn't live the way I had before."

"The poverty got to you?"

"Almost the opposite. Even though they didn't have many possessions, or great housing, or much to eat, people seemed more serene or peaceful or . . ."

"Spiritual?"

"Maybe. I'm not sure how to describe it. As westerners we always seemed so incredibly lucky, but after I was home awhile I began to feel differently. I couldn't put my finger on it. It wasn't the headlines or the social statistics, although they were certainly depressing. What affected me most were little things I would see in the street, or hear in conversations.

"For example, there's this old guy in my hometown who's been standing on the same street corner for years, droning away, 'Let me give you a testimony of what Jesus did.' A few weeks after coming home, I came upon him on my way to lunch, but instead of walking past as usual, I stopped and watched. Over and over he said those few words, all the while staring straight ahead and holding out a small pamphlet. No one stopped, mind you. Not one. Of course, you couldn't blame them either. The guy was a wreck, just a shell of man. If anything, he was a testimony of what Jesus surely did not want, his faith presented in lifeless repetition, his teachings reduced to dull litanies.

"The saddest thing was that the people rushing past him didn't look any more serene than he did. They all seemed bothered or worried. There was no compassion on their face, no joy."

"Too busy."

"Right. Running on the treadmill—making money, spending money, going to church on Sundays some of them—but too often just passing their days and years without thinking that something might be missing."

"It's the traveler's curse, mate. You gain perspective while traveling, and end up judging your own life, your own society, just like you did all the others."

"But I became obsessive about it. I analyzed my life, my travels, my future—the whole bloody world."

"In Australia," Brian said, "there's a tradition of wandering alone. The Aboriginals have been doing it for thousands of years. They call it a 'Walkabout.' When they get the urge to learn or to prove themselves, they take off alone, traveling cross-country, living off the land. They sing out ancient songs as they walk, songs passed down through the generations. They're called *Songlines*, and they not only guide them along the paths of their ancestors, but also into a sort of a hypnotic dimension called the 'Dreamtime.' Over the course of these trials, these internal and external journeys, the young Aboriginals overcome challenges and gradually find the knowledge they seek."

"How do you know about all this?"

"A few years back, I taught Abo' kids up in the Northern Territories."

I tried to imagine him with his startling height and shocking red hair, living among the Aboriginals. It sounded amazing but Brian wasn't missing it much.

"It was bloody hot," he said, "and too many people drank way too much. Most of all, I couldn't stand seeing them get jerked around by white men waving pieces of paper." Perhaps sensing the bitterness in his own voice, he fell silent.

A half hour later we entered Ueno, the huge central train station. We disembarked and waded through the crowds to our respective transfer points. Nobu, Brian, and I were going one-way and the rest another, so we parted with bows and handshakes. As we reached the platform of the Yamanote, the ring line that circles Tokyo, a green train came hurtling in. After the neat lines parted to allow riders off, we boarded smoothly and were soon on our way around the sprawl of Tokyo.

Nobu turned to me, "I hope you will consider our conversation."

"Certainly, Nobu," I promised.

There was concern on his face, as if he were pondering something. Finally, he spoke. "Wisdom is like a cup of water," he said. "Transferred carefully from hand to hand."

I stared at him, noticing his perfect skin and boot black hair. "But what if people aren't ready for that cup?" I asked. "What if they're not even aware that the cup exists or that the water will enrich them?"

"Sooooo," he said, drawing out the sound thoughtfully. "It's difficult, of course, but still we must try."

We stood silently a long while. Finally, as the train slowed at his station, he turned to me. His eyes and face were again like calm water. As the doors opened, he spoke evenly. "If you decide to come, meet me next Saturday at the same time and place."

I nodded.

"If I don't see you, please remember that there are many paths and different teachers. I'm sure you will find both." With that he stepped off the train and bowed deeply. I returned his bow as the doors closed and the train lurched into motion, then watched as he disappeared from view.

At the spotless platform marked Shin Okubo, Brian and I disembarked and descended into the gentle clamor of a Tokyo district at dusk. Two women in kimonos swished past. The vendors pulled down the shutters of their shops. A bicycle deliveryman rang his hand bell as he pedaled past with a load of *bento* boxes stacked high on his rear rack. The sight of the lacquered dinner containers made me hungry.

Brian suggested a nearby shop for a good cheap meal, then led me to it through the narrow back streets. The buildings on either side were wedged tight, with little, if any, room between them. Zoning laws were absent or highly curious, a small machine shop alongside a grocery store and the local shrine. A tiny cemetery, with irregular slate headstones and groves of pine sticks with vertical writings, was sandwiched between buildings on three sides and a railway on the other. Vending machines were outdoors, usually on street corners or in front of shops, selling everything from batteries to beer, from soup to soap. A latticework of bamboo scaffolding covered a new building, built in the same shrunken scale as the surrounding district, and workers clambered up and down wearing white hardhats and work slippers with a separate area for their big toes. Occasionally from a distance, ebbing and flowing like the breeze, came the rumbling of elevated subways, but mostly there was a comfortable and pleasing silence. Over our heads, a deepening darkness forced the retreating orange glow over the horizon.

We reached our destination and ducked under a half curtain to enter. The room was small and square, with a concrete floor, fluorescent lighting, and aged wooden walls with posters that were faded and curled on the corners. A few tired workers in blue suits sat around a horseshoe counter, tended by an elderly waitress in a baggy white smock. As we stepped in, she squinted toward the door, flashed a silver-toothed smile, and called out a cheery welcome.

Her eyes were better at close range, and she cackled merrily to see two foreigners at her counter. She was tiny, and badly stooped, but she chattered while we studied the menu. Finally, we opted for easy-to-order combination meals and a large bottle of beer. Brian filled our glasses, held his up to mine as the smiling woman delivered our soup, and said, "Rub a dub dub, thanks for the grub, yea God."

With that we fell to eating, devouring in quick succession the soup, vegetables, fish, and rice that were laid before us. Between bites, Brian told me more about his travels. Among other adventures, he'd taken an overland trek through Asia, worked a stint in a pub outside London, and spent a year traveling on trucks and local buses through South America. In total, he'd been away from Australia for seven years.

He talked at length about England, and described a hairy truck accident in Peru, but talk shifted again to coming home. For Brian, it seemed to be getting harder. Most of his friends had traveled too, but now they had careers, homes, and families, and diminishing empathy for his continued wanderlust. His alcoholic father was more vocal: "You're a fool. Wastin' your life."

Finally, as if a tap had been turned or a switch thrown, Brian turned the tables. "So how 'bout you. How'd you find the road?"

"Actually, I got the bug twice. The first time, I hitchhiked across Canada the day after graduating from high school, then traveled through Europe the following spring."

"About eighteen were you?"

"Seventeen actually. And coming from the prairies, Europe was about as different as I could imagine." I stopped, considering my words. "But as much as I saw, I was affected more by this weird sense of possibility that I felt when I was traveling. I mean, you set off in the morning not knowing where you'll go, who'll you'll meet, or where you'll sleep, and then somehow, things just work out in some strange and wonderful way."

I stopped while Brian poured more beer. I stalled a bit, finishing the last grains of rice in my bowl. This was always hard to talk about.

"Gradually, I had the realization that I actively attracted, or avoided, all sorts of possible events on a hour by hour, day by day basis, whereas back home, it had always seemed like life went a certain way and I just participated. When traveling, however, I had to make choices constantly, real decisions that brought distinct results. Instead of passive participation, I became aware of cause and effect, and of the need for being proactive. It happened slowly, over several months, but I gradually developed a new sense of *responsibility*."

"Intimidating concept for a young bloke."

"You're right, but I liked it and I came home determined not to slip into my old ways and patterns. But I did, of course. Six months after returning from Europe, it was school, sports, partying—the old routines just pulling me back in."

"Those sweet and sticky bonds." Brian's face crinkled into a wistful smile. "What happened?"

"Well, gradually, as university got more specialized and my social life became hectic, I found myself drawn even deeper into sports. In games, there were rules, objectives, and obstacles I could understand. It was simple."

Brian nodded knowingly.

"By this time I was playing sports nearly year round. I'd reached the top amateur echelon in both football and hockey and the seasons were so long that they ran into each other in the spring and fall. At my size, I would never play professionally, but now I was competing against men who would.

"Anyway, I had fantasized all my life about scoring an overtime goal or the winning touchdown in a championship, so often that these two daydreams became like good books I could slip into. Then, in one year, both my boyhood dreams came to be. After years of bench sitting and fantasizing and fighting my way up the sporting hierarchy, I ran a fumble for the winning touchdown in the provincial football championship, and then in the hockey finals, six months later, in sudden death overtime in the last game, I got a clean breakaway and scored."

"Bloody good, mate."

"But it was a mixed blessing. I went into a funk afterwards."

"Ah wait, I think I know it," Brian said, his voice softening. "The shadow cast by the bright and shining moment."

His smile looked thinner now, melancholic. *What happened to scar him so? Perhaps we have more in common than I thought.*

"It wasn't just that the thrills were gone," I said. "I missed the closeness of the team, all the friends I had. I missed the routine of practicing and playing, and the promise of the next season. But most of all, I no longer had any clear direction. I had lived out my boyish fantasies and suddenly had no replacements."

"It's a common problem, mate. We focus on sports and have tremendous triumphs, and then afterwards real life seems anticlimactic. We derive too much of our identity from sports."

"I don't know about that. I had my own identity."

"Don't get defensive. We all associate with things—groups, places, concepts—it's natural. As for sports, it's easy to devote yourself to them, especially as a young man. They're simple, like you said, and there's room for heroism."

He pushed back his chair and headed for the bathroom, pausing along the way to order us each another beer. Brian was right. I did find sports heroic, so much so that when I finished playing competitively, I struggled to find something else that seemed "worthy." My studies at university seemed dull and obligatory, a far cry from passionate or inspired. My friends, meanwhile, were heading into law, medicine, dentistry, but it often seemed they were either lured by cash or social status or driven by a compulsion to please their parents.

My own mother was a high school principal, herself a counselor to hundreds of students each year, but she never once tried to sway my course. She said only: "I don't care what you do, as long as you do your best." In this advice thankfully, she was specific. It was not the "best" relative to others; this would be a heavy and cruel burden to carry. It was the "best" relative to my own potential that she asked for, that she urged all her kids to strive for. But what constitutes your "best," when the activity in question is your very life?

My current struggles were reminiscent of those back in university. Again I was searching for answers when I wasn't quite sure of the questions, looking for guidance when I didn't know where I was going. Back then the answer had come suddenly, in the form of a vivid memory from that youthful trip to Europe.

When Brian returned I told him the story. "I was on a ferry from Spain to Morocco when I noticed a young man standing near the rail, staring out at the Rock of Gibraltar. He seemed so distant, so incredibly calm, I tried to speak with him. He would say little more than that he had 'Traveled overland from Asia,' but in those few in minutes my imagination was flooded with exotic images. Listening to him talk, bathing in his demeanor, I decided instantly that I would go where this man had gone, learn what he had learned, and attempt to gain the tranquility that I perceived in him. In that brief moment, Asia became my new dream."

"You use the word *dream* a lot."

His bluntness took me aback. "Well, call them hopes then. Or plans or wishes. Whatever you like. I call them dreams because for me most start as daydreams, or waking fantasies that I play out in my head. But over time I have noticed that I often experience things that I have visualized earlier."

"Like your sports triumphs."

"Right. And besides that, or maybe because of that, I often get brief flashes, usually in the midst of a game or some other intense activity, that I'm living out a slow motion dream."

"You're not the first."

"Certainly not. And that's why I'm here, to figure these things out."

"And all this just came to you, on the side of a mountain at top speed?"

"Actually no. What came to me was that the awareness I felt at that moment was important and that I needed to understand and describe it."

Brian sat back and sipped his beer, the froth leaving a generous white ring on his beard. I plunged ahead. "Do you remember the movie, *The Deerhunter?*"

Brian nodded.

"DeNiro's character returns from Vietnam a very different man but his friends all expect him to be the same. It killed me to watch it, especially the scene where he's just arrived home and he stands outside his own house watching his friends prepare a 'welcome home' party. He just can't go in. He can't be like he was anymore."

"I know the feeling." Brian's tone carried a new sadness.

"Anyway, DeNiro goes deer hunting with his friends a few days later. His buddies are drinking beer and carrying on, but he slips away and quietly, methodically begins hunting. Finally, he gets a deer in his sights, dead in the crosshairs. The animal turns to look at him. The moment seems frozen, life and death in the clear focus of a riflescope.

"The situation was different, but I felt that same clarity on the mountain. As if I could taste the wind. And like DeNiro and his deer, it wasn't just the skiing that affected me. It was the poignancy of the situation. My life was changing and I knew it. I couldn't go back to my old life, and I didn't know what else to do."

"What did he do?"

I thought for a minute. "He chose not to shoot and the deer moved on to live his life. But that moment was pivotal for DeNiro's character. He went back to Vietnam to face the fear that had changed him. By confronting it, he came to understand it or, at least, accept it."

"So why did you come to Japan? Why did you go to the monastery?"

"Frankly, I wasn't sure what else to do. I came to have some sort of ski adventure I can write about, but I have no idea where to start. Right now, I'm looking for clues."

"What was Nobu asking you?"

When I described our conversation, he whistled softly. "Live at the monastery. Are you ready for that?"

"I don't know."

"Are your knees ready for that?"

We laughed, having hobbled in tandem from the monastery dinner table. Neither of us could stand the pain of sitting in the Seiza position.

"I want to go," I said, "but I'm concerned what I'll miss."

"Skiing?"

"Sounds crazy, I know."

"Not crazy, mate. Just unusual."

"Right. So unusual I'm not sure how to go about it."

"Well, where's the good skiing?"

"The Japan Alps run the length of Honshu, but the best areas are on the north island, Hokkaido."

"Where they had the Olympics?"

"That's right. Near Sapporo in '72."

"Why don't you go there?"

"Well, I . . ."

The truth was that I couldn't think of a reason. In fact, since Sapporo and my Canadian hometown, Edmonton, were sister cities, Hokkaido was the only region I knew anything about.

"You can get there by train in twenty hours."

"I'm short of money." This was a colossal understatement.

"Hitch then. It's legal in Japan."

I paled a little. The notion of finding and standing alongside Japanese freeways seemed daunting. And what about my gear? I couldn't possibly carry it all. "I've got a lot of stuff," I said.

"If you work something out up there, you can come back and pick it up later."

His logic was relentless but unmistakable. If I got a job in ski country, fine. If not, I would have at least tried before making the monastery decision. Only senseless fears held me back. "I'm dwelling on the difficulties, aren't I?"

He smiled. "So when will you leave?"

I thought a moment. It would take a day or two each way to hitchhike, and I had only a week to decide about the monastery. There was no time to waste. "Tomorrow morning."

"A man of action! Good on ya."

As we paid the check, Brian scribbled a phone number on a piece of paper. "I'll be movin' soon. Give me a dingle when you get back."

We thanked the smiling waitress and then walked through the evening stillness to our lodge. Several men were already in bed, but a few were watching Samurai movies in their bathrobes. I slipped past and explained my traveling plans to the owner. She was most kind, arranging to stow my extra luggage and offering to make me a sign to flash at motorists on the highway.

I washed up finally and climbed into my bunk, but sleep was impossible. The longer I thought about my plan, the stranger it seemed. Thoughts and images flooded my mind, and the walls were so thin that street sounds came easily through the darkness. The seconds ticked past slowly.

three

When I awoke and found Brian already gone, I pulled on some clothes, loaded my daypack, and settled my bill. The owner's wife made me a sign saying: "Sapporo" in big, black kangi characters. She worked carefully, as if the brown cardboard sign was to be hung later in an art gallery. As the placard dried, she showed me on a Tokyo map how to find the northbound highway. I thanked her, stored my extra gear in a clever closet under the stairs, and headed out.

After walking halfway down the block and staring at the confusing map and my scribbled notes, I decided I was hungry. It was partly hesitation, I knew, but I headed on a zigzagging route toward the bustling shopping district, Shinjuku, where video screens and huge electronic billboards dominated the central square and a forest of neon hung vertically off buildings down the broad boulevard. The sidewalks and crosswalks were jammed, people walking and stopping in perfect order, like martial choreography. They all looked so similar too, a virtual army of men in blue suits and young women in dark skirts and light blouses. Each seemed in his or her own world, giving hardly a sideways glance. An open truck, draped in Japanese flags and carrying young men with wide, white headbands, screamed through the central intersection, loudspeakers blaring some nationalistic message, but somehow, people scarcely noticed. Even a monk in full robes walking meditatively down the sidewalk, begging bowl extended, was passed like a boulder in a fast rushing stream.

I found my destination, a small coffee shop that Brian had shown me, studied the plastic food models and the prices in the display window, and then went inside to a well-lit table overlooking the square. After an impeccably polite waitress took my order, I turned and watched the people streaming by. Without exception, their eyes were forward, intently focused. For a moment I envied their determination, their certainty of purpose.

My breakfast arrived looking delicious, a "morning set" of a boiled egg, white toast, and coffee, but it disappeared all too quickly. I returned my gaze to the throng outside, to the earnest faces. I couldn't help but wonder how each of them, how any of them, had come to this point? Were they twists of fate that brought them here and now? Or choices and actions? *Are we leaves floating helplessly downstream or salmon fighting upward, struggling instinctively in leaps of faith toward our unforeseen destiny?*

Finally, I drained my coffee, paid my check, and stepped out into the sidewalk melee. Drawn along by the crowd a few short blocks, I descended into the synchronized frenzy of the Tokyo subway at rush hour. Two crowded trains, a bus, and a long walk brought me to the freeway, but it was under expansion, like most everything in Japan, so I had to walk much further. It was nearly noon and still I trudged, past the land movers, past the piles of wooden forms and reinforcing rods, past the curious construction workers. I saw them pointing at me, and felt their burrowing eyes, but just I kept on walking.

Finally I reached the on-ramp. A thin strip of gravel separated me from wave upon wave of accelerating cars and trucks. It wasn't very safe but my alternatives were rather limited. I held up my sign, stuck out my thumb, and immediately felt foolish. *What am I doing? What if I get arrested? I'll never get a ride.*

Paranoia is natural enough when you're standing alone on a foreign roadside, but hitchhiking is an act of faith. You've got to believe that your ride is coming. You have to be ready for it, looking for it, acting positive, or the opportunity will pass you by. Knowing this however, doesn't make it any easier. You're still standing there, thrown up to fate. You're still smelling the dirty exhaust and feeling the curious stares. You're still alone, holding on by the thinning thread of your conviction.

But then, quite suddenly, my sign worked its charm. A pharmaceutical salesman picked me up to practice his English, then later handed me off like a football to another salesman he cajoled at a gas stop. My sign was a work of art apparently, since both men guessed that the author was an older person, well schooled in calligraphy. I stared at it, trying to perceive the subtleties, but to me it appeared only as black ink swiped on cardboard. Evidently, I had a lot to learn.

Between my late start, driver rest stops, and traffic delays, I didn't get very far the first day. As the blue sky deepened into black, the second driver asked where I would sleep. I'd actually planned to travel all night, but since I couldn't explain this, he headed into a small city and stopped at the train station. A conference ensued with the stationmaster, with me a mute bystander. After a few phone calls and a lot of nodding, the salesman handed me my bag, bowed quietly, and left.

The elderly stationmaster dialed the phone again, spoke a few words, and then passed it to me. A polite woman explained in clear English that they were sending me on the next train to her hostel in a nearby town. She told me which bus to take from the station, where to get off, and how to find her place. It had all been arranged. I had no choice.

An hour later, after wandering down a dark, winding alley with wisps of fog and apprehension, I finally found the small sign I sought. The hostel was small and warm, distinctly Japanese in its design and decor. Although I'd been loath to leave the highway, and I was unsure exactly where I was, it was delightful to be there. After a large bowl of steaming ramen noodles, I crept into a cold, dark dorm room, slid under some impossibly thick quilts, and settled soon into a deep sleep.

My dawning realization was that I had unwittingly come to Nikko, the historic winter palace of the legendary leader, *Ieyasu Tokagawa*.[2]

2   In 1603, he founded the Tokugawa shogunate that would remain in power until 1868.

It was a beautiful day, and from the front of the hostel I could see the temple roofs on a nearby hillside. Curiosity overcame my plans for an early start.

I hiked down a forest path, catching glimpses of the palace as I approached. A few gold and red leaves remained on the trees, accenting the elegant austerity of the ancient buildings. The temple grounds were tranquil, free of the shutter-clicking crowds. Only a young Japanese couple and I wandered the hillside estate, studying the graceful architecture, listening for the faint echoes of history. The bustle of the past week—the turmoil of leaving home, the long overseas flight, and the congestion of Tokyo—fell off me like a weary leaf. Instead, I felt again the feathery calm of my traveling days, the same gentle ease and subtle curiosity I had enjoyed at the monastery. I was floating free of thought, savoring simple things.

But the sun was climbing and I was drawn back by my odd quest to the highway. My luck was good. A truck driver, hauling a load of machine parts, pulled over immediately. He wore a white sweatshirt, oily green work pants, and a tightly rolled bandanna around his forehead. He waggled an unlit cigarette with his teeth. He grunted occasionally but never spoke, and smiled only once when he tossed a small, worn album of family pictures over for my inspection. Finally, he turned up his stereo and drove on through the day.

Hours later at a truck stop, again without warning or explanation, he passed me off to the next recruited driver. I felt like an orphan for which they all felt responsible. The new fellow, another trucker, drove me seven silent hours further, bought me dinner and coffee, even waited at the last rest stop to arrange another lift. But by then it was very late and there were few rigs heading north. He paced up and down in the deserted parking lot. I knew he had to deliver his load, but couldn't bring himself to leave me in the dark. Finally, as midnight approached, I convinced him to go.

As his taillights disappeared on the horizon, I found myself remarkably alone. Without light, I couldn't read; without heat, I couldn't sleep. It promised to be a long night. I collected rocks from the asphalt and hurled them toward a large knot on a nearby tree. My throws were erratic at first, but gradually I adjusted the speed and arc of my throwing motion, then experimented with the exact point of release. But as good as my throws became, I could not groove them into constant perfection. Errant thoughts kept slipping in—hoping for someone to stop, fearing that no one would.

Finally, after countless rocks and a chilly hour, I heard the sweet sound of a decelerating diesel. My hopes rose as golden beams stabbed across the parking lot and a large rig rolled up near the bathroom. A young man in a white T-shirt and jeans jumped out and did a quick double take. He stared at me for a full second, then remembered his pressing concern and dashed into the bathroom. When he emerged, he studied my sign as if it were Egyptian hieroglyphics. I think my hopeful expression said more. He grunted and pointed toward the cab of his truck.

This one was a smoker, but I didn't much care since his only words after jumping in were, "Sapporo, OK," punctuated by a thumbs-up sign and a wide smile. Relief surged through me like the heat from the large dashboard vents. We fell silent and a few sleepy hours later reached the antiquated ferry to Hokkaido. Storing the truck in the hold, we came up into the lounge where there was conventional seating in one section and a huge flat carpet in the other. I stepped outside into the crisp ocean air. It felt good. The cold was delicious now that warmth was so near and accessible. The coastline of Honshu was receding and somewhere, ahead in the darkness, was my destination, Hokkaido. I flashed back on the events of the day, savoring my string of small successes, then went inside for some sleep.

Six hours later, with another big smile and a wave of his hand, the last driver dropped me in downtown Sapporo. It was satisfying to be there finally, but since dawn I had been worried. There was no snow on the ground and very little on the nearby peaks yet it was already late November. *Could I possibly be too early?*

Inquiries brought me to the nearby YMCA where I ate, washed, and headed back out to begin my search. Walking briskly in the cool air, I soon found *Odori-nishi*, the broad central boulevard that stretched toward those disturbingly brown mountains. After a little confusion, I found the office of the Sapporo-Edmonton sister city commission. It wasn't a separate facility as I expected, but simply a bank where officials of the commission worked. I caused a commotion by dropping in unannounced, and after much apologizing and rushing about, two men in their forties, Mr. Suzuki and Mr. Orita, received me in a large second story boardroom.

The meeting was awkward. The two men were painfully uncertain as to the correct protocol for such a visit, and I felt equally embarrassed for surprising them. Our awkward silence was interrupted by a lovely young woman serving tea. She moved so elegantly I could hardly keep from staring, yet to the Japanese men she did not exist. They were concerned only with me, discerning my objective and their attendant responsibility.

As we began talking, I realized my folly. Mr. Suzuki and Mr. Orita were accustomed to trade commissions and patterned protocol, while I sought a bohemian adventure. As gracefully as I could, I let them off the invisible hook of obligation. Realizing this with an almost audible sigh of relief, the older man excused himself after a polite time and suggested that Mr. Orita and I take lunch together.

The younger banker loosened up as we left the building, partly because the situation was resolved, but also, I suspected, because he was away from his superior. He talked now with curiosity and emotion, as if the human being within him could now be revealed. Over sushi in a rooftop restaurant, with a view of the wind-whipped Sea of Japan on my right and a looming range of mountains over my host's shoulder, we talked about skiing and Sapporo.

"I love skiing also," he said. "With my son and daughter especially. That was one reason why I made a transfer here."

"Are any of the ski areas open yet?" I asked, holding my breath.

He shook his head. "Not yet. We need a big snowing. Maybe next week, or two weeks more."

My heart sank. Late November should have been late enough. Then, looking out the window, I realized the problem. The mountains, which were not huge, rose directly from the Sea of Japan, itself still cooling from the heat of the summer. Moderated temperatures and low altitudes were not ideal for early season snow.

Mr. Orita did not notice my disappointment. "Oh yes, soon it is very nice. We have many ski areas that we can drive to. See up there . . ." He stopped and pointed up at a broad expanse of mountainside. "That is Mount Teine, where they held the Olympic Games in 1972. You can see the big ski jump."

I nodded, seeing the distinctively curved structure and several brown streaks where the ski runs should have been. The crests and ridges of the mountain range were soft and rolling, worn down by time like the Appalachians of the eastern United States. Evergreen trees were scattered across the flanks, but mostly it was a leafless, deciduous forest, fuzzy brown like a week-old growth on the jaw of the mountain.

Mr. Orita seemed reluctant to part after lunch, as if our brief time together was more than a break from routine. Perhaps he saw something in my curious quest, a romantic idealism that he had counted out of his life as a banker. After I walked him back to his office, he stood watching as I left, bowing slightly and waving as I rounded the corner and disappeared from view.

A cold rain fell for the next two days, dampening my efforts as I made the rounds of the city, asking for work. My initial idea of applying for work at the ski areas was thwarted immediately. Not only were the resorts not open yet, none of them kept an office in the city. I tried the ski shops next, but my heart took on ballast with each curious shake of the head. It was hard enough to explain in English what I wanted, let alone Japanese.

I kept expecting a break somehow, a chance meeting, but walking from place to place was time consuming and discouraging. My thoughts would slip back to Canada, to the monastery, even to the hostel in Tokyo—any place more familiar and hospitable than

Sapporo. The inspiration that seemed so clear on the Canadian mountainside appeared now as a fading memory.

The last store I went to, a large ski shop just off Odori-Nishi, typified my job searching experience. A young clerk scratched his head, then referred me to his manager. More head-scratching and drawn-out sighs. Although the manager's English was far better than my Japanese, we could hardly communicate. He just kept scratching his head.

Just as I turned to leave, he had a new idea. Holding up his hand, he pronounced, very carefully, "Wait a minute, please."

After a moment in the back room, he reappeared with a stocky, balding fellow wearing a *Sun Valley* work apron, evidently a ski mechanic.

"May I help you?" he asked confidently, with little trace of an accent.

I explained my situation and watched his face cloud over. He waited for few seconds after I finished, as if hoping I would say I was joking.

Finally, he spoke. "Sorry, but I can't suggest anything. You see, Japanese companies are very difficult to . . ." After a pause, he tried again. "Ski areas in Japan are all owned by big companies with personnel offices and strict procedures for hiring."

"I see." The corporate route did not sound promising.

"Do you have a work permit?"

When I shook my head, he shrugged his shoulders as if there were no point in further questions.

I thanked him and trudged out to the street, totally deflated. I had been everywhere, asked everyone. No luck. Now my money and time had run out. If I was going to the monastery with Nobu, I had less than forty-eight hours to make it back to Tokyo. I didn't want to give up but there seemed little choice.

That night, as if to torment me, it began to snow lightly, just a few pale flakes from the dark November sky. After walking the length of Odori-Nishi, I found myself in the oddly comforting confines of a Shakey's Pizza franchise, writing in my journal while listening to a jukebox that was fatefully stuck on Kenny Roger's throaty song, "The Gambler," playing it over and over incessantly. The chorus burned into my consciousness:

Know when to hold 'em
Know when to fold 'em
Know when to walk away
Know when to run

Was this a karmic clue, jackhammering into my brain? Aren't we all gamblers, risking our lives in different ways? Is quixotic searching a fool's life? Is it better to be safe and sanitary, venturing little but gaining nothing? What of those caught halfway, seeking but not knowing why or how? That was my fear too, that I was holding back subconsciously, afraid to let this—or make this—strange adventure come to pass.

That night I had a dream. In it, I heard laughter and gentle admonitions. As I became cognizant, I realized that there were spiritual beings surrounding me, addressing me like I was one of them, just returning home. My whole life, as I had known it, had occurred in a few brief minutes of their time. It had been a test to see if I could piece together the clues and discover the truth about my own existence. They had all tried it before; for them a lifetime was a parlor game. During my time on earth, they had devised situations to tempt, tease, shock, and educate me, seeing where I drew near the cosmic truth, or joke as they saw it, then laughing when the realization slipped away. They could listen, and even influence, my thoughts during the process, and enjoy vicariously my pondering. For them it was the "Hide and Seek" of eternity. The search was everything.

four

I headed south the next morning. I started by hitchhiking, then learned in the nearby port, Tomakomai, of a freighter heading south to Tokyo. The fare was steep but I could sleep on board to save a night's lodging, and I would be back in time for the monastery. Perhaps more significantly, although I didn't want to admit it, my spirit was too beaten up to stand again like a refugee at the roadside.

The ship was dilapidated, with scanty facilities and deck paint that had long ago succumbed to the elements. We were soon out to sea, where I had plenty of time to stare out over the water and consider my options. Too much time, actually, and too few options. I couldn't ski in Hokkaido and I wasn't sure where to try next. My money had dwindled to a hundred and forty dollars, hardly enough for nine sparse days. I had no visa and I couldn't speak Japanese. The only sure thing was that Nobu would be waiting on the train platform the next morning.

A stiff wind sprang up, blowing froth off the ocean chop, buffeting the disparate array of ships that sailed along the coastline of Honshu. Opportunistic seagulls surfed the breezes above our heads, looking for scraps. One gray-white gull soared scant feet from me, synchronized with the ship as if tethered invisibly. The wind rose and fell, snapping the ship's flag, yet on this creature, every feather and muscle was aligning perfectly, adjusting instantly. Its dark, shining eyes were riveted forward, piercing the wind. I stared into them like crystal balls.

It vanished suddenly, hurtled backward by the wind, but the image stayed with me. Especially the eyes, that primal focus. I had seen this before in the gaze of teammates and competitors in full flight. It is a beautiful sight, one of the true joys of sports. Whatever the creature or competition, there is always an optimal state of concentration, of instinctive awareness. I had seen it in others; I had sensed it within myself. Somehow, I would learn to understand it.

Before dawn Saturday, we pulled into Tokyo harbor. A bus and a subway brought me back to the Shinjuku coffee shop where I had sat the previous week. The same waitress greeted me at the door and sat me overlooking the square; the same stout cook bustled about in the kitchen; the same throng streamed past on the sidewalk. Had five days really passed? I looked at my watch. The date had indeed changed. The time too. In just over two hours, Nobu would be at watching for me, wondering if I would show up.

The decision pressed upon me. There was no one to talk to, but I couldn't have expressed myself anyway. Not logically. My options were to go live in a Zen monastery, to try again for an improbable ski adventure, or to stay in Tokyo and wait. I thought again of my strange dream in Sapporo. Were those spiritual beings watching me, witnessing my internal struggle? It seemed that I could hear them laughing.

Realistically, since I had no money to seek another ski area, there were only two choices. I could either live in the monastery or work in Tokyo to save money. At the very least, I would need to earn enough yen each day to eat, sleep, and get around; anything more I could save to try the skiing idea again. The trouble was, Tokyo was one of the world's most expensive cities. Could I possibly earn enough without working papers?

I tried to visualize the two possibilities. Scenes of the monastery came easily to mind—the orange leaves against the rich brown soil, my faint shadow on the wall of the meditation chamber, the Master sitting calmly on the dais. Ski visualizations were more elusive, at least those distinctly Japanese, but I could summon the fluid images of

Canadian winters past. I saw myself bouncing through snowy white bumps, carving long turns on a wide clear slope, swiveling quickly down a steep face.

Strangely, the same emotion accompanied these disparate images. Though the first were of meditative isolation and the others were of rapid action, I felt a deep calm throughout. This was what haunted me, what the Master confirmed but did not explain. How can such different activities yield the same awareness?

I thought of Herman Hesse's book, *Narcissus and Goldmund,* in which the monk Narcissus takes the road of the mind, of meditative contemplation, while the exuberant Goldmund takes the route of the senses, of learning through experience. I thought of the Aborigines, and their concept of the "walkabout" and the "Dreamtime," and of Castaneda too, who said that a warrior must find and walk "a path with heart."

It was late. If I were going to the monastery, I had to get back and arrange permanent storage for my equipment. That would take an hour at least. If I was going to go, I had to leave that minute. I closed my eyes and tried to reason it through, but soon gave up. Why? Because it wasn't reason-able. In such situations, my intuition was in control.

I took a breath, then another, from as deep as I could in my abdomen. I let everything drop away, settle down, fall silent. I listened for my innermost voice, the one I heard in my quietest moments. Gradually, the decision became clear. Though I couldn't yet ski in Japan, and didn't know how, or even if, I ever would, I couldn't ignore the strange vision that had drawn me there. Whatever the game was, I had to play it through.

So I sat still, staring out the window as the minutes ticked past, not moving, not even thinking, until finally the choice existed no longer. Despite the pang I felt imagining Nobu looking fruitlessly down the platform, the stronger reaction was an almost palpable sense of relief. The die was cast.

I opened *The Japan Times* and studied the classified ads. Almost immediately, my heart sank. Several English schools were listed, but nearly all requested specific teaching credentials. With growing concern, I circled those that didn't and plotted a route to visit them. Next, I checked the rooms for rent, adding a few more stops along my way.

Finally, armed with coins and newspaper, I found the public telephone, one of the stubby beasts throughout Tokyo that consumed coins greedily. I dreaded this. Besides the cost of the calls, the ultra-polite requests for the correct change were spoken in Japanese. Since I couldn't discern the deposit, I had to repeatedly ask the waitress for assistance.

Judging from the English of those answering my calls, it was no wonder that they hired foreigners to teach. But not me necessarily. Several schools rejected me outright, citing their need for the proper documents. Others let me waste valuable money on the subway, as well as time spent searching through labyrinthian neighborhoods, before giving me the bad news.

My quest for an apartment didn't go much better. A tiny room by a subway would have been loud but acceptable, if only I could have persuaded the landlady to waive the necessary deposits and advance rent. A "room" with some Australians turned out to be a cot in the common area where they drank every night. Staying at the hostel wasn't feasible much longer, since the daily rate was eating my funds in giant bites.

By early evening, the carnage was complete. I was twelve dollars and six leads poorer, and only marginally wiser. Feeling battered, I fished Brian's phone number out of my address book and prayed he was home.

"*Moshi, Moshi,*" came the standard phone greeting.

Damn! I couldn't even attempt Japanese, so I tried English. "Is Brian . . . ," I stopped, realizing that I didn't know his last name.

"Yes, may I help you?" came the reply, now in perfect English.

Thank God! "Do you have an Australian named Brian living there?"

"Brian-san. Yes. One moment please."

I waited, reveling in this minor victory. After a minute, footsteps approached and a familiar voice answered, "Hello?"

"Brian, it's Rick.

"How was Hokkaido?"

"No luck."

"Too bad, mate," he said softly. After a moment's silence, he added, "Passed on the monastery too, did you?"

"I'm afraid so."

"Where you stayin' then?"

"That's what I called about. Any room where you are?"

"Hold on. I'll check."

I heard his footsteps recede and then voices in the distance. My breath sounded loud and I realized I was nervous. I needed a break.

The footsteps returned until Brian again held the phone. "Good timing, mate. A French chap moved today. Come out and take a look. I'll meet you at the local station."

Elated, I took down the details and headed for the subway. The trip was easy, a few quick stops on the ring line to Ikebukero, the mammoth shopping center/train station complex, where I navigated a complicated route to my transfer point. I soon boarded another clean, modern train and traveled outward about thirty minutes to a neighborhood called Toshimaen, known for its small amusement park.

As promised, Brian was waiting to escort me. The carnival grounds stretched alongside the subway, and offices and shops lined the winding main street, but once onto the side road, the district was more like a sprawling village with garden plots and fruit trees and no building higher than two stories. The darkened street was nearly deserted, just a pair of pensioners shuffling slowly and a housewife with a baby bundled to her chest.

He pointed out shops and services as we walked, telling me the pertinent data: "It takes eleven minutes to walk from the house to the station. From there to Ikebukero takes thirty-seven minutes, then another five minutes to walk to the transfer point to catch the ring line. Don't be late because the trains never are."

This precise summation was unlike the casual Brian I knew. Evidently, he had learned the commuting ropes quickly.

We stopped before a two-story house. Like most others in Tokyo, it was built within a foot of the property line. The young owner, Jun Yoshida, came out to meet me. He was a spry fellow with round wire-rimmed glasses, a wispy goatee, and evident ease with westerners. It turned out that he had once lived in Banff, the Canadian mountain town where I had received my ski instructor's certification. He even knew Kohei Yokura, a Japanese-Canadian who had been in my class. This was an extraordinary break. Even though I sensed Yoshida was friendly to everyone, I had learned already that introductions and mutual friends are invaluable in Japan.

Laughing about Kohei and Banff, we donned slippers in the entrance and padded down the darkened central hallway. Although shadowy and somewhat drafty, the house felt comfortable immediately. The interior was of traditional design, with sliding paper doors opening off the hallway onto bedrooms on either side. The kitchen, tucked alongside the staircase, was tiny but fragrant and warm. As we climbed the creaking, wooden stairs to the second floor, where five doorways lined a narrow hallway, I knew already that I wanted to stay. But would I like the room? Which one would it be? He walked midway down the hall, slid back a door, then gestured for me to look. Every step pushed my anticipation higher. I reached the door and peeked in.

It was small but not tiny, plain but not stark. The floor was covered with *tatami* mats, a futon with bedding was rolled up in the corner, and a low table sat by the window. I stepped out of my slippers and entered. The clean walls, the single bamboo shelf up high, the tall window with its flower box and view of the neighborhood—every detail agreed with me. It was peaceful, private, and very Japanese.

I wanted it, a place of my own. A refuge. But could I afford it? I swallowed hard to hear the price, which worked out to a hundred dollars a week, but since Kohei was a mutual friend, Yoshida offered to waive the security deposit. That was a break, but it was still nearly all the money I had left.

How would I eat? Where would next week's rent come from?

Brian noticed my concern and pulled me aside. "Not what you're lookin' for?"

"No, no, it's great, but . . ."

"Too steep?"

I explained my situation, embarrassed that I was stretched so thin.

Brian was unfazed. "Look, it's a good room. Take it. At least that problem will be settled. Then come down with me tomorrow to ESS, that coffeehouse I told you about. Maybe you can get a few shifts. At the least, you'll meet some other foreigners. Something will come up."

I took a breath and turned to Yoshida. "I'll take it."

The next morning, I checked out of the hostel and dragged my skis, backpack, and monstrous gear bag to the subway. It was torturous, first carrying my luggage through the enormous stations, then along the small, winding streets. I stopped repeatedly, my shoulders aching and fingers burning. Finally, I staggered stupefied into Yoshida House and collapsed in the kitchen. I just sat there for a long while, recovering my strength, listening to the sounds of my new home. Already it felt good, the warmth of the stove, the smell of the food, the bustle of people coming and going.

Finally, I went upstairs and began getting settled. I arranged my books and writing implements on the small table, laid out my clothes on the shelf overhead, and made up my bed with the sheets provided. I stood my skis up in the corner and stowed the rest of my equipment into a storage area downstairs. As I worked, I hoped this room would be my home for longer than the week I could afford.

Next came a careful visit to the grocer. I had parceled out my remaining yen, leaving enough for subway rides and allocating the rest for food. I walked the aisles, looking askance at the strange assortment of dried, canned, and refrigerated foods on the shelves. Eventually, I ended up with meager amounts of milk, bread, eggs, and coffee, as well as assorted fruits and vegetables that were familiar. Back in the kitchen, I staked my claim on a cupboard shelf and a corner of the refrigerator. My first act, enormously satisfying, was to throw chopped vegetables into some instant noodles, then devour the fragrant mixture in the warm corner of the kitchen.

There was little other activity in the house. I faintly heard a television in the common area and the occasional sound of footsteps, but it seemed that most of my ten roommates had gone out. That was fine with me. I was exhausted and looking forward to the peacefulness of my room.

I washed my dishes and climbed the creaking stairs. I loved the polished smoothness of the hardwood floors and the texture of the *tatami* mats in my room. I savored the quietness of the evening and the exquisite coolness of the air. I opened my window, lit a candle, and sat at the low square table, called a *kutatsu*, which had an electric heater underneath and a quilt on the fringe that I wrapped around my waist. The heat seemed to radiate up from my legs to my torso, which was clad in a turtleneck and sweater. I felt comfortable and relaxed.

I took out my notebook and began writing. Between the monastery, the ill-fated Sapporo trip, and the job searching, it had been a difficult and eventful week. But things were looking up. Quite suddenly I had a great room, and Brian would be taking me to his workplace in the morning. I looked over at my skis in the corner. They would have to wait.

five

I woke in heaven. The sun poured in my open window, filling the room with light. A bird chirped nearby and the neighbor's hanging chimes added their breezy accompaniment. There were no men snoring or grumbling as in the hostel, no bunk to climb down from, no congestion of clothes, suitcases, and bodies—only me, my single futon, and my low table by the window. It was bliss.

I folded my futon mattress and began stretching on the floor. The sunlight had warmed the *tatami*, making its fibrous texture especially pleasant. The radiance embraced me also, nourishing my skin, lifting my already buoyant spirit. A private room seemed already to be the best decision I had yet made in Japan. The only trouble was that now I had to pay for it—somehow. I needed to hook on at Brian's workplace in order to pay another week's rent and buy some more groceries. If not, well, Plan B wasn't too clear just yet.

I forced myself to focus on my stretching, mostly on my legs, back, and shoulders, then went downstairs for breakfast. Brian stood cooking at the stove while a Frenchman named Claude sat at the small table reading the classified ads.

"G'mornin' mate," said Brian. "How'd you get on last night?"

"All set up, thanks."

"You still comin' in with me?"

"Absolutely," I said, pouring hot water over some instant coffee. "Tell me about this place."

"It's called the English Speaking Society, or ESS, but that's just a fancy name. Basically, it's a club where Japanese pay by the hour to practice their English with foreigners."

"You just sit there and talk?"

"That's it."

"Does it pay well?"

"Not bad. And they're always looking for fresh *gaijin*."

I looked at him. "*Gaijin?*"

"*Gaijin* means foreigner, or non-Japanese. To them, we're not Australians or French or American, just non-Japanese. It's a simple reckoning, a kind of *'them and us'* mentality." He let me digest this, then continued. "Anyway, teachers burn out."

"What's so difficult?"

Claude put down his paper and looked at me with the condescending weariness of the French. He took a pen from his pocket, held it in front of me and said in a tortuously slow voice, "This . . . is . . . a . . . pen." Turning to Brian, he repeated, "This . . . is . . . a . . . pen."

I got the point. Numbing repetition.

"He's just jealous," Brian laughed. "He's not a native English speaker, so he has to flog old kimonos for a living."

"I reclaim treasures," he retorted. "You babble on command."

Brian grinned. "Don't mind him. It's not so bad at ESS. The newcomers drive you a bit bonkers, asking the same questions all the time, but the regulars are OK."

"What about teaching individuals?"

"Private lessons pay better and are more interesting, but they take months to line up. The trick is to accept whatever group classes you can get at first, then gradually improve your schedule. Commuting time is a big factor. Classes in the suburbs pay well, but you to travel an hour each way. Sometimes it's not worth it. Overall, it's like playing bridge—pick up a good class, discard a bad one, pick up, discard— over and over until you have a tight circle of schools and clients."

"Sounds like a long process."

"Can be, unless you get lucky. If you know any foreigners leaving Japan, you can sometimes pick up their private clients."

Brian had inhaled his breakfast, rinsed his plate, and moved to the door. "Ready?"

"Right with you," I said, downing my coffee.

We set off for my first lesson in Japanese style commuting. With me in a half jog to match Brian's long stride, we reached the station in the prescribed eleven minutes. The train departed immediately, and we rolled into Ikebukero exactly thirty-seven minutes later. Brian walked briskly, weaving through the crowds, navigating without hesitation the halls and escalators. He had perfected the transfer route to the Yamanote, Tokyo's ring line, down to a fast five minutes, but I made a mental note to allow a few minutes more.

A few quick stops, high above the low gray buildings and bustling streets, and another brisk walk brought us finally to the English Speaking Society. The less regal abbreviation, ESS, was far more appropriate, for it turned out to be a dreary second story room with decrepit furniture and the reek of old smoke and bad coffee. Japanese began arriving in ones and twos, and arranging themselves in rings around Brian, a drawling Texan at the next table, and myself. They all assumed I was a hired tongue as well, and I stayed for Brian's entire shift, drinking several cups of wretched coffee and trying to be as talkative and interesting as possible.

The owner, Mr. Tanaka, was a wizened old elf who smoked and coughed on alternate breaths. He sat motionless in the corner, eyeing me like an old tiger would some fresh prey. He made no attempt to talk to me; he just sat there, smoking one cigarette after another. If silence was his bargaining stance, he definitely had the advantage. Finally, as it came time to leave, I could wait no longer.

He studied me as I approached, likely sensing my situation. At least he opened his mouth. "You want working?" he asked, squinting through his smoky wreath. I nodded and began to speak, but he cut me off, "You can work anytime?"

I nodded again.

"Native speaker?"

"Yes, of course. I come from Canada."

His eyes narrowed. "You speak French or English?"

"Oh, I'm from western Canada. The English-speaking part."

I felt ridiculous, attempting to transform simple words into a pronunciation sales pitch. Mr. Tanaka wanted native speakers, but after listening all afternoon to the thickly accented speech of Brian and the Texan, I knew that was a flawed selection criterion. I stood silently, waiting for a long plume of smoke to be thoughtfully exhaled.

"OK," he said finally. "Work here is talk English, especially to new customers. Start tomorrow. Ten o'clock."

That was it. I was in. He gave me three shifts to start, six hours each, at the equivalent of eight dollars an hour. Not a king's ransom, especially for the sacrifice of my pink lung tissue to that noxious, smoke-filled air, but at least I could buy groceries and pay rent.

I came away relieved, almost jubilant, but also surprisingly tired. To listen and respond perceptively took a lot of focus. The Japanese were appreciative, of course, and it was satisfying, but I knew already why the English Speaking Society burned out so many foreigners.

Over the next week I met hundreds of Japanese men and women, all keen to practice their English. They were of all ages and income groups but they came and left alone, united only by their desire to speak English and meet foreigners. Groups of four or five would gather around each native English speaker, most of them shy and unaccustomed to casual chatter, even in their own language. Although I tried to manipulate the topics to satisfy my curiosities about Japan, discussions often degenerated into textbook-style conversations like "Why did you come to Japan?" or "Do you like Japanese food?"

The regulars, who came as if the place were a clubhouse, made the repetition with newcomers bearable. One was Honda, a moon-faced professor at the illustrious Tokyo University, who talked excitedly about quantum physics. Jun was a concert pianist with a dog-eared dictionary and a penchant for new English words. A tiny, childlike woman was nicknamed Miss NHK because she constantly discussed the NHK television network. Chang, a Korean student in Japan, was friendly amongst the others, but privately he described the prejudice that he faced.

I came away on Friday with Mr. Tanaka's praise, four days on the following week's schedule, and an envelope full of cash. Things were definitely looking up. I had enough now to pay Jun Yoshida for another week, stock my cupboards, and have a little left for subways. Better yet, I had been given two leads by the Texan about English schools that weren't strict about credentials or working papers.

I went the next day, and sure enough, Mrs. Takahashi, a kindly woman in the Shibuya district, put me to work teaching a group of five-year-old kids after school on Wednesdays. At another agency, I arranged to commute an hour and a half to a Monday evening meeting with junior level managers of a regional Matsushita factory. My income was not impressive, but already I could save a little money.

That night I treated myself to a hot bath at the neighborhood *sento*. Fortunately, Brian knew the location and the procedure, which saved me some embarrassment. We washed ourselves *before* getting in the tub, each of us sitting on a little plastic stool, lathering up, then dumping small buckets of water over our heads. Once clean, we then had to choose one of two tubs for our soak. I soon learned that *hot* is a relative term in a Japanese bathhouse, measurable by the pinkness of the bathers' bodies when they emerged. These baths would have been better labeled as "Scalding" and "Unsafe."

But in we went, feeling every inch like lobsters, until finally we were immersed. My body was engulfed with sensations. Each time someone moved in the tub, the underwater currents pushed the hot water against me, through me, in wave after wave of extraordinary feeling.

Finally, I climbed out and wove, quite unsteadily, to the outside garden. It was small, just a tiny pond surrounded by trees, rocks, and a high wooden fence. I stood alone, steam rising off my skin into the blackness of the night, the cold air caressing my naked body. I felt tired and wonderfully peaceful.

My mind, so active all week, could barely sustain my thoughts. They were like blossoms on a cherry tree in late spring, so thick and full that they fell and floated to the earth. I had been in Japan just three weeks. The things I had seen and done already, the thousand ideas I had pondered, they were all too heavy now. *Let them go,* I counseled myself. *Give yourself a rest.*

But the mind is stubborn, resilient. I thought again of Nobu up at the monastery, sitting on the small black cushion, facing the wall of his consciousness. I imagined the mountains above Sapporo, awaiting the cold Siberian winds and the snow that would soon come. I saw myself skiing too, carving wide turns on white snow beneath a biting blue sky. Somehow I still felt sure it would happen.

six

Sunday brought a much-needed day of rest. Over breakfast and while doing my laundry, I gradually met my housemates. Like any cross-section of foreigners in Japan, they were an odd bunch. There were three Israeli women, just out of the army and en route to America. Three mustachioed Pakistanis were washing dishes at a nearby restaurant and saving collectively for a business back home. Claude and another Frenchman were buying used kimonos at estate sales and shipping them to California boutiques. There was an English couple studying Japanese pottery, a German woman who had just spent two years wandering with the holy men in India, and a young woman from Toronto who built custom guitars. And there was Brian, who seemed already like an old friend.

Most of the women worked as hostesses in private clubs, dancing and making conversation with the male clientele. Like others new to Japan, I wondered about this, but I was assured that it was purely business.

"We're social facilitators," said Elizabeth, the English woman, describing how they sat with Japanese businessmen, poured outrageously priced drinks, listened to drunken attempts at English or Karaoke, then pocketed their hefty cash wages each night. Her husband, who sat next to her, didn't seem the least perturbed. He currently had several of the truly odd jobs held by western men in Japan—English teacher, proofreader, model, and film extra.

In the late afternoon, Brian poked his head in my door. "I'm meetin' a friend for a drink. Want to come?"

Rick Phipps

I didn't really have money to spare, but it seemed time to celebrate. I grabbed my jacket and we headed out, me jogging to match Brian's long stride. We made the subway perfectly, and a few minutes later were walking through the entertainment district, *Roppongi.*

"We're a bit early," Brian said. "Want to whack a few?"

I looked in the direction he was pointing. There was a pie shaped, multi-level driving range, with dozens of golfers on each level sending a cascade of white balls out into distant nets. I was a Sunday golfer at best, but I loved the feeling. It was tempting but I simply didn't have the extra cash. "I'll just watch."

But Brian had already read my mind. "Look, I'll spring for a bucket, and we'll share it. Right?"

That settled it. Brian went into the shop and came out a few minutes later up with a driver, a three-six-nine iron package, and a large bucket of balls. A spot came open on the second level beside a guy that was driving balls an astonishing distance. He was dressed head to toe in black, with a massive bag, also black, and an impressive set of clubs.

There were several men gathered near, smoking and quietly watching the man in black. Both Brian and I hesitated, neither of us particularly desirous of the extra scrutiny and inevitable comparison. Finally, Brian said, "Bloody hell," and stepped on to the mat holding the driver. From the first swing, it was evident that he too had played the game. There was surprising suppleness in Brian's lanky frame that provided a smooth transfer of power. With a few notable exceptions, he cracked the balls out with authority.

My turn. I stepped up and selected the nine iron. Less chance of a misfire, I thought. I took a few practices, felt the rust in my movements and the slight slippage of my sneakers. I placed a ball on the green mat, stared at it until it swelled large, then took my swing. Click. It lifted easily, rocketing up into a perfect trajectory that looked magnificent against the darkening sky. The beauty of it filled me, the smoothness of the motion, the sweetness of the impact, the resonating joy of watching the tiny white ball soar into the darkness. Of the rest, I hit a variety of bad and good shots, but none so memorable as the first. I had known what I wanted, what the club was supposed to do, and that was exactly what happened.

Thought of it filled my mind as I stepped back to the bench and let Brian shoot the last few balls. The intriguing thing about golf is that in every given situation, there is a potentially perfect shot. Within your bag is the club with which to do it. If you've played much, you've surely made that shot before, perhaps thousands of times. In theory, if willing alone could make it so, you would make it again, every time. The reality, however, is that something slips into the mind or muscles of even the best golfers. You tense up, mentally or physically, and affect somehow the path or the angle of your club head. It needn't be much. A hundredth of an inch can make the difference between a good and bad swing. It is this that makes golf such an aggravating yet enticing sport. A golf shot is so difficult to do perfectly that we revel in the moments when we come close.

The man in black was a superb golfer, in apparent control of his game, but the true test couldn't be seen. It could only come on the course, against others of equal or greater skill where tiny errors loom large. In such situations, even professional golfers miss shots they could otherwise make blindfolded. Why? Because they fall prey to the same demons as the average golfer. They start thinking about their shots, trying to consciously control them, and that just doesn't work. The mechanics are too complicated, the control mechanisms too sensitive. Strange as it seems, you simply have to trust yourself.

Brian ripped a low rising drive with his last ball, then stepped back to join me on the bench. We watched the ninja golfer ply his trade, just two of a dozen appreciative onlookers. The man never spoke, smiled, frowned, or otherwise displayed emotion. He just worked his way through his clubs like a musician practicing scales. Each instrument sounded a pure note, a tiny sweet sound that all golfers know and love.

I studied his every move. His hands were soft, with a grip gentle enough to hold a small bird. His pre-swing preparation was subtle, yet as thorough as an airline pilot. He coiled slowly, evenly, then flowed seamlessly into a powerfully fluid release. His swing was kinetic perfection; the ball was an incidental detail, encountered and dispatched along the way. Indeed, the man in black seemed almost oblivious to the result, a white bullet streaking out into space with that beautiful, vanishing sound.

With each such display, the crowd murmured softly. Some fingered their own clubs, checking their grip against his. Others stepped back into open areas and drew back imaginary swings. The rest of us just stood there, staring at this slight magician who made golf balls disappear so gracefully. My eyes weren't skilled enough to fully grasp his physical techniques, but I could appreciate his attitude. He had the calm beyond confidence, the unerring movements, the bearing of a champion.

We peeled ourselves away finally and headed to our rendezvous. Brian gave a low whistle. "That fellow could really hit the ball. So effortless."

"That's the secret, I think. He didn't force it."

"Just let it happen."

"What about those guys watching? Didn't move. Didn't say a word."

Just then, Brian grabbed a handrail and bound up a flight of wrought iron steps. I followed and soon found myself in my first Japanese jazz club. It was narrow and smoky and on one wall there were huge posters of Ella Fitzgerald, Duke Ellington, and Thelonious Monk. Behind the bar stood row upon row, perhaps a thousand bottles, of J&B whisky, each with a numbered tag hanging from it. There were at least as many records around an elaborate stereo, and music from the current album, prominently displayed, sounded crisp and clean. The crowd listened seriously.

"How'd you find this place?" I asked quietly

"The girl we're meeting, Yumi, it's her favorite. I bought a bottle, so now it's my favorite too."

"You bought a bottle?"

"Yeah. It's called bottle keep. All those bottles on the shelves are privately owned. You pay a hefty sum to buy it from the house, then they bring it each time you come. You can drink it as fast or slow as you like."

"Good for repeat business."

"Yeah. Like your private club."

"This girl Yumi. Is she your girlfriend?"

"Nah. Just a friend I made my first week here. She's lonely, I think, and she finds me interesting or amusing or something. I can't quite figure it out."

"She's Japanese, I take it."

"Yes and no. She was raised here, but she lived for years in New York."

"Doing what?"

"She was a translator at first, but now she's some kind of artist."

"Why'd she come back?"

"Bit of a long story. Her father's quite sick, but apparently there were hard feelings when she went away, and they're both pretty stubborn."

Brian's bottle arrived, complete with ice, glasses, and water. We poured our drinks and sat back listening. After a few minutes, a small woman entered wearing a billowing black outfit and an eccentric hat. "There she is," Brian said, waving.

I watched her approach with great interest. It's hard to teach or define a *sense of style*, but Yumi definitely had it. She exuded it, defined it. Eyes turned in the room, but she paid no mind. Her gait was not jaunty but strong, not demure but subtle. It indicated physical skill, likely dance training, I suspected, enhanced by poise and flair.

We stood as Yumi arrived, Brian introducing me, and then settled into our seats. She asked for water without ice, and as Brian poured it, her eyes moved around the room. Her face was elliptical and softly sculpted. Her skin was perfect, her lips full. As she unwrapped her shawl and took off her hat, I saw long straight hair, well down her back, and a slender athletic body. Yumi was beautiful.

And blunt. We were hardly settled when she turned to me and said, "Brian told me that you're an athlete."

I nodded but before I could reply, she stared straight at me and asked, "Don't you think that sports are contaminated now? The athletes make so much money they forget the essence."

It was hardly subtle, but her topic intrigued me. "What's the essence of sport?"

But she didn't answer. She just settled back, listening to the music. Brian and I glanced at each other, eyebrows arched quizzically. I was intrigued, perhaps even a little intimidated. As the song concluded, I asked Yumi about her artwork.

"A bit of everything. I play guitar and flute. I paint in oils and watercolors. I make pottery and wood block prints. Sometimes, I combine the various aspects together into a show or a performance piece."

"Why is your father so upset with you?" Brian asked.

"He was furious from the day I left home. It got worse when I went to New York." Her voice dropped slightly. "You don't realize that the hurts don't go away. That angry words are remembered."

Brian tried to console her. "I've had harsh words with my father too."

"But your father's not dying."

That froze the conversation. A low saxophone filled the air, a long melancholy note that seemed sadly appropriate. Yumi turned and said quietly, "My father has cancer. I've come home to be with him."

I nodded. "How is he now?"

"Quite well today. Thank you for asking." With this she met my eyes for the first time. They were dark and pure. Intense. Mysterious.

"How are your classes, Yumi?" Brian asked, shifting the subject.

She shrugged without speaking.

"What kind of classes?" I asked.

"Traditional," she said abruptly, but after a few moments she added, "Flower arrangement and tea ceremony right now."

"For a performance piece?" I asked.

"I don't think so. I've just become newly interested in the ancient Japanese arts. In New York everyone tries to be new and creative, always *avant garde*. And I liked that at first. It was edgy, unpredictable. The people were different, the ideas seemed original."

"That's New York," I said.

"But after awhile my feelings changed. The art was innovative, but so much was no good. It was *only* different. Young artists, some with little real training, were suddenly big stars, with huge openings and fantastic prices. They were innovators sure, but nothing like, say, Picasso. He didn't break the rules until after he mastered them.

"So that's my other purpose here," she said. "To look again at the traditional arts. To study the inward improvisation."

"You better help me with that."

"Me too," Brian added.

"Listen to this music," Yumi said.

A saxophone wailed over an undulating backbeat, with subtle strength from a low bass melody. The notes came out crisp and clear from speakers hung high in the corners.

"This is a familiar piece," Yumi said. "These musicians know it so well that they either improvise within it, adding to it, or play something different, then smoothly return to the original melody. They listen to each other and react to the different moods and musical ideas. With good jazz musicians, a song is never played quite the same way twice. Which is why Japanese are such jazz lovers. They love the individuality of the players, adding their interpretation."

Typically, I thought of her words in the context of sport, of great players inventing creative responses to routine challenges. Her words also gave me a new understanding of jazz, or at least the theoretical possibilities of jazz, but I didn't know the songs or the instruments well enough to perceive the improvisations.

Yumi shrugged. "It takes years."

"So what is inward improvisation, as opposed to outward?"

"Just my way of labeling it. Outward improvisation is to improve something by creating something new. Inward improvisation goes deeper into an established style. Adding nuances."

For the first time, I noticed the silver strands in her hair. She was older than I had first realized. Her voice was soft now.

"The Japanese way has always been study and emulate. We studied the Chinese for centuries, then westerners. Except that we never take anything 'as is.' We always adapt it slightly, make it more appropriate or pleasing to our needs."

"Often you improve it," I said. "American companies have repeatedly developed products that the Japanese subsequently make better, stronger, and cheaper."

She smiled. "We are not so strong on original ideas, but we are masters of detail."

"What you call inward improvisation."

"It applies to everything, from companies to individuals. We study the master."

"We saw that at the driving range," Brian said. "Wouldn't you say, Rick?"

I nodded and described for Yumi the skill of the man in black and the crowd of golfers watching him. When I mentioned his implacable poise, Yumi seized my words instantly. "You asked me what was important about sports. It is just that, what you saw today, something so much easier to watch then to describe. That is *essence*."

I knew instantly what she meant. I had seen that utter focus before; I felt it myself at times. It was wonderful, like a cocoon of concentration that settles over you to muffle all distraction. Your senses become heightened and you can detect the subtlest of details about your game. Best of all, you feel a strange connectedness that extends even beyond the game and your immediate surrounding.

"In Japan," Yumi said, "that attitude, that state of being, is an important part of what a master conveys. It is beyond mere technique. In fact, it is what eventually elevates technique into mastery."

"In art or sports?" I asked.

"Sport is an art when properly performed. That's why we call judo and karate the martial arts. There is also the Art of Tea, the Art of Flower Arranging, and so on. We believe it is the attitude and not the activity that is important."

The attitude. I remembered Pursig's[3] last conversation with his son as they discussed him maintaining his own motorcycle. "Is it hard?" the boy asks. "Not if you have the right attitudes," Pursig replied. "It's having the right attitudes that's hard."

I confess to seeing Yumi in a new light. Until that moment she was a beautiful, fascinating woman. Suddenly, I wondered if she couldn't teach me, or at least, help me learn.

But this thought made me instantly self-conscious. I wanted to say the right thing now, but I simply blurted out, "Are your classes open to visitors?"

"I don't think so. Why?"

"Well, I . . . I'd like to learn more about this."

"I've already loaned Brian some books. Perhaps he will pass them along to you." Brian shrugged and nodded amiably.

"That would be good, thanks." I searched for the next words. "Perhaps we could meet for a drink sometime and talk about them?"

A trace of a smile crossed Yumi's face. She turned to Brian and said, "Is he asking me for a date?"

Brian laughed. "I think he is."

Yumi didn't press the teasing. "I'm busy most evenings," she said. "But if you want, I'll meet you here next Sunday afternoon. There are a few things I can show you."

I agreed, of course, feeling the excitement rise. I'm not sure which of my urges was stronger. Brian winked and refilled my drink, then we sat back and listened to more "inward improvisations."

In the coming days, I was ever more aware of Japanese culture. I learned that most of my housemates, the longtime residents at

3   Robert Pursig is the author of the landmark book *Zen and the Art of Motorcycle Maintenance* (Corgi/Bantam).

Yoshida House, had one thing in common; to satisfy the require-
ments for an extended visa, they were all studying some traditional
discipline. Classes in the various arts—flower arranging, calligraphy,
pottery, judo, karate, *aikido*, and in the Japanese language—were all
accessible and reasonably priced. Some amongst us welcomed this as
an opportunity, but I knew already that many foreigners regarded this
cultural stipulation as a nuisance. So much to learn in Japan, but too
few had the thirst.

Everywhere I went, it was highly apparent that the Japanese
attitude toward learning was quite different. Diligent study, both of
visitors and of their respective traditions, was evident in merchandise, architecture, transportation, sports, fashion, food—in virtually
everything. This was an historical pattern, I learned, reading Brian's
dog-eared copy of *Zen and Japanese Culture* (Valore Books), by the
acclaimed Japanese scholar Daisetz Suzuki. The Japanese studied
China through most of her history, adopting her ancient ideas, then
did the same with the Western nations, first in the fifteenth century,
then again after United States forced open her borders in 1853. But
in ancient times as now, the Japanese modified ideas, products, and
processes, and along the way adapted them to their own needs and
preferences. Very often, as the world has discovered, these hybrids
became better than the original.

Only once, for 250 years in the Edo period, did the Japanese close
their doors to foreign influence. After the "barbarians" were expelled
in late sixteenth century until the "black ship" of Admiral Perry in
1853, they used the work of their own Masters as guides for emu-
lation and innovation. In a process of steady, if somewhat bizarre,
evolvement, they attained the artistic and cultural refinement that
not only characterizes this period, but largely epitomizes the aesthet-
ics and discipline of Japan.

I was drawn in by Suzuki's book, and by others I found about
Japanese culture, and I spent long hours reading them while commuting through Tokyo or sitting at my low table by the window in
my room. In fact, as my money concerns subsided, the days took on

a calm, orderly flow, and I found myself increasingly enjoying the peaceful rhythm of Japanese life. Facilities were clean and functional; people were polite and considerate; events occurred on schedule. Seen as a whole, there were very few distractions.

Were it not for my skis, standing tall in my room like sentinels guarding my dreams, I could have easily passed a peaceful winter in Tokyo. But every night, coming home, those skis reminded me that days were slipping past, and I had no better idea than before about a skiing job. The ski resorts were opening now, as the colder Siberian air brought snow to the mountains, and skiers were often riding the subways with their luggage. Sports stores bulged with the latest para-phernalia, and ski advertisements tormented me in shop windows and the subway. Was I crazy to torture myself with vague hope?

seven

Thoughts of Yumi orbited my mind constantly during that week. The image of her—the supple walk, the lustrous black hair, the slender neck—remained with me as I rode in on the subway and talked my way through the slow sessions at ESS. I tried to focus on my customers, but I was beset by wisps of memory. Even when it's a pleasant image or thought, it is exasperating when some idea or worry or hope lingers long in your mind, like a visiting friend who overstays his welcome. When you need to focus, these distractions are like raindrops on the surface of a pond, each marring the waters of reflection. My work, my relationships, my finances—these were all easy enough to fret about, but nothing could distract me more easily than a woman. Whether biological or psychological, it wasn't logical.

On Monday evening, fortunately, I had something else that demanded my attention. At 7 P.M., I had my first group lesson at the Matsushita factory. I went out early to beat the rush hour, riding a quiet, immaculately clean subway for seventy minutes to a small suburban district. It was growing dark as I arrived, and I walked the main street while the evening bustle mounted. The sidewalks were full with students in uniform, mothers with babies, grandmothers in kimonos, and, finally, wave after wave of businessmen in blue suits, known as "salary men," descending haggard from the raised subway platform.

The community felt comfortable. It was modern, like Tokyo, yet there seemed to be more civility, more community, here. People shopped, walked, and talked on the street, waving and bowing to friends and customers. There was haggling and gossiping going on, as there usually is in the marketplaces of the world. Except in North American cities, that is, or in pockets of 'modernity' patterned after America, where people too often go to massive shopping centers where they seldom know the vendors or meet their neighbors. Sadly, that is shopping devoid of its social aspect. The mall environment, however convenient and profitable, cannot replace the Main Street as a place where one can go and simply be amidst other people. Many of us live alone in our houses and apartments, and too seldom enjoy this familiar social place where we can see and hear others in a neutral setting.

Finally, it came time for my lesson. I went to the guardhouse at the gate to the Matsushita factory. I gave my name, received a visitor's badge, and was led to second story room in a plain brick building. My group was already waiting. There were ten men in all, middle-aged managers in blue factory overalls and ties. Judging from their faces and postures, it was apparent that they considered themselves still at work.

I introduced myself and asked them all to do the same. One by one, they stood up straight, not quite at attention, and performed this feat in the fewest number of seconds possible.

"Fine," I said. "Now let's go more slowly and say, 'My name is' beforehand."

This took considerably longer, but I could tell immediately who had language confidence. They all had books in front of them, and there was a teacher's copy for me. I opened it to the marker and found extraordinarily dry lesson material. When I glanced up, no one looked too excited about it. "Is this the book you always use?"

A slim man stood up. "Yes, sir."

I clapped the book shut and said, "First of all, my name is Rick, and you don't have to stand up to speak. Secondly, if you don't mind, I think we should forget the book for now and get to know each other. We'll worry about lessons later."

The group looked at each other and then together closed their workbooks. Several sat up with new interest. *Now what?* I thought.

"Why don't you tell me your position, and what kind of work you do?"

You could almost hear the foreheads creasing in confusion. Talk about their work? No one looked happy at the prospect. *Bad choice,* I decided.

"I've got a better idea. What sports do you like? Sumo? Karate?"

They looked at me like I was crazy, until the slim man spoke again. "I like baseball."

"Me also," said another nervously. Around the room heads nodded.

That broke the ice. Now we had a topic we all knew and cared about. From there it grew much easier until, a few minutes later, we were actually having a little fun. We talked first about Japanese professional baseball, and about the legendary hitter, Sadaharu Oh, who had surpassed Hank Aaron in home runs. When the topic shifted to high school baseball, and then to Japanese players on U.S. professional teams, the group became much more vocal and opinionated. I had no idea baseball was so popular, or the fans so passionate. By now, everyone was talking with something close to enthusiasm. When I looked at my watch, the hour was nearly gone.

The most heated discussion was the last one: "Which bar should we all go to?"

Apparently it had been decided that their new teacher, who they now addressed as Mr. Rick, or Rick-san, should come for snacks and drinks. "Please be our guest," they implored.

Sushi was weighed against tempura or noodles, chefs and hostesses were compared until, somehow, a consensus was reached. We set out immediately, walking the darkened streets in buoyant spirits. The restaurant was small, tucked away in a back alley. The waitresses and cooks sang out a welcome as the warmth and aroma enveloped us. Saké and beer appeared instantly and took swift effect. Within minutes, faces were red and ties and tongues were loose.

The quietest amongst them became bold. "We work six days a week," said Hibino, a large man with soft jowls that grew pink and then scarlet as he drank. "We don't want to, but we have no choice."

The others nodded and murmured the national mantra of agreement: *"So, neh."*

"Our offices are open rooms so everyone can see," Hibino said. "When the quitting bell rings and others keep working, we cannot leave in front of them. Eight, nine, ten o'clock goes by sometimes. Only when the older workers leave can the junior members go."

I watched for a reaction from the others. Hibino was speaking very boldly now, with much more vehemence than I had yet heard in Japan, except from Yumi. But instead of shocked silence, I saw nods of agreement around the table. I ventured a question. "What about Saturday. Isn't that a holiday?"

"Yes, but if someone says he is coming in, which is always, then it's bad team spirit to let him work alone."

I looked over at the youngest man. "How long does it take you to get home?"

He looked at me blankly. "I don't go home," he said. "Single men stay in the company dormitory. We must save money to get married."

I digested those notions, then looked back to Hibino. "Well, you're married, right. You can go home?" He nodded. "How long does it take?"

"One and a half hours, each way."

"If you work ten or eleven hours, six days a week, and have that traveling every day, when do you see your kids?"

"On Sunday," he said glumly, downing his beer in a long guzzle. I sat back in my seat, considering this. Hibino used the words "team spirit," yet he used them with a strange emphasis. It wasn't the "team spirit" I knew.

None of them owned a house. "Impossible," they said emphatically. Speculation, once unthinkable in Japan, had driven prices well beyond a workingman's reach. Everyone lives in apartments, or "rabbit hutches," as they are scornfully known.

As the evening wore on, we all got quite drunk. I couldn't help myself. Every time I put my glass down, somebody was filling it up for me. Meanwhile, the grumbling was getting louder and louder, and I wondered again if such talk was appropriate. The complaints had shifted to the younger workers at the factory, to the younger generation. Hibino, who was by now alarmingly red, spoke for the group. "We have a saying for these people. We call them 'a new kind of human.'"

The others agreed noisily.

"They have poor attitude," he said. "They won't work hard. They don't care about quality. They don't give us proper respect. It's terrible. We have to obey our superiors but we don't get the same support from below us."

This set off another round of nods and sighs. Youthful rebellion was a popular topic of late, and much was written in the newspapers. Students struck or openly defied their teachers, they cut classes, and they often refused to yield their subway seats to the elderly. This generation was accustomed to affluence, with no firsthand knowledge of the hardships of the post-war era.

I escaped in time to catch the last train, suffered the next day with a hangover, and then on Wednesday evening saw the other end of this societal assembly line. Seven pre-school children poured into my tiny classroom, each with his or her own cartoon-covered backpack and a loud excited laugh. They were well behaved for the most part, opening their books as bidden, parroting phrases on cue, but it was obvious, particularly as the lesson wore on, that they were bored. They repeated words and sentences dutifully, but not one of them cared about English. They were just obeying their parents' orders.

Childhood tutoring. I had read for years about the Japanese system, but never imagined the pressure or the process. As I looked at the young faces around the room, it was hard to comprehend that they were preparing for examinations that would determine their future. How could that be?

After my class, Mrs. Takahashi called me into the closet she called an office. I swallowed hard, hoping my performance had been satisfactory. She had come in about half way through my class, watched expressionless for ten minutes, then left without a word or a sign. Was I to be praised or admonished?

Mrs. Takahashi sat me it down, clearing the only other chair in the office of its stack of workbooks. At first, she shifted them to her crowded desktop, then she changed her mind and instead created a precarious pile on the filing cabinet. When the phone rang in mid-stack and she glared at it, I felt sorry for her suddenly. Mrs. Takahashi was middle-aged and dignified, and the demands of her business were wearing her thin.

Still, she answered with the poise typical of Japanese woman. Her voice was melodic suddenly and completely receptive, totally belying the frustration I had glimpsed. After a short conversation, with protracted "Thank yous" and "Good-byes," and an extra pause to make sure that she was the last to set down the receiver, she turned to me.

"We have a problem in your class today."

My heart sank. "My lesson was . . . "

She waved her hand in front of her face, fingers upward. This meant no.

"Your teaching was fine. Very good actually. This problem is quite different."

I waited, much relieved.

"You remember the boy I brought in late today?"

I nodded. When she had come in mid-lesson, she had escorted a fresh-faced youngster who sat quietly the rest of the class.

"His mother came to see me today. Her husband, the boy's father, is being transferred to Osaka."

"He has to leave?"

"Quite the opposite. He and his mother are staying in Tokyo. The father has chosen to live alone in Osaka and visit on holidays."

"Why?"

"In Japan, we worry about children's relationships. The boy is familiar with his friends and his school situation here. The parents don't want to disrupt that."

"But he would make new friends in Osaka."

"Perhaps. But perhaps not, also. Making new friends is not so easy in Japan. And the danger of not being accepted by his schoolmates is very great."

"But he's only five years old."

"That is a difficult and sensitive time."

The phone rang again. Mrs. Takahashi removed her left earring and lifted the headphone, "*Moshi, moshi.*"

I was stunned by the notion that a five-year-old boy couldn't adapt to a new environment! This was far from the prevalent thinking surrounding my childhood which was, pretty much, "Kids are flexible. They make new friends." I suppose this was largely true, but I remembered the hard good-byes, sometimes tearful, when a classmate walked out of our lives. I also remembered the painful awkwardness that newcomers felt, standing by the door as the principal introduced them to their new class. In time we would all know them, but at that moment, they looked like the loneliest people on earth.

Mrs. Takahashi hung up the phone and turned to me. At the mother's request, I was to keep an eye on the boy and to report any unusual behavior. I wasn't sure if I would even recognize it, but I agreed. In the remaining few minutes, I asked a few questions about her school and generally tried to schmooze my way into another class. But it was too soon for that, or there was nothing else available, for she remained quiet on the subject.

After leaving her office I swung by the jazz club in hopes of seeing Yumi. Sunday seemed far away, too long to wait. I wanted to ask her about those kids and the men at Matsushita. I want to hear her frank opinions and unusual insight. Most of all, I suppose, I wanted to look at her again.

But she wasn't there. I ordered a beer, and chose a stool at the bar where I could watch the door. Every time someone entered, I looked to see if it was her. The beer was cold and it tasted good going down, and before long I ordered another. I let the music fill me, lift me, carry me off on its magical transport. It felt good to relax.

After the second beer was gone, and I had glanced several more times to the door, I decided I'd had enough. I zipped up my old leather coat and headed out into the cold evening. I wasn't nearly drunk but the beer did change my perception. I looked around me at the shops and the people rushing past and saw it all again with fresh eyes. It is so easy to grow accustomed to things, even Tokyo on a winter's night when you're 9,000 miles from home.

There was a bright noisy place with rows of glass boxes that looked like vertical pinball machines, each with a zealot on a stool with a basket of silver balls. Further down were several shops and cafes with signs like "Lucky Spot" or "Good Time Place," or some other name that looked silly in literal English translation. In a quieter section, there was a Torii gate and a flagstone path toward a darkened shrine. At a restaurant window, I stood and watched a sushi chef slicing fish and preparing sushi. Even from a distance, his concentration was evident and his swift, sure strokes with the knife were mesmerizing.

I reached the subway and climbed to the platform. The green Yamanote train roared in shortly and carried me off around the city. On the broad boulevards there were cars and colorful lights, but great patches were slumbering in darkness. Tokyo was like that. Divided. Organized. Everything in its place. There was a pattern too, a flow, that I was already finding so very easy and comfortable to slip into.

eight

Sunday finally arrived. I headed down early and found the club just opening when I arrived. A waitress was wiping down tables and the bartender was polishing glasses, both working with the overpowering moodiness of Miles Davis on the cranked up stereo. Noticing me, the bartender moved to lower the volume, but I waved him off.

I sat at my usual stool, ordered a coffee, and sat back to wait. I'd worked in restaurants and bars myself, and there was something so pleasant about the start of a new day. When you open the doors and walk through the empty tables, you can feel, almost hear, the energy of the night before. The staff arrives gradually, exchanging greetings and laughter like teammates coming to a clubhouse. Everyone gets in uniform and performs his preparations, then the doors open and the game begins again.

I had just purchased an English version of *The Japan Times*, so I fished it out of my pack, scanned the headlines, then turned to the sports page. Like many men, I read the sports page first, before the world and business news. At least there you find victory and defeat in equal proportion, with frequent emphasis on the successes and triumphs of the human spirit. There are characters in sport greater than any movie or soap opera, and heroes who become so without a single life lost. You follow your favorite athletes for years, thrilling in their victories, sharing with them their setbacks. Teams, too, capture our imagination, whether they represent our city or our nation. Through them, with them, we get vicarious thrills and associative joy, enhanced even more by the delicious details in each day's newspaper.

The Japan Times' sports section consisted of summaries and game scores of overseas competition, as well as brief articles on local sports. Seeing, in the top corner, a photograph of a hockey player, I quickly scanned the story.

A familiar name caught my eye. A friend of mine from Edmonton, Randy Gregg, was the playing coach of a Japanese professional hockey team. His club, the Kokudo Bunnies, was due to start a tournament that week in Tokyo. I couldn't believe it; Randy was playing hockey in Japan!

I looked up to see Yumi in the doorway, backlit by the afternoon sun. Given my anticipation, such an entrance was appropriately dramatic. She greeted me coolly however.

"Ready to go?" she asked, her voice strained.

I nodded, threw down money for the coffee, and followed her out. We had walked barely fifty yards when she said, without looking up, "I'm not quite myself today."

I stopped walking. Yumi stood ahead of me, staring at the leafless skeleton of a young tree. "Let's just grab a coffee," I suggested.

She averted my gaze, and spoke in a quavering voice, "It's all right. Let's go."

She resumed walking and I fell in beside her. After awhile she apologized. "I had a bad night with my father. He's in pain so we didn't get much sleep."

"Let's do this another day."

"No, it's good to get out. He feels better in the daytime."

"Is your mother with him?" I asked.

"My aunt is visiting. My mother died last year."

"I'm sorry."

"Me too," she said softly. We walked silently a little further, then she added, "I was in New York at the time. Another sin in my father's eyes."

"Is this your first time back?"

"No. I came back for the funeral. But he was so mad and hurt he wouldn't talk to me." Her replies came slowly. Each phrase was sad, and seconds elapsed between them.

"He was afraid too. He'd been with my mom for fifty years."

"Fifty years!"

"They married early and had me late. The only child. I think I was a mistake."

The silence hung heavy. Finally, she continued. "So I went straight back to New York, and didn't talk to him for several months. Then my aunt phoned and said he was sick."

"When was that?"

"Three months ago. I called right away, but he wouldn't speak to me. Stubborn male pride. I had to get the details from my aunt, and basically, it wasn't good. A few months, maybe more, and meanwhile, he's cooking and cleaning for himself and doing the books at his school, things my mother had always taken care of."

"What kind of school?"

"A tiny pottery studio with a small shop to sell his work. But it's a shambles now, and that's partly what I'm doing, getting his things in order."

We had come to a busy street lined with billboards and signs. We were walking fast now, and Yumi evidently had a destination in mind.

"Where are we going?" I asked.

"To a painting exhibit."

A gallery. Not something I would've sought out myself. We strolled along, looking in shop windows, going in occasionally to check merchandise more closely. Almost in passing, Yumi asked, "How was your week?"

I described my baseball talk with the Matsushita managers and my young student who couldn't be relocated, but she said nothing. When I told her about the regulars at ESS, however, and how I tried to collect opinions and impressions, she reacted strongly.

"You're wasting your time. Anyone coming to a place like that isn't thinking like a typical Japanese any longer." Yumi said this with conviction, with the vigor of our first conversation. "As for the frustrations of those managers, take a look at these women instead."

We were in a small shop, and she was alluding to the uniformed sales clerks, all bustling about. "This is what most Japanese women have to look forward to. Their most important function is to bow correctly and welcome customers perfectly. You find them in every store and restaurant."

We stepped from the store onto the busy sidewalk. Yumi was fully transformed now, back into "social analyst" mode.

"Their equivalent in the big companies is the 'office girl,'" she said. "It's changing a little now, but basically, women in Japan have no power, no responsibility, no real hope of advancement. They are expected to work a few years, then get married, raise children, and take care of their husbands, men like your overworked Mitsubishi managers. Tell me, who has the better life?"

As she spoke, Yumi turned into a large department store and moved at a lightning pace through the aisles. We came to an elevator where a young attendant was demonstrating Yumi's point perfectly. With her waist on a hinge and her mouth in constant use, she bowed and welcomed, bowed and welcomed continuously. When the elevator was full she came in, closed the doors, and began reciting what was on the next floor. The process was repeated on every floor, the girl thanking and bowing like a well-wound doll.

When we left the elevator, Yumi continued. "It's the same everywhere. That's why I left Japan."

I didn't know how to respond, so we walked on in silence through the tasteful and impeccably clean store. We came to a line-up, a single file snaking back fifty yards through the store. Yumi joined in at the end. "This is it," she said.

"What is 'it,' exactly?"

"Impressionist paintings."

"Here? In a department store?"

"This is a very wealthy company."

I wracked my brain, trying to remember more about the Impressionists, but I couldn't pull back much. French. Late nineteenth century. That was about it. But the line was moving steadily, so I'd learn more soon.

We shuffled past elaborate displays in each department, Yumi pointing out the newest versions of clothes, toys, and appliances. "This is just unbelievable," she said. "Japan has become the trendiest country in the world."

"How about the French or the Italians?"

"This is far bigger than clothes or cars. It's a total culture thing. Whatever is popular here, becomes incredibly popular."

"That's not so different. In the States—"

"But it's much easier to control and manipulate in Japan. America is so big, with so many types of people and such different attitudes. Here everyone thinks alike. And if they're not sure what to do, or to say, or to buy, they just follow the expression, 'Do as the person on your right.'"

"Isn't price a factor? And quality?"

"Yes, but not in the way you would think. At least, not like America. Price comparison is just starting in Japan. Until now, people would gladly pay a high price to buy from a prestigious company, to carry their purchase home in a well known shopping bag, or to present a gift wrapped in distinctive paper. It was worth it, just to associate with the prestige of a famous company."

"Why is it changing now?"

"Discount chains, either American or patterned after American. People are choosing to get the same product for less money."

"Why wouldn't they do that before?"

"The old thinking was too strong. It still is, really, but it's eroding."

"Sorry. I don't get it."

"Sociologists call Japan a *vertical society*. Everything here is organized up and down, top to bottom. Hierarchy is very important.

Japanese attach great importance to the number one thing, what we call *Ichi-ban*. This attracts more respect."

"Why would that affect a man when he's shopping?"

"Because he wants to buy the number one product at the number one store. If he wants a watch, he wants a Rolex. If he buys Scotch whisky, he wants imported Scotch, preferably Johnny Walker Black or some aged single malt. You see, it's not just the physical product. It's the reputation of the product or the company or the country. If it is the best, the *Ichi-ban*, then you gain respect by associating with it."

"Isn't it the same everywhere?" I asked. "People in every country want quality."

"True. But in Japan the process has been reduced to a science."

I thought about this awhile, and then replied, "Or elevated to an art form."

"Association with quality is why your young students are taking tutorials when they're only five years old. If they're accepted into good primary schools, they will later enter similar high schools, and eventually, the top universities."

"Doesn't their performance have something to do with it?"

"Of course they must do well. But everyone does well."

"But some students are smarter," I pointed out.

"That's not so obvious here. Teachers here value the progress of the class more than individual brilliance. Your final test scores are far less important here than the name and reputation of the schools you have attended. That's like a pedigree."

"So it's this 'respect by association' thing?"

"That's right. Graduates from top universities go almost automatically into the government or some highly reputable company."

"Into social status."

Yumi nodded.

And then, I thought, even though their adult work schedules would be arduous, like my Matsushita managers, the respect accorded them would make their lives more tolerable. It was an incredible concept.

"In the West, it's quite different," I said. "You have to prove yourself as you go along. Qualify at each level."

"You're right. It is different. More than you realize. You were controlled carefully as a child, but given responsibility as you got older. More and more freedom coming with age. In Japan, it is the opposite. You are never more free than as a child. Children are adored here. Almost never punished. But as you have seen, as soon as children enter school, they enter a system that places more restrictions and obligations on them as they grow older. Reaching adulthood in Japan means accepting a tightly prescribed role, whereas young Americans are expected to think and act for themselves when they graduate."

Yumi's insight was amazing. Where had she learned all this? And what if she had not rebelled and gone to America, and was today one of these sales clerks, seething with frustration and unrealized potential?

She was still talking. "You have to be patient, hard-working, and self-effacing in Japanese society, and that is exactly what students are taught in school."

I interrupted her. "Whereas in North America, you're told that you are an individual, free to form your own point of view. Work habits are important too, but we stress personal ambition and initiative."

"Here they don't want individual thinking. They want consensus."

"But my students say the new generation is different. They call them a 'new breed of human.'"

Yumi nodded, checking her watch. "After this, I'll take you to see some of these 'new humans.'"

We had reached the head of the line and were heading into the exhibit. There were twenty or so paintings, each with a soft spotlight and an attentive guard. I recognized several of the canvases and wanted to stop, but the relentless surge of the line behind us prevented much discussion. It seemed incredible, works by Monet, Degas, Renoir, and others, all extraordinarily valuable, hanging in a temporary gallery between rugs and home furnishings.

I tried to memorize them, to let the images imprint on my consciousness. They were simple in composition generally, women working in a field or a basket of fruit on a sun-drenched table, but in each there seemed to be a distinct mood, a warmth of light and spirit. Also interesting, to my untrained eye, was how seemingly random patches of paint were quite effective and recognizable as part of the larger painting. I asked Yumi about this as we left the exhibit.

"You're right," she said. "The techniques were different. The subjects were different. Almost everything about these paintings was different."

"This would be 'outward improvisation.'"

Yumi smiled. "That's right. One of the largest shifts in Western art history. And it was influenced by Japan."

"How is that?"

"Look over there." Yumi was pointing toward a sales clerk carefully wrapping a shopper's purchase in colorful patterned paper.

"I don't understand."

"Wrapping paper. After Japan was opened to the West in 1853, merchants exported things to Europe wrapped in paper that they considered worthless. But these wood block prints, very common in Japan, were totally foreign to Europeans. The Asian use of line, the flat perspective, the subject matter—it was all very different to the Western way of seeing. These French painters were the first to incorporate that."

"How did they get the name *Impressionists?*"

"There are lots of opinions. For me, their paintings capture mood. They were all were very interested in light, and some of them painted the same subject over and over at different times of day, trying to preserve the feeling as it changed."

Capturing the moment, I thought. How interesting. My thoughts shifted back to Yumi, who was examining a blanket. Her hands were delicate and they moved with soft sureness. Her hair was pulled up under a velvet hat but a wisp draped softly over the nape of her neck. Trying not to stare, I instead asked, "How do you know about art history?"

"In university I studied to be an art teacher, like my father."

But at the mention of her father, she changed the subject. "Let's go. I want to show you something else."

We dropped on the elevator to a sparkling clean subway station. A train whisked in and shuttled us quickly to our destination, *Harajuku*, where we came above ground into a festival atmosphere. There were people everywhere, with hundreds of costumed teenagers milling about.

"This way," Yumi said, pulling me down a boulevard that was closed to traffic.

"What's the rush?"

"This only lasts until five o'clock."

I wasn't even sure what "this" was. There were ten or more groups, ranging in size from a dozen to a hundred, spaced along a three-hundred-yard street. They stood in circles around portable stereos and a pile of their knapsacks. Some kids were dancing, but most were watching their leader in the center. There were hundreds of onlookers on the sidewalk, several with cameras. The first group, the largest, appeared to be a James Dean look-a-like contest. They all wore black leather jackets and slicked back hair. As we passed, each member was down on one knee, listening prayerfully to the leader. Another group was dressed like elves in airy costumes and glittery make-up. Beyond them, pseudo-punks and gays and a host of other groups stretched down the street, all gathered or dancing around in circles. Were it not so staged, so evidently self-conscious, the groupings would have had the appearance of tribal behavior. Their stereos were their ceremonial flame, warming them to their ritual dances.

The most telling moment came precisely at five o'clock, after police removed the barricades at the end of the block and a wave of traffic sent the groups scattering. Several dancers disappeared into the trees of the nearby park, reappearing minutes later in street clothes.

The implication was clear: Before five, they could stand rebelliously with the group of their choice, but when it came time to go home, they had to appear as expected before their parents.

I kept expecting a commentary on the dancers and their sudden identity change, but Yumi had fallen silent. She was off in her thoughts, walking and watching the scene around us. It seemed I was a pleasant distraction, someone that reminded her of New York and the life she had left on hold.

The young dancers were everywhere on the crowded sidewalks, walking in small groups, now carrying their radical personalities in paper bags. To me, they appeared as bohemians of convenience. They weren't rebelling; they were acting—imitating people who actually lived those lives twenty-four hours a day. That's the one thing about true individuality. It's not part time. It's not always pleasant either.

Yumi was a perfect example. She had acted on her urges, left her home and father, forged a new life. It couldn't have been easy, a woman, a solitary child, resisting her father in a culture based on obedience. And now she was pulled between two countries, so changed by America that she could never again fit back into Japan.

Of course, I was now caught in this same bind. Like Yumi, I'd left virtually everything behind—old friends, old attitudes, old expectations. And what did I get in return? Where had my stark individuality taken me? I was alone in a foreign country. My family and friends were worried about me. I had more questions than answers. And I couldn't go back.

We wandered toward *Roppongi*, the entertainment district. The streets were brightly lit now and crowded like a carnival midway, with couples arm in arm or in groups of six or eight. Everything seemed clean and orderly, except that far too often we saw drunken men staggering down the street. On one corner, a young man was vomiting horribly in the gutters.

Yumi was disgusted. "The drinking is very bad right now. Everyone gets bonuses in December so they can afford too much alcohol."

"Don't Japanese men drink all the time?"

She nodded. "Drinking is important in Japan, especially in business. It promotes communication."

I thought immediately of my Matsushita group, and how anxious they all were to get me drinking. And undoubtedly, they did become more vocal. There was just one question. "But Japanese get drunk so easily. Isn't this embarrassing?"

Yumi turned to me. "This is hard to explain but important to understand. Since Japanese people are sensitive about shame, we have an understanding that if you have been drinking, even a little bit, you are no longer responsible for what you say or do."

The glow of the neon sign was on her face, and some flashing advertisement was reflecting in the glassiness of her eye. At once I was seeing all this, the drunken man in the background, and the revelry of passers-by. I had heard what she said, but it didn't seem possible. "Say that again please."

"If you've been drinking," Yumi repeated, "you don't have to worry about embarrassment or loss of respect. This point is very important for Japanese."

This stunned me. "How much do you have to drink?"

"If you have even one sip of whiskey, beer, or sake, you can talk without fear. Even if you throw up or insult someone, the next day it is like it never happened. Everything is simply forgotten."

"You mean ignored."

"No. I mean forgotten. Never spoken of again."

To hear her describe it, alcohol was like a safety valve, letting steam out of the pressure cooker of Japanese living. The ramifications were astounding. All those businessmen, suppressed all day like my Matsushita students, could suddenly speak truthfully, release the opinions and anger they had been building up. All it took was a drink.

The notion that this was a 'national understanding' was equally bizarre, like it was an enormous family secret that wasn't to be discussed, a massive, collective, and individual denial process. Essentially, drinking had been ritualized, adapted in a weird way to meet a cultural need.

Suddenly we turned a corner and were back at the jazz club where we started. I was taken by surprise, but quickly suggested that we have a drink. Yumi waited a moment before responding, her face bathed in the streetlight. A smile came to her lips, and I thought she would agree. But she didn't.

"Thank you for a nice day," she said. "But I should go home to my father now."

"I understand," I said. "Would you like to meet again?"

Again the smile. "Perhaps," she said. "I'll call you."

With that and a small wave, she was gone. I watched until she disappeared around the corner, then went inside for a beer. I needed it. The whole day was a blur—the paintings, the dancers, the insights of Yumi. I now had a tutor of sorts, but what was I learning exactly? About the process of learning partly. About Japanese culture certainly. But about myself too, and Western culture, for every time I turned around, I heard or saw something that put my own society in a different light. And it wasn't just me anymore, being overly analytical. Yumi was straddling two worlds also.

nine

At breakfast the next morning I pulled the sports page out of my pack and reread the hockey story. Randy's team would be playing Monday, Wednesday, and Friday night in some kind of round robin tournament. I had to teach Monday night, but I could see either of the second two games. Brian was sitting across from me. I told him about Randy and asked if he'd like to go.

He feigned sarcasm. "Stand in the cold to watch grown men fight over a piece of rubber. Sounds like fun."

"Wednesday or Friday. Take your pick."

"Have to be Wednesday. I'm starting *Aikido* on Friday."

"*Aikido?*"

"Yeah, at the main *dojo*. I checked it out last week. Mostly Japanese but several French and a few other foreigners. I wanted to start right away but they had to special order my get-up. Over here I'm a triple extra large."

My curiosity was piqued. "How much are lessons?"

"By the month, about forty dollars, I reckon." It was apparent that Brian and I were both newcomers to Japan. We still thought in dollars not yen.

"Too rich for my blood," I said, and turned back to the sports page. "Says here that the games start at seven. I teach Wednesday afternoon, but we can meet at the rink. I'll call Randy to see if he can meet us for a drink afterwards."

"Hold on," Brian said, looking up from his plate. "Wednesday won't work. I'm meeting Yumi for a drink."

This was news to me. I hoped my surprise didn't show. "What time?"

"Nine."

"Come anyway then. You can leave after two periods."

Brian nodded. "Why don't your bring your hockey friend and join us?"

"We'll see," I said. I was surprised at not knowing about their "date," hurt at not being invited earlier, and mad at myself for both unreasonable reactions.

I heard Jun Yoshida's voice in the hall, talking to his wife. Since it was Monday, they were changing all our bed linens. Clutching my newspaper, I went out and asked for help contacting Randy. Jun agreed easily and picked up the hall phone. Three calls later, after much mention of Canada and my name, he handed me the receiver.

A little surprised, I said a cautious, "Hello?"

"Rick, it's Randy. What are you doing here?"

"Me? What about you?"

"I played a tournament here in university. After I graduated they called me." He went on to tell me the story of his recruitment, then asked again about me.

"My story's more complicated. Why don't we get together after your game Wednesday night and I'll tell you about it?"

"That'll work. Come down to the bench afterwards."

"Fine. See you then." I hung down, a little amazed. Randy had always been an extraordinary fellow. He hadn't just played in university. He had captained his team, the Golden Bears, to the national title, and then gone on to play in the Olympics for Canada. He could likely have turned pro but had instead come to play in Japan. Besides this, he was a tremendous baseball player, one of the best in Canada, and had just graduated from medical school.

Looking to thank Jun, I found him in one of the rooms, making up the bed. He straightened as I entered, saying, "Ah, Rick-san. I've been wanting to talk with you. Kohei is coming next week."

"Coming from Banff. Now?" It was surprising since our mutual friend ran a charter company and this was prime tour season.

Jun shrugged. "Just a short trip, I guess, to see his parents. I told him you were here and he wants to meet with you."

"That's great," I said, but I could hardly believe it. Out of the blue, I suddenly had another friend in Tokyo. Jun was going to set up the meeting and call me, so I thanked him profusely and went to get ready for work.

The days were picking up speed now. Before I knew it, I was down at ESS, holding court for timid newcomers, back on the subway to go talk baseball and eat sushi with my Matsushita group, then back to ESS all day Tuesday, then over to my young pre-schoolers on Wednesday afternoon. I finished with just enough time to make it to the arena for the hockey game.

Brian was waiting at the entrance, drawing a few stares. We bought tickets and entered, coming through the grandstand tunnel near ice level where the teams could be seen at close range performing their warm-up. The sounds were so familiar—the rhythmic biting of steel blades into ice, the thumping of pucks against boards, the smack of sticks against the ice—they reminded of how intimately I knew the game of hockey. After twenty years, I knew how to play a "four man box" or stymie a "two on one," how to reverse in a corner and escape a thundering blow, or how to visualize a pass through a swirl of moving players and make real that possibility in an instant. But I also knew how difficult these things were, how infinitesimal were the margins, how great the pressures, and how very easy it was to hesitate and be beaten. This, too, was a world I had explored.

The teams skated swiftly in large circles, peeling off one at a time to fire hard shots at the goaltender. Brian flinched several times as pucks or bodies struck the glass in front of us, but his eyes were wide and he was obviously enjoying it. His reaction wasn't surprising. Men can skate faster, and with far more agility, than they can run. The puck travels more quickly yet, and with a degree of control that is uncanny.

"Is that your friend?" Brian pointed to a huge player standing by the bench talking to the coach. I nodded. His size was unmistakable, as was his red hair. Brian realized the coincidence at the same instant I did, for he said, "Poor bugger looks like me."

It was true! I had probably united the only two 6' 4" redheads in all of Japan. But Randy looked even bigger on skates, with pads and a helmet adding to the effect. When he left the bench and skated gracefully around the rink, he towered over his teammates.

The referee blew the whistle to start the game. Brian and I moved up into the stands. It wasn't crowded so we could get almost perfect seats—high enough to see most of the ice above the fiberglass protection, but still close enough see the facial expressions of the players. The teams lined up for the opening face-off and the game got underway.

The play went up and down the ice, with good scoring chances coming early at both ends. Brian was riveted. "This is outstanding, mate. I had no idea."

I was less impressed, but I wasn't yet sure what was bothering me. Finally, a whistle blew and both teams changed lines. "What's going on now?"

"Fresh players."

"Really? But the other blokes just started."

"It's tiring."

"All sports are tiring."

"Not like hockey. Look at the speed of the game."

We watched quietly for a couple of minutes. "It just seems strange, Brian said. "Getting all warmed up, then coming in for a rest."

"But because they're rested, they can skate hard for the minute or two that they're out there. They don't have to pace themselves."

"Aren't they supposed to smash into each other?"

"Different teams have different styles. In Canada you'd see a lot of body checking, but there's not much out there tonight."

"What's happenin' over there?"

He was pointing to the two large clusters of fans in the building, one behind each bench. They were cheering alternately in well-rehearsed routines, each guided by a uniformed leader. We thought at first that they were fan clubs, but gradually realized that they were employees of the parent company of the respective hockey teams. When Brian looked at me quizzically, I shrugged and said, "Japanese thing."

Down on the ice, things seemed just as odd. Although the skating and passing were crisp, and the shots were hard and accurate, something intangible was missing, something more evident from what didn't happen than what did. The attacking team would repeatedly skirt the periphery of the defense, passing tentatively, even when chances to shoot or drive to the net appeared. It looked like half-court basketball, where patterned plays are preferred over spontaneity.

Bothered by this, I moved down by the glass to get a closer look. The opposition had just been penalized, so Randy's team had a man advantage and the puck in the attacking zone. Repeatedly, the puck snapped from stick to stick, out of reach of the boxed defenders but no closer to the goal either. At one point it became ridiculous, as the center, traditionally the playmaker, passed back and forth with his defenseman on the blue line. Half the penalty time had expired and they hadn't even attempted a shot. Finally, seemingly out of desperation, the center made a tentative move that was quickly repulsed. Instead of frustration, the center's face seemed to show relief. At least he had done something.

No one in the stands seemed to notice. They couldn't tell that the flow of the game was wrong, that the thrust and parry was missing. But then, they could likely detect things that I could not, like the fine calligraphy of my hitchhiking sign to Sapporo. While that was lost on me, hockey was a form of creativity I knew well.

The game was tied after two periods, and Brian was enjoying it, but it was time for him to meet Yumi. "Say hello for me," I said, trying to sound nonchalant.

"Why don't you join us later?"

It was tempting but I had already decided against it. "I'll just catch up with Randy."

Brian shrugged and waved and soon disappeared under the grandstand. The teams reappeared and resumed their struggle. It was the weirdest thing to watch, quite unlike watching youngsters who were just learning. These were men out there, and they had all acquired the necessary physical abilities, but they just couldn't execute the plays effectively. Perhaps I was thinking of Yumi, sitting in the club, but the comparison that came to mind was an out-of-tune piano. The instrument was capable and the notes were being played properly, but the sound wasn't right. The result weren't harmonious.

After Randy's team scored a late goal and won the game, I went down to congratulate him as he came off the ice. We chatted briefly near the bench, then Randy directed me to a nearby hotel. "I'll meet you in the lobby," he said.

I was confused. Normally, I would wait near the dressing room. Randy explained. "We change in our rooms at the hotel and walk over."

"Really?"

He shrugged. "It's different here."

It certainly was. I went to the hotel and waited as directed. After a half hour, Randy appeared. "Hungry?" he asked.

"Thirsty, for sure."

We headed out and soon found a good-looking *yakitori* house. We had hardly ducked through the curtained entrance when the owner, a short bald man with a thin silver beard, rushed over and made a big fuss. A professional athlete, in his restaurant! A *gaijin*, no less, a gargantuan redhead. Heads turned throughout the room. By now, I was accustomed to Brian's notoriety, but Randy's celebrity status added yet another dimension.

We were escorted to a prominent table where Randy positioned his long legs carefully and tried to ignore the fleeting glances and hushed talk around us. If he was flattered or annoyed it didn't show.

Two tall beers with frosty mugs appeared. We toasted his win and selected appetizers from the menu. "So, what's it like," I asked finally, "playing with the Japanese?"

He shrugged. "Totally different than Canada."

"I can see that."

"Their approach is so methodical," he said. "Today, for instance, we skated early, ate lunch together, had an afternoon meeting and dinner, played the game, then had a formal post-game meeting. That's standard. I'm with them almost every hour of the day."

"Sounds intense," I said.

Randy described other quirks: the tournament format instead of season-ending playoffs; the media circus surrounding the foreigners; the weekly strategy meetings with the team owner, one of richest men in Japan. As Randy spoke, our food arrived and we set to eating.

I ventured a comment. "Your guys are good," I said. "They skate, pass, and shoot beautifully. But if you don't mind me saying so, there's something missing."

He lifted his huge head, clearly interested. "Like what?"

"Initiative. Teamwork is critical, but eventually someone has to see a chance and go for it. Players have to make things happen."

"It's true," he said, stabbing at his food. "They won't assert themselves, the young ones especially."

"Why is that?"

"Hard to say. It's complicated and frustrating."

Randy put down his chopsticks and moved both his hands as he spoke. "This fall, for instance, a few of the young guys came back from hockey camps in Canada. They had scrimmaged and hung out with university players and pros all summer and the difference was incredible. They were confident and aggressive, especially around the net."

"So what happened?"

His voice sounded puzzled. "It just didn't last. The veterans didn't like sharing their spots on the power play or seeing the young guys get attention. A little grumbling and a few meetings—it didn't take long for the younger players to get the hint."

"Stop rocking the boat," I said.

"Pretty much."

I whistled softly. "The status quo was more important to the vets than winning." I cringed trying to imagine the young guys getting this painful social message, one so contrary to the spirit of sport.

Randy resumed eating, his voice sounding a little resigned. "Within days, they were as timid as before."

"Didn't that bug you?"

"Well, it put me in a tough situation. Normally, the two foreigners on each team are strictly players, no coaching duties, so they can complain about things. But since I have the title of "Playing Coach," I have to toe the line. Do it the Japanese way."

"What if you didn't?"

"That's not really an option. I like the Japanese. They treat me well."

I respected his disciplined temperament. The Japanese evidently did as well, judging from the responsibility they had given him.

Randy went on. "I'm certainly not the first foreigner to wrestle with this approach to sport. Baseball players have been coming over for years, and there are lots of stories about their struggles or refusals to fit in."

"It's one extreme or the other, right?" I had heard about foreign baseball players from my Matsushita group. Just like Randy's hockey league, each team was allowed two foreigners. Some were heroes; others were pilloried in the Japanese press.

For the first time, Randy's tone seemed exasperated. "Some of us really try. We adjust our behavior constantly. Other guys get fed up. They start saying and doing what they want, not caring what the press will make of it. The smallest things become headlines, causing embarrassment for the manager and resentment among their teammates."

"What bugs you most? The Japanese system or the foreigners who won't try to fit it?"

He thought about that, leaning back in his chair with a full glass of beer. Clearly this issue troubled him. Finally, he replied. "Both. I think most of us could handle a different system if we could figure it out. If we were given some guidelines, some rule books. But instead, it's all hush-hush. Everyone treats the foreigners with kid gloves, fully expecting that we can't understand them and are likely to make mistakes—"

"Which you then perpetuate."

"Right, without even knowing it. Sometimes you don't even realize you've blundered until you read about in the newspaper. Then everyone waits to see how you'll react. If you get mad or try to ignore it, things will get worse. If you seek Japanese advice, then you'll understand what you've done wrong and how you can smooth things over."

"How do you that?"

Randy shrugged. "Depends on the situation. An apology sometimes. Just doing it correctly the next day is often enough. Everyone notices these things. They don't say anything, but they pay attention. They know that you're trying."

"It's strange," I said. "We know so little about them yet they know so much about us. In hockey and baseball, like everything else, they study other cultures and adopt what they want. They bring in experts like you, study your ways, then work to perfect and improve on what they've learned."

"But like you said, it's not just technique. You need initiative."

"Which brings us back to your team. There's no spark, no spontaneity. Everyone's just sitting back, waiting."

I thought of Yumi suddenly and her notion of "inward improvisation." It seemed applicable here. I tried it out. "Great players are constantly improvising, especially goal scorers. They assess a situation, the tempo and probabilities, then they . . . they just *imagine* a possibility and go for it."

Randy was nodding so I pressed the point. "You know where that comes from. From trusting yourself. From spending thousands of hours on the ice, seeing every possible play. You become so skilled and so familiar that anticipation merges with reaction. Your body simply takes over. And you don't worry about making the perfect play. Only one try in three results in a shot, and only one shot in ten is a goal, so you just keep trying, improvising, adjusting. Lots of goals come on rebounds and mistakes that one person reacts more quickly to."

Randy cut in. "Remember those Saturday morning free-for-alls at the local rink back in Edmonton? Twenty on each side, all ages and sizes."

"Sure. Nobody was worried about losing or making a mistake. You were just playing the game, up and down, all day long."

Randy shook his head. "Here they don't start playing until thirteen or fourteen, and even then with a short schedule and strict practices."

I made a suggestion. "It might help your team to just scrimmage for fifteen minutes every practice. No whistles, no face-offs, no stoppages—just action and reaction. The players—particularly the younger ones—would learn to improvise more. They'd have to. They might even have some fun."

"You might be right but there is no way it could actually happen." Randy said this with resigned certainty.

"Why not?"

"The general manager would never go for it. I'm the coach but he's the boss. I'd have a hard time convincing him that a free-for-all was important. These practices are carefully planned and run to the minute."

"Too bad," I said, "when random play may be exactly what they need."

Randy shrugged and waved for the bill. I looked at my watch and realized it was late. I hated to cut off the conversation but I had to rush to catch the last subway. As we left the restaurant, I wished Randy good luck with his team and success in the tournament, then sprinted toward the station. I caught my train on the dead run, just squeezing in the doors, then paced the empty car as I rolled homeward.

Randy's words disturbed me, as had Hibino's when he described youthful workers as "a new kind of human," but their perspective on the problem was diametrically different. On Randy's team the younger players were suppressed by older players invoking their rights of seniority. In the Matsushita situation, the senior managers complained that their young staff members were no longer providing the proper respect and obedience.

In this light, Randy's situation seemed particularly bizarre. He was held responsible for the success of the team, but he had limited cultural understanding and little real power. He was a smart guy, and he was clearly trying to learn and adapt to a strange social microcosm in which athletic and cultural norms were intertwined and compressed.

I got off the train and walked past the darkened amusement park, past the shuttered stalls and looming fences, past the figurines that now looked more lonely than cute in the moonlight. Reaching home, I made a cup of tea and sat quietly in the kitchen. I resisted the urge to knock on Brian's door and ask about his time with Yumi. It was late.

I climbed the creaking stairs to my room and sat a long while at my table. With the candle flickering in the breeze of the open window, I took out my journal and began to record and organize my thoughts. To see these Japanese teams and groups was to remember the ones within which I had grown up. Among my teenaged friends, I wanted to be accepted, respected, liked, maybe even loved. Like most kids that age, I would dress differently, talk differently, act differently—anything that would help me fit in better. But it wasn't that easy. It was exceedingly difficult to know what or how to change. That was it really. No matter how badly you wanted to, discerning cool was as hard as acting cool.

That was partly why I played sports. Whatever the season, there was always a group of friends to spend time with. We always had a clear objective and respect could be won with effort and skill. As years passed, being an athlete gave me both identity and social status—both appealing aspects in those turbulent times.

It's about acceptance, I realized. Whether Eastern or Western, we all want to belong, to feel like we are a part of something bigger than ourselves.

ten

I lay in bed the next morning, psyching myself for a double shift at ESS. I would work the next day also, then again on Saturday. I accepted the extra shifts gladly, trying to build my cash reserves. I now had two hundred dollars saved, but hardly enough to try the ski gambit again. Frankly, in that regard, I was at a loss for ideas. Nothing had changed in my situation.

To make matters worse, the girl I was covering for at ESS was going skiing, part of a weekend tour at another English-language school. The news that the ski areas were open now and getting lots of snow didn't make me feel any better, nor did the sight of ski merchandise in the store windows or in the bulging bags of shoppers.

Balanced against these anxieties was the realization that I'd grown accustomed to living in Tokyo. Quite comfortable, actually. Since I found jobs and a place to live, life had assumed a calm and orderly flow. I was reading and writing every day, exploring Tokyo, enjoying my room and my times with Brian and Yumi. I almost didn't want to admit it, but I was peaceful.

There was a knock at the door. Jun Yoshida poked his head in. "Kohei has arrived. Can you join us for a drink tonight?"

"I have to work late."

"In that case," he said, "I'm supposed to invite you to his parents' house for dinner Saturday evening. It's in Kamakura so you would stay overnight."

I thought quickly. I had hoped to see Yumi Sunday, but she hadn't called yet, and besides, an invitation to Japanese home was an honor.

"Please tell him that I would love to."

Jun smiled. "I'll arrange the details."

He had scarcely left when Brian arrived. "Want to come and watch my *Aikido* class tomorrow night?"

"Sure, if it's not a problem."

We arranged our meeting place and Brian left. I shook my head. Hardly out of bed and I had a full weekend planned. Life was getting busy!

Between the subway rides and two very slow days at ESS, I had a chance to read several sections of my book on Japanese culture. I was struck frequently by the historical background of so many things I was seeing and hearing about modern Japanese society. So many of my group experiences—the Matsushita managers, the schoolchildren, Randy's hockey team, Yumi's many lessons and observations—were rendered at least partly understandable by Suzuki's tome.

I even carried it with me when I went to watch Brian's *Aikido* lesson, and had appropriately arrived in the section devoted to the martial arts. Brian met me on the platform and we walked together to his *dojo*. It was housed in a plain, two-story building in a residential neighborhood, evidently old but well-maintained.

We removed our shoes and entered. Brian went to change, but advised me first, "The only thing you must remember is to bow to the master's photograph when you enter and leave the *dojo*."

"Where's the photograph?"

"At one end. You'll see." With that he disappeared. I walked over to the practice hall and peeked in. It was rectangular, mat-covered, and utterly unadorned save for a small black and white picture on the end wall of *Aikido's* founder, Morihei Uyeshiba. As students began appearing, I noticed the solemnity with which they bowed to the Master.

When there was a gap in the procession, I stepped in myself. I felt strangely nervous, as if people might watch me bow. I felt awe too, for the silver-haired man on the wall and the concept he had created. It was odd. I knew only a little about *Aikido*, but the people I saw around me, and the way they carried themselves, filled me with surging respect.

I read a small pamphlet I had been given at the door. It quoted Uyeshiba: *"The secret of Aikido is to harmonize ourselves with the movement of the universe and bring ourselves into accord with the universe itself. He who has gained the secret of aikido has the universe in himself and can say, 'I am the universe.'"*

The pamphlet explained the word *Aikido*. *Ai-* meant mutual, *-ki* meant the energy of the body, and *-do* meant "the way of." The basic strategy was to harmonize with the strength and momentum of your opponent, then use his own force to negate him.

The lesson began and a pattern quickly emerged. The teacher displayed a technique twice, then the class divided into pairs and practiced it for ten minutes. The master walked around, occasionally demonstrating some nuance, seldom saying a word. In fact, there was little sound at all. There were no blows, kicks, or blood-curdling, chi-summoning screams, only thumps coming regularly from the mats as the students landed from their various throws.

Over the course of the class, the students worked on six techniques, each designed to negate a different threat. Care was taken to prepare students for the same type of attack from different sides. Typically, this would be a grappling hold, a charge, or a blow. Since the strategy is to blend with an opponent's energy, the first step is to recognize what's happening. This is critical if you are to react properly. No matter how skilled you are, if you are terrified by the flurry of the fight, then your trained abilities are useless. Your mind is overwhelmed with distraction.

A huge benefit of these drills was that the students were familiarizing themselves with the look and feel of an attack. They were learning to sense the tactic, the direction, the weight, strength, and skill of their opponent, and then react accordingly. Although these drills were conducted at three-quarters speed, the students were nonetheless laying neural pathways.

I thought back to the hockey game the night before, to the pained look on the center's face as he tried to imagine a play. His expression was of confusion, panic. There was too much possibility and too little certainty. His mind was a blur of images, thoughts, and fears, like a traffic intersection out of control.

I recognized that terror because I'd felt it myself, in my early years especially, but in lesser degrees later. It was only when I'd gained confidence and perspective that I understood not only the intricacies of the game, but the "hall of mirrors" psychology of that awful moment.

The *Aikido* teacher was isolating the possibilities and techniques of a hand-to-hand struggle. It made perfect sense, like practicing passing and stick-handling in hockey. It was like saying, "In this situation, do this, and if he reacts this way, then do this."

I thought of Yumi and her notions on improvisation. It wasn't applicable here, not at this level anyway. What I was seeing was not improvisation. These were the basics, the notes of the scale, the colors of the palette.

I glanced again at the pamphlet and reread the definitions and terminology. I noticed that the suffix -*do* at the end of Japanese martial arts, such as Ai-ki-do, ju-do, ken-do, meant "the way of." Conceptually, they were all linked together by *Bushido*, the ancient military code that has demanded and provided honor in Japanese culture for centuries. Bushido is broadly defined as *"The Way of the Warrior."*

As I watched from the perimeter, I was struck suddenly by a vague sense of loss. We have no equivalent in Western society, I realized, no sport that is termed an art form, or thought of as a path of personal development. After twenty years on ice, I could say that I had learned "The Way of Hockey," and the same was true of football after ten seasons. But we think of our activities differently, not as Football-do, Hockey-do, or Ski-do, but as mere games.

As Yumi had reminded me, and I had read in Suzuki's book, the Japanese consider their skills to be arts, as in the "martial arts," and expect from them spiritual, as well as physical, learning. We in the West assign to our sports no such role in our lives, at least not consciously, yet we play sports in unprecedented numbers, and often with more passion and devotion than we bring to anything else. Why? Because when we play sports we forget the past and the future, and just focus in on the now. It doesn't matter what the sport is. Whatever activity demands of us this devotion, and brings us to this same pure attention, is capable of giving us this same meditative benefit. If only we understand it as such. Honor it as such. Allow it this place in our lives.

These thoughts were still brewing when we got home. While Brian nursed his new bruises with a few beers in the kitchen, I went upstairs with a cup of tea and my book. I sat at my table, my window open to the sounds and chilled fragrances of the night, and peered through the pages into the history of the Samurai.

I learned how they embraced Zen in the thirteenth century, partly because its strict precepts helped them rule the country, but also because of its mystic insights. They trained their physical abilities to legendary degrees but discovered that the key to victory was mental control. No matter how skilled they became, they realized that fears and even thoughts would hamper their abilities. The key to survival lay in the ability to bypass their thinking minds and trust entirely on a state of unfettered and unforced concentration. The greater the threat, often of imminent death, the more complete their focus needed to be.

As the Samurai cultivated this single-mindedness, they found that their descriptions of this state of being was closely mirrored by what the monks said about sitting meditation. Just as the monks concentrated on their breathing, the warriors focused on the thin strip of steel in their hands. All else was forgotten save the inner edge of the blade and their intention to use it. The monks and Samurai called this state of awareness *Mushin,* or "White Paper Mind."

These notions rang true to me. Although I hadn't literally faced death, I had faced injury and the seeming death of defeat for many years. And in the process, I had felt moments so very similar to these descriptions they could only be the same. At times in hockey, football, and skiing, the three sports I excelled at, I felt so completely dispassionate it was as if I had gone on automatic pilot. I was, in these moments, more intensely involved than ever before in my life, but somehow I was able to detach myself, disassociate myself from my "normal" concerns. It was almost like watching myself play.

At these moments I performed better than ever before in my life, playing, quite literally, "out of my mind." But I couldn't retain or prolong this clarity, particularly if I was trying to. I couldn't forget or explain it either. This had always been the most fascinating and frustrating aspect, and it was doubly intriguing to learn now that the ancient Japanese felt the same way.

I worked long into the night, reading, taking notes, comparing these old ideas to my own experiences. It felt good to be piecing thoughts and intuitions together, reveling in the silence of the night and the glowing heater beneath my table. Finally, I lay back on the *tatami* mat, listened to tinkling chimes in the distance, and drifted off to sleep.

eleven

I met Kohei at a statue in the Shibuya station. He was small, even for a Japanese, but just as cheerful and kind as I remembered. We climbed to the platform and boarded the subway, all the while chatting about mutual friends from Banff and our ski instructor's class the year before. After a long ride, we arrived in historic town of Kamakura on the eastern coast. As we walked through the narrow, dimly lit streets to their family home, I practiced the polite expressions one should say before and after eating.

Kohei was amused by my efforts. "It doesn't matter," he said. "You are a foreigner. They don't expect you to know this."

But that just made me more determined. I didn't want to rely on a blanket excuse or to perpetuate a stereotype about foreigners. I detested that laziness in others. Wherever I had gone in my travels, I always made an effort to behave appropriately. Even if I could say little else, I at least tried to learn "Thank you" in the local language or dialect. This simple respect invariably caused smiles to widen.

Kohei's home was fragrant with cooking aromas when we arrived. His family was overwhelmingly kind, meeting us at the door and hanging on my every word and gesture. While Kohei's mother and sister finished cooking, Mr. Yokura showed me their rear garden. It was compact, the size of the patio in my Canadian home, and bordered on the rear by a sheer face of rock, but it was immaculately tended and painstakingly landscaped. Everything was small in size, but viewed with the right perspective, the trees and shrubs could have been imagined as much larger plants in the wild. A wooden walkway, bordered by sliding wooden wall panels, united the house and garden.

Dinner was served. Two of the low tables, the *kotatsu*, were pulled together and we all knelt or sat cross-legged around them. Dishes of fish, rice, vegetables, seaweed, and pickles were passed, all aromatic and beautifully presented. The food was delicious too, but I had trouble eating since almost all of the conversation involved me, and I was trying hard to be attentive and polite. On top of that, Kohei's father was almost constantly refilling my beer mug, urging me to drink.

As we talked, laughed, and toasted repeatedly, the evening cold invaded the house. Like most Japanese homes, the walls and windows were neither insulated nor sealed as in North America. We were nicely warmed by the electric elements below our tables, but these were the only heating sources in the house besides the kitchen stove. I'd read that the Japanese typically do not heat their houses; that they find it more economical to bring people to heat, rather than heat to people. Besides its practicality, there is social warmth in a family gathered together instead of being off in separate parts of the house. So it was for us. Wearing thick sweaters, sitting cross-legged with the quilted table apron wrapped tightly around our waist, we ate, drank, sang, and pantomimed our way through the evening.

Evidence of conservation kept appearing. Kohei's sister and mother, as they cleaned up the kitchen, were careful to separate their paper and metal garbage for recycling. The small water heater, suspended above the sink, heated the water just before it passed through the faucet—no thought of keeping a large tank indefinitely warm as in most North American houses.

When later, as their houseguest, I was given the first bath, I fortunately guessed correctly that others in the house would use the same hot water after me. That meant dousing and scrubbing in the cold night air—not an appealing prospect—but I did the right thing. It may have been the fastest scrub and rinse on record, but I slipped into the soothing waters with both my conscience and my body clean.

By the time I was out of the bathroom, four futons plus piles of bedding had appeared, transforming the living room into a collective bedroom. Kohei, his parents, his brother, and I would all sleep side by side. With their urging, I climbed immediately under the heavy quilts and waited while each of the family had their bath. Kohei explained that if you get directly into bed after a bath, your body heat will be retained long into the night. I believed him; since my body was glowing and deliciously comfortable.

What a relief it was to simply lie there and listen to the rattling windowpanes, with no need any longer to make conversation or strain to be polite. Kohei was kind and his family's generosity was touching, but there were many unspoken rules to observe. Kohei had coached me on a few—the donning of the slippers at the entrance, the right way to praise the food, the left-over-right wrapping of the bathrobe—but God knows what other mistakes I had made.

In so many ways, life in Japan seemed as metered as the flow of electricity. It was one thing to merely talk with the Japanese at the ESS—to objectively observe and discuss their behavior—and quite another to be actually living amongst them. Exhausted, I fell off to sleep, grateful for the reprieve.

Kohei had a strange request at breakfast. "Would you mind spending a few hours with my father? I have a tennis meeting with a friend."

"Of course not," I replied, but I was a little concerned. His father's English was worse than my Japanese.

After Kohei left, Mr. Yokura and I went for a long walk, highlighted alternately by tourist spots and favored watering holes. At the first, he ordered beer and introduced me to his retired buddies as they wandered in. It took awhile, but with some help from his friends, Mr. Yokura shared with me his deep regret that his son didn't drink. It was a huge disappointment that he and Kohei could not rise up and float together on the forgetful, exuberant cloud of alcohol. He wanted to "get to know him better."

In his youth, Mr. Yokura worked seventy hours a week to help rebuild Japan after the war, leaving the child rearing to his wife. Now, when he was retired, his son was living abroad and would likely be home only a few more times in his life. His sudden desire for closeness made alcohol seem that much more appealing. To drink together might bridge the gap of absence—his formerly, now Kohei's—and melt the stiff patriarchal relationship they had sustained for decades.

Mr. Yokura took me from the huge bronze Buddha on the Kamakura hillside to a sushi and sake lunch, followed by a visit to a long fishing pier and another drinking spot. The pace was relentless. We were half drunk already with no end in sight.

Wobbling back into the daylight, I learned that we were now to meet up with Kohei's mother and some of her friends. This seemed odd, but again I went with the flow. At an elegant, split-level home, we were graciously ushered in by Kohei's mother and four other ladies in their early sixties. They led us to a living room where a long low Japanese table, stretched incongruously between Western chairs and sofas, was sumptuously set with food and more drinks. I learned that this was a *Bonnen-kai* party, which, literally translated, means "forget the year."

Kohei's mother explained that friends gather in December and discuss the good events of the year, typically assisted by alcohol. Fond memories are described in great detail and supported by the commentaries and approval of others. Since no mention is ever made of bad occurrences or misfortunes, the result is a reinforcement of the happiest memories only. It was an interesting notion, like prioritizing the filing system of your memory. Good events were highlighted and stored prominently for easy grasp, while memories of pain or sorrow were allowed to recede and gather dust.

Although they had been drinking, the women remained exquisitely poised. They held their glasses delicately, with the fingertips of their free hand touching them softly near the base. Before eating an orange, they would peel the outer skin and remove any stringy white detritus, placing all this in a tidy pile on a napkin. Even in these simple movements, they displayed such exquisite dexterity, such grace in posture and conversation, that I felt conspicuously awkward. On top of this, I felt increasingly tired. During this marathon day with Kohei's father and the previous evening with his family, the strain of constant attention had gradually worn me out. I felt ungrateful, but still I wished silently for the peace of my own small room.

My hosts had other plans.

Mrs. Yokura asked me quietly, "Have you seen a tea ceremony, Rick-san?"

I saw it coming. Such questions in Japan were never casual. Mustering enthusiasm, yet adding what I hoped was the proper tinge of regret, I replied, "Not yet, I'm afraid."

Beaming with pleasure, she asked, "Could my friend, Mrs. Morita, perform one for you?"

The small lady on my left protested. "I am only a beginner," she said, but the other ladies all clucked and smiled. Kohei's mother assured me that Mrs. Morita was renowned. Despite my hospitality burnout, I couldn't refuse. The situation was obligatory, and I really did want to see a tea ceremony.

Minutes later, accompanied by Kohei's parents, Mrs. Morita led me through the lengthening shadows to a small wooden house amidst a well-tended garden. Moving deliberately, she pointed out various trees and shrubs, adorned now in autumn colors, and spoke deliberately about each. She was so graceful, so controlled as we examined the various details, I wondered if the performance had not already begun.

Clambering through a small square portal in the exterior wall, we entered the tearoom. The entryway seemed odd, but she assured me that every detail was designed especially for the tea ceremony. Using hints rather than direct suggestions, she helped me notice the variations of the ceiling, the calculated imperfections of the hand-built walls, the small fire pit for the heating of the water, and especially the *tokonoma*, the recessed area adorned with a single hanging scroll.

Sitting in a circle with Kohei's parents, my legs tucked gingerly beneath me, I watched Mrs. Morita prepare the tea. Using both hands in slow, deliberate motions, she put a small, evidently cherished kettle onto a rack above a low flame. While waiting for it to boil, she handled the tea like it was a precious spice and delicately laid out her utensils. I tried to sensitize myself, to perceive the small details denoting mastery, but it was difficult. Were I versed in the ceremony, I may have recognized the skill of her technique, but as it was, I could only note the utter simplicity and economy of her effort.

Once the tea was prepared, we each had our turn to drink. I studied Kohei's mother and tried to do things correctly: to hold and admire the bowl, to drink from it serenely, to wipe it clean and pass it on with humility. The precise and purposeful movements, the earthy yet elegant aesthetic—it all reminded me of the monastery. Apparently, from what I remembered in Suzuki's book, this was evidence of Mrs. Morita's skill, since the tea ceremony was an offshoot of the Zen aesthetic and approach to life. Properly considered and purposefully done, every activity constitutes an art form to be simplified and perfected.

The day still wasn't over. Kohei was waiting when we returned to their family home, and I sensed immediately that something was up. Kohei's mother was very excited.

Kohei saw my confusion. "Let's go," he said. "I want you to meet the girl I played tennis with."

Had I known Japanese culture better, his "tennis date" and his behavior would have been clues. On the train, after some stammering by Kohei, I learned the truth.

"The girl we are going to see," he said nervously. "I am going to marry her."

I was speechless. After a moment, Kohei spoke again. "Sorry I didn't tell you," he said, "but today was a special date."

Then it dawned on me. Kohei hadn't come to Japan to visit his parents. He had come to find a wife. I asked Kohei if he had met this girl before.

"I saw her picture and read about her—she's the daughter of a man in my father's company—but I only met her today."

"And you decided to get married?"

He nodded sheepishly.

Realizing that my incredulity was embarrassing him, I thought up a few questions. "She had seen your photograph? Read your biography?"

He nodded again.

"And she wants to live in Canada?"

"Of course. She vacationed there last summer and enjoyed it very much."

"Was it prearranged that you would marry?"

"Oh no," he said. "Our families just helped us meet."

He paused for a moment. Over his shoulder, out the train window, I saw the gray sprawl of Tokyo flashing past. There were so many people, yet they moved in their own circles only. How would they meet otherwise?

"I considered four girls," he said. "Junko, that's her name, actually met two other men before me. But . . ." his voice tailed off.

"They didn't like each other."

He shook his head. "Though it's an arranged meeting, nothing is certain."

"Except that you both felt ready to get married." He smiled and shrugged, and I sat back and let the notion settle in. The more I thought of it, the better sense it made. By distributing their photographs and biographies on an informal network of friends and close relatives, their bids traveled subtly and selectively. Only candidates with mutually suitable credentials—interests, social status, and family background—were actually met. In this way, overt compatibility problems, which often surface later in "love marriages," could be largely avoided. Compared with singles bars, dating services, and the personal ads in newspapers, these Japanese introductions made good sense. What shocked me was how quickly Kohei and Junko made their decision!

As we disembarked, I congratulated Kohei and tried to set him at ease. He relaxed gradually and we walked, laughing through an evidently prosperous suburb to Junko's home. She greeted us at the door and I was charmed immediately. Junko was pert and pretty and quick to laugh, and I was astounded by the seeming ease with which she talked and related with Kohei. It was their second date, their first time together in her family home, yet they both seemed relaxed.

Junko had asked a girlfriend to join us, so we all sat in chairs around a Western-style coffee table looking at their family photo albums. I watched with amazement as Kohei learned about Junko's personal and family history. What a concept! Here was a woman he had never even seen a day earlier, and now he was to share her ancestry. Talk shifted to their wedding, which was planned already for spring. After a Tokyo ceremony, they would honeymoon in Hawaii on the way home to live in Banff. Kohei had an established travel business, and Junko hoped to find some sort of retail work, but it was clear they would start a family soon.

It was dark by the time we said goodbye and walked through quiet streets to the subway. I was exhausted; I couldn't even imagine how Kohei felt. Still, he was as polite as ever, asking when my nights off were and what I would like to do in Tokyo.

"Don't worry about me. You've only got a few days to see your family and arrange things with Junko."

He nodded, a little relieved, yet it was clear he felt responsible to me.

Suddenly he stopped and flashed a wide smile. "Let's go skiing."

My heart leapt as I imagined it, Kohei and I on the side of a snowy mountain, looking down a mogul field. My stomach bubbled already with anticipation. My fingers tingled. Skiing had begun to seem like an unreachable dream and now suddenly, out of the blue, I would get my chance.

We quickly made a plan. Kohei would borrow his father's car the following Sunday, two days after Christmas, and we'd drive up for the day. There were several good areas within reach, and he would check the snow conditions at each. Two days would have been better, but Kohei's time was obviously limited. As for me, the expense would be hard on my meager budget, but it would be worth it to finally ski in Japan.

We boarded the subway, Kohei for a short hop only to Kamakura, me for the long haul back to Tokyo. It would take two more hours to get home, but now I had thoughts of skiing to keep me entertained.

twelve

It was a long week. Work schedules were light near Christmas and several roommates spent the week lounging around Yoshida House. I wasn't alone but Wednesday came without anyone knowing it was my birthday. I didn't feel like dropping hints, and everyone seemed to have plans, so after work I treated myself to a hot bath and some sushi at a small local restaurant. I returned feeling good and settled in at my low table to write, but people downstairs had the television turned up loud. The sound, particularly the commercials, carried up through the floor easily. Accustomed to quiet evenings, I resented this annoyance. It seemed like second hand smoke, polluting the air.

Since my return from traveling, I had developed a distinct bias against television. It seemed too prominent in people's lives, too powerful in their minds. The news was usually bad, playing on our latent masochism. The entertainment programs were often violent or moronic. Even the sports programming which, of course, I liked best, were over-hyped, over-commercialized, and far too prevalent, tempting people to watch sports instead of playing themselves.

But the most annoying aspect was advertising. Tempting people. Creating desires. Making people want *things,* even if they don't need or can't afford them. No matter how much they have, or how well they live, advertising works with almost sinister effectiveness to make everyone want *more*. It has to. People will only buy if they feel dissatisfied with their present state.

At first, these observations hit me hard. I'd grown accustomed to no media at all, or relatively primitive exposure in many parts of

Asia, where multiple small newspapers vied with limited radio and television coverage. It was stunning to return to North America and once again encounter saturation exposure—hundreds of television stations, a full spectrum of radio broadcasts, hundreds of newspapers and magazines—all trying to grab and hold my attention so as to sell me something. How could anyone not be affected by this onslaught?

In time I would regain the psychological armor that would shield me from this information radiation, but was that a good thing? I'd just spent a year alone, traveling the earth to gain a fresh perspective and gradually feeling a subtle but distinct *peeling away* of tension that was both physical and mental. Only when I recognized my own spirit, and felt it lithe and limber, did I realize how it had shrunken and stiffened amid the pressures of my former lifestyle. Did I want to be psychically callused once again? Hardly. Quite the opposite.

Despite the noise from downstairs, these ideas all found the page over the course of the next few days. I wrote all Wednesday night and most of Thursday, interrupted only by an afternoon walk with Jun Yoshida's dog, who was over for a visit and looking forlorn. I talked to him as we walked, doubting the dog was bilingual but guessing he would welcome the chatter. It was good for me too, the fresh air and exercise mostly, but also the fascination of watching this dog explore the neighborhood. He was earnest in his gait, pulling me along, and utterly insistent in his sniffing. At every fragrant post he would first smell, then add to, the canine guest register.

Afterwards I grabbed a few snacks from the kitchen and sat with him on the front step. He was clearly appreciative, both of the treats I fed him and of the massages I applied on his flanks. Under my touch he sprawled and stretched in luxuriating bliss. I stopped after awhile but stayed there anyway, just sharing the time with him, watching the afternoon shadows lengthen.

That night was Christmas Eve, only the second I'd ever spent away from my family. They would soon be sitting around the dining room table, talking quickly to get their comments, jokes or jibes in, often speaking over one another. It was the regular dinner hour raised to a festive pitch, to be outdone only by Christmas dinner the following night. I hated to miss it, to imagine my regular seat empty.

I returned to my room and wrote for a few more hours, then shared a beer with Brian when he came in around midnight. He apologized when he heard that I'd spent the day alone. "I should have said something, mate. You could have joined us."

But it was fine really. The time alone had been good for me, giving me a chance to settle down and think. The weeks of December had been so busy, and I had experienced so many new things, that it felt good to slow down and digest what I had learned.

There was another benefit too. I was feeling my traveling self again, regularly now, for hours on end, not just in bursts like sunbeams through scattered clouds. The clues were subtle. Physically, it was the relishing of simple pleasures, the warmth of my morning coffee cup, the pleasing texture of my towel rubbed against my skin. Sensually, it was noticing the fragrance of my candle or the random notes of my wind-blown chimes. Aesthetically, it was appreciating the texture and frozen vitality of landscaped yards or the pleasing shapes that my letters formed as I wrote. Mentally, it was the gentle alertness I felt, the certainty with which the words came, each one perfect, as if formed first by God.

This is my natural state, I thought, my original self, the one I'd lost touch with in my busy life, felt in flashes of clarity during sports, then learned or regained while traveling. I couldn't yet understand or explain it, but this was a higher form of awareness. I knew that for sure. The challenge was to prolong these periods, to evoke them more frequently, to connect them eventually, or rather, to slip not from their subtle grace.

Then I caught myself. That wasn't right. Consciousness was not like a binary code, on or off, yes or no. It was more like an undulating curve on a graph, rising and falling as time passed. When both the peaks and the troughs rose together, trending upward, the low points in an evolving conscious were getting higher also, so even when one slipped from the most gracious state, the slide was not steep or long and the rise returned soon enough.

And so it went, on and on into the night, thinking about thinking, peering through prisms for the truth, until finally my eyes closed, and I dreamt the sleeping dream instead.

Christmas dawned cold, and I lay awhile under the warmth of my thick quilt. There was no reason to get up early—no fireplace downstairs adorned with stockings, no tree with presents underneath, no goodies around the house or turkey dinner to look forward to. Nonetheless, it was Christmas and I could hear people rustling in the kitchen, so I rose, dressed, and went downstairs. It was actually quite festive, Brian orchestrating six others in an ambitious breakfast effort. We sorted out the various foods we had, decided on breakfast and evening menus, and set to work. Since space was limited, and we needed milk for coffee, I offered to go to the local store.

It felt great to get outside and it gave me another chance to walk the dog. Or run the dog, as it turned out, since he was straining at the leash like an Alaskan sled dog. So off we went, as fast and far as I could, which was only the three blocks to the store. I arrived breathing hard and feeling a little dizzy. It was shocking. I was hardly in shape for skiing and my trip with Kohei was in two days.

I bought milk and a bag of oranges, the kind I'd grown up enjoying on Christmas morning, then ran with the dog back to Yoshida House. I was just in time. The fresh ground coffee had just finished percolating and the smell filled the kitchen. I poured a cup and sat back. Real coffee! What a pleasure after the instant powdered variety I normally used or the swill I drank down at ESS. I offered oranges all around and took two myself. As a kid, I loved the fun of peeling them almost as much as their delicious taste. The first orange disappeared quickly, but with the second, I imitated the women at the bonnen-kai party I had attended with Kohei's parents. It took awhile, but gradually I removed all the stringy white bits, including the spine. I tasted a piece. Pure flavor exploded in my mouth without a hint of the pulpy remnants. Good idea.

Brian looked over from the stove. "Yumi called. She invited us out to her house tomorrow."

My pulse quickened. "What about her father?"

"He's feeling better apparently. Anyway, it's set for one o'clock if you want to go."

"Absolutely."

Brian returned to his stove, and I bit into another succulent piece of orange. What a twist! An invitation to Yumi's house. I hadn't heard from her, and as the days passed I had tried not to think of her either. It was hard though. I saw her at night sometimes, when I closed my eyes, or even in my thoughts, when I allowed my mind to wander. It wasn't surprising. She was an exceptional woman.

We feasted on our communal breakfast, with omelets, pancakes, fruit, various breads, and more delicious coffee. Hearing and smelling our festivities, others in the house woke up and began the cooking and eating cycle all over again. It got crowded in the kitchen, so the first group moved into the common area where the television was blaring the channel designed for American military personnel.

Soon we were watching a replay of some college football game. It was an odd thing, sitting in Tokyo with people from Pakistan, Israel, Australia, and Germany, explaining American football. They liked the spectacle—the color of the uniforms against the green turf and the exuberant cheerleaders and raucous fans—but the game itself was a mystery. What were the hats for? Why were some players so big? What did they talk about in the circles?

I explained a little but their interest was superficial. Before long everyone had wandered off except Brian, who once again wanted to know why the game stopped and started so often, and why players kept coming off and on?

"Kind of a part time thing, isn't it?" he joked. "Play a little, relax for a bit, have a drink, play a little more. Christ, there's more players on the bench than the field."

I explained the notion of offense, defense, and special teams, and how the substitution in football was so different than the rotation in hockey. Brian it took all in, nodding and thinking. "So they have a different plan each time they come out of the meeting."

"Out of the huddle. That's right. Both teams have a play, one designed to score, one designed to defend."

"Then it's a quick bit of action, a pile of bodies, and back to make another plan."

We laughed and went for another cup of coffee. The kitchen was crowded, so I filled my cup and took it up to my room. I opened my notebook to write but instead sat staring out at the neighbor's small garden.

I hadn't watched football for years, and now it was easy to see the humor of Brian's mocking summation. In fact, it was far easier to see this than what really happens, which is a kinetic flurry of astounding complexity. Every time the ball is snapped, physical battles erupt all over the field. On the line, behemoths fight using willpower and brute strength, while in the open field, agile predators match foot speed and guile. The success of each play depends on these smaller contests, especially when they're close to the point of attack. The overall momentum swings to the cumulative winners of those individual struggles.

The fast, violent drama of those one-on-one battles is what football is all about—two men matching their skill and will in forty or fifty intensive flurries over three hours. In most respects, especially at the college and professional level, such combatants are remarkably equal. They're both big and strong; they're both well coached and in good condition; they both tire as the games wears on. What's left—the defining factor—is their courage, their human spirit.

To understand this you have to play the game, or at least witness its intensity and violence at close range. I sometimes advise people who wanted to learn more about football: "Go to a practice. Stand ten feet away from the full impact collisions. Only when you're close like that do you realize the ferocity of the game, the sheer force being expended. When you hear the impact, and feel it in your stomach, that's when you start to understand. What has gladiatorial appeal from a distance may prove frightening in close proximity.

How can players stand it? Basically, they adjust to it over time as they and their opponents get bigger and faster, just as competitors do in all other sports. At each new level the competition gets tougher and a certain number of athletes are somehow more able to cope with the new challenges. For every one that makes it, however, there are several others who quit, get cut, or ride the bench. As for me, I rode that bench early on, hanging on at ever-higher levels until suddenly something clicked and suddenly I was a starter and then, a few years later, a captain.

God, it was exciting and frightening to be out there finally, trying not to embarrass myself! When the ball was snapped all hell broke loose, with big guys trying to crush me into the dirt, followed by bull-dozing fullbacks with high, hard knees or light-footed tailbacks who could easily leave you lonely, foolish with empty arms. But gradually I sensed that others were scared too, and that the calmest ones played best. The realization settled me down and I found strength in rallying the others, inciting them to action: "Come on. Let's get these guys."

The intensity in football was amazing, the courage too. So often I watched players get crushed, yet somehow get up and limp back for the next play. Of course, they didn't always get up. One or two got carted off every game that weren't looking or got unlucky. That was part of it too. Luck. You had to trust it. You had to bust your ass every play, but you had to be lucky too. You had to believe you'd get through it, that some big guy wouldn't fall against your knee and blow it out. Again. By the time I was eighteen, thanks to both football and hockey, I'd already had two operations and spent six months in casts.

Was football worth it? Depends when you ask. As the years pass, and the injury piper is demanding his due, I'll no doubt be more conflicted, but during my playing days there was no doubt. Football was life vividly lived, partly because I was thrilled, but just as much because I was terrified. In the heat of the game, I was supercharged, overflowing with testosterone, adrenaline, and team spirit. When I hit someone clean—buried my helmet into his chest and felt his wind and strength whoosh out—I felt this extraordinary rush, like a drug pumped straight into my veins. Often I bellowed like a wild man, utterly primal.

Most intriguing were those magical moments when time slowed down and the game became a violent ballet. It always happened when I was playing my best. I was running, blocking, and tackling at high speed, yet somehow it was all in slow motion and I was performing perfectly. It was thrilling, yet remarkable also because I felt dispassionate, aloof, interested but delicately so. This was understandable in a twisted way. When it mattered most, I seemed to care least. I needed to. If I cared too much, I would try too hard. That had always been my weakness. Trying too hard. Thinking too much. Success came finally when I learned to let go.

I brought this state of mind to my hockey too, or perhaps it was vice versa. Maybe I developed this gentle focus while skiing and transferred it to both my other sports. That may well be, for it was the year after I took up skiing that I got off the bench and began playing regularly in hockey and football. Likely it was a synergy, one supporting the other, for my seasons overlapped by that time, and I was stronger and in better shape than ever before. As I gained more confidence, I played better, relaxed more, and trusted myself more completely.

It was precisely this state I was curious about, when the body is relaxed and ready for action and the mind is empty yet lucid. My search to understand this subtle state had pulled me to Japan, but was I learning anything? Perhaps. I was sorting out past thoughts. I was studying historical descriptions. I was seeing different types of perception and an entirely new way of learning. This was all good, but having more pieces doesn't make a puzzle easier.

thirteen

Yumi's home was farther from the city than I expected. It took three subways, a bus, and a fair hike to reach it, and I marveled that Yumi came to Tokyo as often as she did. The compensation was the space they had, a large plot with high trees overhead and a thick draping of bamboo around the multi-building compound. The largest structure, which we guessed to be the workshop, stood out front, adjoined by a small hut with shelves of finished pottery in the window. To one side was an open shed with stacked baskets and pots and several tools hanging neatly on the wall. Past a small immaculate garden was the house, ringed by a wooden walkway and protected overhead by a thick thatch roof. All the buildings were old in design and appearance, yet each was well tended.

I followed Brian up the flagstone walk, carrying the colorful flowers we had purchased in Tokyo. We'd explained to the shopkeeper that our friend was experienced in flower arranging and trusted her to choose flowers that Yumi would approve of. The woman asked what style Yumi was schooled in? Style? We didn't know. So she gathered and wrapped four long stemmed flowers, of a species I didn't recognize, and tied them tastefully with a ribbon.

Her choices seemed to be excellent, for Yumi expressed delight in receiving them. Or it may simply have been the appropriate response to a visitor's gift, since her father stood behind Yumi at the entrance area, and she was functioning in Japanese mode. We bowed low as she introduced us, making polite talk about the tall, twisted vase he had on display in his *tokonoma*.

Lunch was to be served in the next room. We donned house slippers to shuffle down a hardwood hallway, past empty *tatami* rooms on either side, then removed them as we stepped into a small, sparse dining area with four cushions around a low kutatsu. Yumi showed us where to sit but we waited until her father got settled, hoping fervently he wouldn't sit in the Seiza position. If he did, then we would have to also to be polite, and I wasn't sure my knees could stand much of that. Fortunately, he adopted the cross-legged position and we happily followed suit.

Yumi first served us beer, pouring delicately from a tall bottle. She then brought four lacquered platters, each complete with miso soup, sandwiches, tofu with soy sauce, pickled mackerel, sliced vegetables, sliced yellow pickles, and white rice. It looked delicious. Either Yumi had a cook hidden in the back or she had been well schooled by her mother in traditional cooking.

We admired the bowls, all hand-made, each subtly different in size, shape, color, and texture. The wizened potter watched quietly, listening to our comments, but since he couldn't speak English, and we couldn't speak Japanese, it was difficult to converse. I wondered what he thought about us, especially Brian with his size and beard. Did he wonder at Yumi's motives, bringing us here? Were we to show him, by our presence, that she maintained foreign contact and intended one day to return to New York? It was a strange thought, that Brian and I might be pawns in a silent struggle between father and daughter.

His face was expressive, but in the way of weathered stone, shaped by the forces of time and nature. Thick black glasses perched on his nose. His hair was silver and well receded, but it was trimmed and combed neatly. He wore simple, sturdy, oft-washed garments. He hardly watched Yumi as she bustled quietly about us, but I could see his pleasure in having her near. His tone was soft when he spoke with her, even cheerful at times. He smiled to see the small pastries she served for dessert, and nodded with distinct satisfaction as she served his tea. Even if we were foreigners, having his daughter home and entertaining guests was evidently satisfying.

As our meal concluded, he spoke briskly to Yumi and looked toward us. She translated. "My father is going back to work. You may visit the workshop if you wish."

We thanked him and bowed as he left, then tried to help Yumi with the dishes. She refused us twice, the second time more strongly. "You really are foreigners aren't you? First off, men don't help in the kitchen. My father would find that . . . well, I can't imagine what he'd think if he saw you washing dishes. Secondly, an invitation to his workshop is not a casual thing. He's expecting you in there."

Duly chastened, we retreated to the entrance and donned our shoes. It was a gorgeous day outside, a pale sun in a flawless blue sky. We entered the workshop through an open door, stepping carefully over large and small pots, and walked between stacked shelves to a large square working area. Shelves lined all the walls, except where a large door opened to the driveway, and on either side where tall windows let shafts of light into the dark room. Large tables filled the center area while in one corner, like a chained beast, loomed the kiln.

He was tending some small bedding plants on a sunny window ledge. He signaled for us to look around, then returned to his plants. Examining each in turn, he pulled away dead leaves and unwanted sprouts, then watered them with the care of a chemist. Finally, he held each plant in his hands and rotated it, inspecting its details as if monitoring a miracle in progress.

When Yumi's father came finally came over, we all stood there for a moment, no one quite sure what to do. Then, quite abruptly, he began a pantomime where he pretended to pick up clay and carry it to the potting wheel. He gestured with his hands as if making something, then moved to a shelf where the new pieces were stored. He put his imaginary piece down, paused to indicate waiting, then moved it to a table near several large cans and jars, evidently glazes of various color. He showed us the glazing motions, stepped to a different set of shelves where other pieces sat waiting, then took his piece to the kiln where several items were already stacked and wedged in place. After a final pause, he carried his imaginary masterpiece out into the adjoining store.

We stepped from the dusty clutter of the workshop into a tiny, crowed showroom. All around were the creations of this man's hands, arranged tastefully on glass shelves. It was a stunning display. My respect was suddenly amplified into awe, and with it came a desire, almost a yearning, to learn this myself. Yumi said he taught students, but hand-chosen ones only, and with the motive, I suspected, of passing on knowledge rather than earning money.

He left us in the showroom inspecting his wares, and when we returned to the workshop he was sitting at his pottery wheel with a fresh hunk of clay. We stood near as he centered it and began shaping his piece. It quickly became round and then cylindrical, and he began working it upward, ever thinner. The shape seemed to change miraculously within his grasp. The slightest touch could do it, maybe less. With both his hands and the clay wet, his merest thought seemed enough. He worked with such concentration that he almost willed the pot to transform itself. It was as if his hands and the pot merged in that creative instant. No distinction. His life flowed into the clay, giving it the subtle energy of a handcrafted item.

With a grunt, some swift movements, and a couple of tools, he finished the details of the base and removed the finished pot from the wheel. After placing it on the appropriate shelf, he turned to us and gave a palms-up shrug. That was it. That was the tour.

We thanked him and stood around for a while longer, but then realized that we were supposed to leave and let him work. We slipped out and headed back to the house.

"Christ, did you see that?" Brian muttered. "Like bloody magic."

Before I could reply we were back inside, putting on slippers and finding Yumi at the low table where we ate lunch. She had lain out the flowers we brought and had a tall slim vase ready to arrange them.

She stopped to get us another beer, an idea strongly encouraged by Brian.

I was still in shock. Those few minutes in the pottery studio taught me more than a dozen art lectures in college. To see the beauty emerging, to witness the effortlessness of the creating, to feel the wonderment rising within my chest, it was beyond description. It was like alchemy, transmuting formless mud into gold.

In my mind's eye, I kept seeing his fingers, touching the clay. I imagined what it would feel like, the clay moist, my fingers soft.

But you don't see with your eyes, I thought.

You see with your fingertips.

No, you see it with your mind, and your fingertips take over and do it.

No, your fingertips are your mind. Your consciousness shifts completely to your fingers, much as it does when caressing a woman's breast. You feel only that, and revel in every nuance. It was like sex, using or making love with your art, fusing with it.

Yumi came in with the beer and poured us both a glass. I half expected her to revert to Western ways and say, "Pour it yourself," but she maintained her Japanese deportment flawlessly.

Brian toasted her father's work, and we sat back to watch Yumi arrange the flowers. She examined each of the four stalks, comparing them in size and characteristics. Finally she selected one, snipped it at the base, and set it into place. It looked stark standing by itself, but somehow beautiful already. Yumi stared at it a long while, then held up two more stems in succession, as if confirming her vision. She took the shorter one, cut it down an inch and placed in the center, but angled it forward slightly to create a third dimension.

Again she paused and looked at her remaining flowers. I swear I felt the suspense building. She was so careful with those first two choices, and the result was so lovely, that I was curious, excited actually, to see what she would do with the others.

In that instant, I grasped the appeal of flower arranging. Out of the myriad species of flowers, and the almost infinite variation of shape, size, combination, and spatial juxtaposition, you have the challenging pleasure of finding a harmonious compromise. Even with a limited number of flowers, such as these four we presented to Yumi, the options are still vast. Seeing her select the third and fourth stalks, measure and cut them, then set each gently into place, I realized how truly creative it was. Like her father, imagining a pot then creating it, she assessed her components, visualized her arrangements, and then made it happen. It was remarkable.

Just as fascinating was Yumi's rapt attention. I wasn't surprised, since flower arranging was another of the Zen arts, but in the face of it I was humbled, intrigued, and envious. Why? Because Yumi and her father both displayed what she once referred to as "*essence.*" It was how they did it as much as what they did and in their respective disciplines they were standard holders of a long tradition. It wasn't about art. It was about the process of making art, and the attitude they brought to—and carried from—their endeavors. What a wonderful legacy!

fourteen

Early Sunday morning, I stood outside Yoshida House with my bag packed and my skis leaning against the fence. Right on time, a blue Toyota came round the corner with Kohei behind the wheel. We loaded quickly and took off, weaving excitedly through the deserted streets, but gradually, as we found the freeway and headed for the mountains, our chatter fell silent.

I closed my eyes but not for sleep. As always before skiing, I thought back to past ski trips and re-imagined my best runs. Snips of action, like a highlight reel, flashed through my mind. I saw myself skiing, the scenery flashing by, the different combinations of pitch and terrain. Although this was imaginary, the excitement in my stomach felt real.

It grew cloudy and cold as we climbed. A long line of ski-laden cars formed ahead of us and the Japan Alps rose from the plateau like huge battlements stretching north and south into the mist. As we wound into them and saw advertisements for various other ski areas, I wrote the names and locations into my notebook. At each turnoff, I studied the signs and access roads, looking for something propitious.

When we arrived at the Naeba ski resort, the parking lot looked like a ski-industry convention. Or a fashion show. Everyone wore the latest in equipment and clothing—even obvious beginners were decked out like pros. To me, this seemed as incongruous as the *kangi* lettering on a Bavarian-style lodge, or the skiers using vending machines to buy lift tickets. The strangest thing was to watch Japanese enjoy themselves, laugh out loud even, since I had only ever seen them working and commuting.

Finally we stepped into our skis and slid over to the chairlift. The lift line wasn't crowded, but once we were scooped up I saw clusters of people everywhere on the hill. Sometimes they were talking and resting; usually they were looking uphill toward a sprawled figure. Often skiers were bunched so closely it was impossible for others to ski through them. I saw a collision, then another. No one got upset or alarmed; it was as if this was a normal part of the skiing experience. The skiers simply brushed themselves off, laughingly bowed to each other, and then took off again. It would have been funny if it were not so dangerous.

By the time I reached the top, however, I didn't care if a million skiers were scattered below. I was finally on skis in Japan. We stood awhile, surveying the long gray valley and the irregular peaks that disappeared into the cloud. The air was fresh, cold on my tongue, and I drew it in deep.

Kohei took off and I watched him descend. He was nimble, almost weightless on his skis, and I smiled to see traces of our ski instructor's training in his movements. I pushed off to catch up, angling toward the right side of the run. Here, as in most ski areas, there was loose snow and room to ski. People get nervous near the trees and stay a safe margin away, but I loved to weave down the edge of the scraped-up snow. I found a good line, steep but smooth, where the snow was soft. I slipped into a rhythm, the wind feeling good on my face, my skis shifting easily beneath me.

A fallen teenager forced me into the mogul field, so I slowed myself on the first bump, compressing fully as the resistance grew. I rose gently over the top and began a bobbing weave through the last few mounds. The turns felt tight. My balance was good. I was calm.

I found Kohei waiting on a crest. Like me, he was beaming. "*Sugoya*, Rick-san," he said. Great.

He set off again, this time down a steeper section that curved around the mountain, but I had another idea. There was a good side hill, completely empty, so I angled onto the left flank. As I came further over, I saw more and more space opening below me, all dusted in fresh snow. It seemed strange to have so many skiers on the main run yet none here.

People on the chairlift were turning in their seats as they rose, waiting to watch me ski. I felt conspicuous suddenly. Exhaling slowly, from deep in my abdomen, I tried to release my thoughts.

Forget it, I thought. *Forget everything. Time to ski.*

I pushed off. A small bump came quickly. I cut it sharply with my downhill ski and bounced around into loose snow beneath. I aimed for the next mogul, drew it in—ooomphf—and felt the icy crystals explode up around me. Pivoting on the crest and dropping fast, I swept left in a wide turn. I was beneath the lift now and the eyes from above were on me. The steel tower loomed. At the last instant, I bounced into a reversal and curved just beyond its metallic grasp. Accelerating into the last stretch of moguls, I took one, brushed over two, then—uuuggh—compressed hard on the last. My knees, up near my chin, took the strain, releasing me gently onto the main run.

I stopped, chest heaving, to let Kohei catch up. I looked upward through my billowing breath and relived those turns, that flooding of adrenaline and exhilaration. Even if I didn't ski another run, the trip was already worth it. I was again filled with that exquisite aliveness that skiing brings; I saw it also in the excited expressions of the skiers around me. At our own level, we were each challenging the mountain, reveling in the energy it brought out of us.

I thought back suddenly to Tokyo. I had been comfortable, even happy in the routine I had forged. Until that instant, I could have spent my winter there. But that one run changed everything. I remembered vividly why I had come to Japan. To settle for pleasant time in Tokyo would be a cop-out, not at all what I had foreseen.

But my renewed determination was soon bruised. With Kohei's help at lunchtime, I found the ski school and asked to see the director. He looked confused as Kohei explained my situation. He asked a few questions, and I watched Kohei shake his head. Translation wasn't necessary. Without working papers or the ability to speak Japanese, what could I do? What service could I offer?

In the afternoon, I skied like a man possessed. Kohei was returning to Canada, and I wasn't sure when or if I'd ski again, so I opened the throttle wide on every run. My eyes were tearing up, even through my goggles, and Kohei was laughing hard when he caught me each time at the bottom. Up we'd go again, agonizingly slowly, then down in a blur. My legs were dangerously tired, but my desire was stronger. Even on the last run, when the lifts closed and the mountain lay cloaked in a cold blue light, I still skied lustily, with serpentine turns interspersed with swiveling staccato bursts.

But then, all too soon, the slope ended and the day was gone. I stepped out of my skis sadly, wondering if I would use them again that winter. It was hard to believe. It wasn't even January and my season might be ending on the day it began.

On the long drive home, I kept seeing those runs in my mind's eye. They renewed my certainty that something would happen. But what? With the hum of wheels underneath and headlights stabbing the darkness, I stared down the highway. Where was the right road now?

fifteen

Luck, karma, power, fate, synchronicity, or the stars—whoever, or whatever, gets mentioned in the credits, the next few days were like a Hollywood movie. It began the next night with an offhand comment from Brian.

"By the way, Rick," he said. "I was down at that job placement agency for Australians today and I heard something about a Canadian bloke getting work at a ski area in Hokkaido."

In my surprise, I bumped the table and spilled my tea. "Really?"

He nodded. "Sorry I didn't get more details, but I reckon you could go down yourself and ask. Here, I wrote out the address and directions for you."

"Thanks," I said, taking the wrinkled piece of yellow notepaper. We were in the kitchen, with cooking and washing going on around us, but suddenly it all seemed far away. Out of nowhere, I had a ray of hope.

The next morning I followed Brian's instructions to a third-story office on a quiet side street. It was an open room with dark hardwood floors and wooden desks that looked like a newspaper office in the thirties. Three ladies looked up from their desks. The oldest, a slender, silver haired woman, rose to greet me.

"May I help you?" she asked, in perfect English.

"I hope so," I said. "I'm a ski instructor. I'm trying to find work at a ski resort."

It sounded far-fetched, but she nodded kindly and asked, "Are you Australian?"

"No."

She nodded quietly. "Do you have working papers?"

When I shook my head, I saw, in her confused expression, my hope flickering.

"I'm very sorry," she said sincerely. "I can not help you. This office is for Australian citizens with working papers."

I was crushed. I wanted to ask, 'Didn't you already help a Canadian?' But I couldn't. She was only doing her job. It wouldn't help to make her feel awkward. I bowed and moved to the exit. Just as my hand touched the door, she chose to speak again.

"Wait a moment, please," she said. I turned and stepped back into the room, feeling my heart rise like a yo-yo.

"There is a man coming this afternoon from Sapporo who may be able to help you. I'll explain your situation. If you call me tomorrow, I will tell you what he says."

"Yes, of course. Thank you." Mere thanks seemed insufficient. She was assisting me when she had no reason to. I bowed again.

Suddenly, as she rose from her return bow, I saw surprise cross her face. She was looking over my shoulder to the door, where a middle-aged, athletic man was entering. He called out a cheerful greeting that the office women answered in unison.

As she moved toward him, the woman said to me, "Wait here a moment. This is the man from Sapporo."

She greeted him warmly and exchanged pleasantries, but I heard her tone of voice shift as the topic came around to me. The man looked at me just once, but it was the careful gaze of appraisal. I met his eyes and bowed.

He nodded toward me, bending slightly, then their talk shifted to other business. She led him to the desk of her coworker, then excused herself and returned to me. "Thank you for waiting. If you'll please call me tomorrow, I'll let you know."

I felt helpless and anxious, but I knew better than to press for details. Whatever was happening, it was clearly out of her hands. I thanked her again and left.

The day dragged on. The night was worse. I was in the kitchen, nursing a cup of tea, when Brian popped in.

"How did it go?" he asked.

I shrugged and described the fateful exchange. "Ask me tomorrow."

He slapped me on the back and went to bed. I turned off the lights and climbed the stairs to my room. The window was open and the heater was on beneath my small table, so I pulled up its fringe around my waist and lay back, listening to the chimes. The wind breathed gently through my room, bringing a melody that set my candle dancing. I watched the golden interplay of shadow and light on the ceiling, imagining my own life in the whimsical exchange.

I woke early and cooked myself an omelet. I was hungry, but even more, I wanted to stay busy until it came time to use the telephone. I ate and washed the dishes and cleaned my room. I put in a load of laundry. I took a shower. It was still only nine o'clock, too early to call.

Finally, at nine-thirty, armed with my coins, my notebook, and my hopes, I went to the phone. I made the connection and recognized the woman's voice immediately. With my breakfast doing back flips inside me, I identified myself.

"Oh, good morning," she said. "Have you a pencil or pen?"

"Yes, go ahead."

She gave me a name and a phone number, saying, "If you go up to Sapporo, this man might be able to help you."

There was a long silence on the line. I waited to hear more. Sapporo was a thousand miles away and I hadn't much money. Would there be a job for me there? A place to stay? I needed answers but I couldn't ask the questions. I contorted mentally, like a bowler trying body English to influence the roll of his ball.

"I'm sorry I can't say anything else, but this man may be able to help you."

Once again, I understood her position. She was able only to suggest a possibility off the record and, as much as I wanted to, I could hardly ask for more. I thanked her as profusely as I could, then hung up.

It was a long walk back to the kitchen. The piece of paper seemed huge in my hand. I looked again at the name I'd written.

Miura Yuichiro. I wasn't even sure which was the surname.

I drained the last of my tea and headed out the door to work. Faced with this new decision, the day was agonizing. I thought about Yumi—her beautiful features and graceful body, her sharp wit and unusual wisdom. I thought of Brian too, and the hours we'd spend around the kitchen table, talking and laughing. I'd already taught my classes that week, so if I left I wouldn't see my Matsushita fellows again, or the fresh-faced kids.

Every place I went, everything I saw, I wondered if it were the last time. In a matter of days, hours even, I could be heading north to Sapporo. But how could I pull it off? I had saved barely enough money for a one-way train ticket and a few days' expenses. It meant giving up my teaching jobs and leaving the home and friends I had found. All that for a gamble, a long shot at best.

That night, as we walked to the local bathhouse, I asked for Brian's advice. With a wit as dry as the desert that weaned him, he summed up my situation. "Well, let's first weigh the facts. You've been given a man's name in Sapporo and you're to travel a thousand miles in the hope that he'll help you before your money runs out. How much do you have, two hundred Yank dollars? Well, yes, it does seem daft.

"But on the other hand," he continued, "You came the same way to Japan, didn't you? A one-way ticket, a paltry amount of cash and all that ski gear in hopes of having—how did you describe it? 'Some sort of ski adventure.'"

I nodded.

"You could do worse than to follow your dreams, mate. I'm home-spun, mind you, but from what I've seen there's too few people who dare to dream these days, and fewer still living them out."

We were now at the bathhouse, standing near the entrance. His eyes were fixed on mine and I felt a surge of gratitude. "Thanks," I said. "For everything."

"No worries, mate. Rip a few turns for me."

We left our shoes by the door and entered. We undressed, lathered, and scrubbed, then stepped to the bath. I eased myself in, ignoring the heated protest of my feet, legs, stomach, and chest. Gradually, my swirling thoughts were forgotten, evaporated. There was only this piercing sensation, wave upon wave of exquisite agony. It was worse when someone moved, generating underwater currents that pushed the hot water against me, through me. My tension melted; my cares faded to their true, relative unimportance. There was just me and the water. Nothing more.

Getting out finally, I moved to the exterior garden. I stood there naked and steaming, my vapor rising white into the black evening sky. I was peaceful finally. I knew what to do.

Once the decision was made, there was no time or money to waste. The next morning I told Jun Yoshida of my plans and said my room would be available Saturday. I swung by my English schools to give notice, pick up my wages, and leave notes for my students. The kids likely wouldn't notice or care much, but the Matsushita gang would miss their baseball talks. With that in mind, I slipped a second note into the envelope for them to give their new teacher, explaining the success of my impromptu strategy.

I put in my last shift at ESS, drinking more of the horrid coffee and saying good-bye to my regulars. They were surprised, astounded really, that I was taking such an enormous gamble, and explaining it repeatedly didn't do much for my confidence. When it came time to leave finally, and the group gathered around me at the door, I found myself remarkably sad. As tedious as the routine had become, I had made several good friends at the English Speaking Society.

But when my feet hit the pavement, and I took those first steps toward my new adventure, I was clearly looking forward. That night was New Year's Eve, and I was to meet Brian and Yumi at the club.

Yumi had arranged this early in the week, not knowing it would be our last time together.

I arrived at the club first, then Brian, and we took a table. It was good we were sitting down, for when Yumi walked in, wearing a beautiful blue kimono, I might well have fallen over. She looked radiant, like Japanese femininity personified.

That day I had noticed many more women than usual wearing kimonos, and Yumi explained the tradition of dressing up on New Year's Eve and visiting the shrines to give thanks and offer prayers. In fact, she wanted to take us that evening to the nearby Meiji shine, one of the largest in Japan.

I agreed, of course, scarcely able to take my eyes off her. She seemed so mysterious suddenly. With the traditional garb, she donned also an exquisite discreteness. Perhaps it was always so, and my eyes were blind to the subtleties, but in these amazing garments, Yumi's every move seemed perfect. I felt clumsy in comparison.

Yumi couldn't stay late, so Brian and I downed our drinks and headed out. The streets were busy now, even more so as we passed through the huge red gate into the sprawling forest that surrounded the Meiji shrine. There were thousands of women in kimonos now, and men in their equivalent finery, all around us in a long procession through the trees, and for a brief moment it seemed we had slipped back in time.

Yumi walked between us, and spoke with her head down. "I understand you are leaving."

"Tomorrow," I said.

There was an awkward silence and I suddenly recognized her sadness. This thought flooded me with confused emotion. Yumi was an exotic woman, a friend, and a teacher too. Her insight and compassion were as attractive as her perfect skin and flowing movements. I would miss our time together, our long walks and intriguing talks.

She spoke again, softly. "Who is it you will seek in Sapporo?"

I fished the crumpled paper from my pocket and read the name haltingly: "Mi . . . Miura . . . Yui . . . Yuichiro."

"Miura Yuichiro?" she asked, her voice rising.

She turned to face me. "Do you know who Miura Yuichiro is?"

As I looked into her widened eyes and shook my head, I felt the first tremors of destiny. Time slowed down. Over her shoulder, I saw the procession toward the shrine, moving with thanks and prayers as Japanese had for centuries, but they seemed frozen in that instant, like the backdrop of a play. There was only Yumi and I and the words that tumbled from her mouth: "Miura Yuichiro is the most famous skier in Japan. He is *The Man Who Skied Down Everest.*"

Time stopped. The moment hung there about me. I had gone from a ludicrous plan to the sudden knowledge that I was to meet, out of a hundred million people, the ideal man. I felt like God was reaching down to touch me, like my dream was unfolding in slow motion. My head fell back and I laughed, a huge long laugh from the depths of my being that echoed into the night and started again the forward motion of time.

sixteen

I collected myself as the train gathered speed. My chest heaved, my left knee ached, and my clothes were soggy with perspiration. I'd been struggling with my skis and duffel bag for an hour, stumbling stupefied with exhaustion from subway to subway, rushing onto the platform mere seconds before the train started to roll. Now I lay slumped on my bags between cars, too tired to move. Raising my head finally, seeing through the glass of the doors that both cars were empty, I laughed weakly. No worry about a place to sit.

Moving forward, I stored my luggage and collapsed into a window seat. I peeled off my coat and sweater with relief, feeling foolish for misjudging the time, amazed at how adrenaline had overcome both pain and fatigue, and dismayed that my peace of mind had so quickly given way to panic. In the rush for the train, I'd completely lost the calm of my Tokyo days.

As the train lurched however, and rolled slowly out of the station, I felt my excitement returning. I propped up my leg, then took out my journal and read the previous night's entry, my last from the privacy of my room. Half of it concerned what I was leaving behind, the rest with excited hopes and expectations. Yumi's news about Miura shocked me, as did her summation of his background. He became famous for skiing Mt. Everest, but before that he was a world-class speed skier and racer, and had skied major peaks on all the continents, including Kilimanjaro and the revered Mt. Fuji. While such feats were already growing more common, his deeds came years before the notion of extreme skiing existed. Yumi was emphatic. Miura was Japan's most respected ski Master, the venerated Number One.

Brian had seen me off that morning, sharing a last cup of coffee in the small warm kitchen under the stairs. I would miss him, especially his straightforward approach and hearty laugh. I would miss our talks too, long rambling affairs over tall beers, trading stories of distant adventures and occasional insights.

I'd written most of them down in my thick and tattered notebook. I glanced through it now, reading select passages. Perhaps the most interesting talk was our first, on the night Brian and I returned from the monastery. We seemed to understand each other immediately, having each taken our 'walkabout' to the same place. We both played sports, traveled to learn, and outgrew our lives at home. Different stories, same result.

Having described for Brian my circuitous path, I returned from our talks and wrote it all down in great detail. As I relived those moments through my writing, I found myself understanding them better in light of my latest adventure in Japan. Each of my past challenges was distinctly different, but looking through them together revealed not only a similarity, but a lifelong pattern.

I first rushed for a train the day after my high school graduation, except then I was hopping a moving freight car for a free trip across Canada. I ran with a friend, Troy, across a young wheat field, leapt a barbed wire fence, and clambered up the rail embankment. Sprinting alongside the train as it gathered speed, we tried vainly to open the huge doors. Finally, as the caboose came into view, we grabbed the metal ladders of the last car and pulled ourselves up onto the roof. After laughing hard and catching our breath, we spread out a picnic of cheese, fruit, and bread and had our first taste of the traveling life on top of a boxcar hurtling across the prairies.

Troy viewed our graduation trip as a lark, but I was standing at a fork in the road, taking a serious look down the less-worn path. Could I see then the adventures, the struggles, the consequences of a wider world view? Hardly, but I took the first step anyway. Nine months later, I landed in Lisbon, Portugal, ready for whatever adventure four months and nine hundred dollars could bring in Europe. When Portugal's historic coup d'état occurred on my second day, it seemed to be a good omen. In the naïve expectations of an eighteen-year-old romantic, things like coups simply happen when you travel. Everything was exotic—espresso bars, cobblestone streets, the winding country roads with herds of sheep, and castles perched high on hills. At the Algarve, I had my first view of the ocean, and ran with a friend alongside the crashing surf, drunk on the excitement of the moment. I was hooked.

A week later, on a ferry steaming south toward the Moroccan port of Tetuan, I met the man who unwittingly changed my life. I first noticed him as he stood near the rail of the ship, looking out through round, wire-rimmed glasses at the Rock of Gibraltar. Ken was about twenty-eight years old, dressed in light cotton clothes, carrying only a small burlap bag. I tried to strike up a conversation but he was reluctant to talk. He had an implacable calm that fascinated me, and I fidgeted around him as a playful pup might around a wise old dog.

When I asked finally where he had come from, he focused his stony blue eyes on mine and said, "I've come overland from Asia." Ken turned back, silent again, but I imagined the rest: trains, trucks, buses, temples, mosques, marketplaces, deltas, and deserts. A sudden certainty filled me: However and wherever he had gone, whatever he learned that filled him with such serenity, I decided in that moment that I would go there and learn it too.

I ended up hitchhiking with Ken through Morocco, getting my initiation to the road. He was a keen observer, often detecting details or behavior that astounded me. His kindness and equanimity were unfailing, and even the hard-bitten Moroccan traders warmed up to him. There was always time for kids, to talk and play simple games. Above all, he was less concerned about where we were going, or where we had been, than he was about what we were doing at that moment.

We parted company in southern Spain but he remained with me in spirit. I emulated him as I traveled on through Europe, imagining how he would act, what he would say in different situations. Since he was so different from anyone I had known, I realized, for the first time perhaps, how influenced I had been by my peers and their opinions. Alone and away from that finally, I enjoyed the freedom to experiment with new ideas and possibilities. This was no radical transformation, more of a gentle and pleasing sense of personal growth. I learned to be myself and to trust myself.

The train gathered speed as we exchanged the grays of Tokyo for the patchwork fields of the outlying farmlands. An elderly woman shuffled into the car, pushing a food cart. She looked downcast as she passed row after row of empty seats, but her face brightened into a silver-toothed smile when she saw me. I looked over her wares and selected a *bento* lunch box with a colorful assortment of bite-sized morsels. They were delicious, and I ate several immediately, but I forced myself to save most of this precious food for later.

Besides money, my immediate concern was the tightness in my knee. I got up to walk and stretch, and could tell immediately that the torturous run to the subway had taken its toll. Without looking, I knew the skin around the kneecap would be puffy with gathering fluid, the sore, spongy reminder of injuries past. The familiar discomfort drew me back to my earlier reverie.

I had returned from that European trip feeling distinctly changed but soon found myself doing all the same things. My friends were in university, so I went too, even though I was unsure what to study and generally doubtful that an eighteen year old could yet know what to do with his or her life. My social activities were just as confusing, trying to reconcile my new individuality within my old groups. I felt independent but yearned also for friendship and belonging. This was not new behavior and I was certainly not alone; I had already observed, among friends and classmates since my early teens, that we all wanted to fit in, that we feared embarrassment and rejection, the relegation to loneliness. Like trees leaning in a constant wind, the desire for acceptance shaped our behavior.

Simpler then, and far more immediate, were the familiar challenges of athletics. Sports had always been a constant, particularly when other things were turbulent or doubtful. Games provided specific goals, time frames, and criteria for improvement. You had friends and teammates sharing a common cause and, hopefully, something wonderful called team spirit. Best of all, even if you failed or lost, there were always other days and chances ahead.

I had a secret motive too. As long as I could remember, I had been playing out football and hockey games in my head, working backward and forward through my fantasies like a film editor. Since I was small and quick in football, I savored the thought of running back a fumble or interception for the big touchdown. In hockey, I enjoyed the fantasy, unlikely for a defenseman, of a breakaway goal in the dying seconds of a championship. Before Europe, my prior seasons in both sports ended in knee injuries, and surgery was definitely not how I envisioned concluding my careers.

But football was not to be. Not that first year. I made it to the last day of tryouts, to the final cut, but was released. With the news came a flood of emotions—disappointment, frustration, and embarrassment. Although this was the perennial champion, star-studded team, loaded with players that were fifty to seventy pounds heavier, it was still hard to face my friends and family. To fail in isolation was bad enough, but to fall short before others was gut-wrenching.

I filled the void as best I could, first with my studies, then with hockey. The tryouts were again difficult, the cream of the city brought together. As always during my sporting career, everyone was bigger and better technically, and several had impressive statistics and press clippings from prior seasons. But I fought my way through training camp, compensating with pure hustle. The coach noticed that. He knew of my recent injuries, saw that I was small and a step behind at first, but apparently he liked my attitude. When the final roster was posted, my name was on the bottom.

I justified his faith, growing stronger as the season progressed. My knees held up, even the right one which had suffered torn ligaments and cartilage. Besides a regular shift on defense, I began drawing extra duty for penalty killing and power plays. I was thrilled but nervous. When we entered the playoffs, my stomach was in my throat before every face-off, with each chance to touch the puck.

Between games meanwhile, while in class or at the library or driving in my car, I still played out hockey scenarios in my head, indulging occasionally in my fantasy of a championship goal. It wasn't a likely scenario, since I had scored only a handful of goals in sixty games that season, but I enjoyed it nonetheless.

By late spring, we were in the finals. It was a grueling series, game after game of hard-hitting hockey. The more intense it became, the more frequently I noticed a strange tornado-like phenomenon: although outwardly in fast and furious motion, I was inside filled with a curious inner calm. The faster and more critical the action became, the deeper my focus grew. I was so dispassionate that I wondered at times if I was even present, if some other force wasn't controlling my actions.

The last game ended in a tie, and we went into sudden-death overtime. The first goal would win the championship. We had five minutes in our dressing room to catch our breath and talk strategy. The coach, studying me from across the room, announced that he was moving me from defense to left wing, a position I hadn't played all year. He patted me on the shoulder and whispered that he "had a hunch." Again I felt this icy calm settle over me.

As we left the dressing room, the huge arena erupted. People were cheering, banging on the glass, and waving banners, but as we slid up for the opening face-off, the noise of the crowd fell away. I could hear only my breath and the scraping of skates on the ice. The puck squirted back to our defenseman, who quickly fed it across to the far winger. He raced across the blue line, then cut back sharply and blasted a hard shot. The goalie splayed his legs in a scissors save, kicking the puck to the corner. Their star defenseman whirled to retrieve it, then snapped it quickly up the boards to the breaking winger. He linked up with his teammate and broke in on our defense, two on two. He drew wide, faked a pass, then ripped a quick shot. Clunk! The puck ricocheted off the goal post.

Attackers swarmed into our end. The puck slid back to their defenseman on the left point. I started rushing toward him but my other winger was already there, reaching to block his shot. The sound of the puck striking his pads gave me my cue.

I charged alone up the ice as my teammate reached the loose puck and flipped it up ahead of me. It was a clean breakaway. I was crossing the blue line with only the goalie between me and victory, the whole play happening in slow motion. But the puck hit a bump and started rolling on its side, just as the goalie rushed out to cut down the angle. Things started speeding up; I felt my panic rising as I fought with the puck. My big moment. I couldn't blow it.

Suddenly I knew what to do. I had been there so often in my mind. I looked down one last time, calm now, and saw the puck fall flat. I looked up, saw my long-awaited chance, now real, and snapped my wrists. With the puck gone, speeding slowly toward the top left corner, the arena fell eerily silent. My momentum carried me past the net, where I saw, almost magically, the unmistakable black bulge of the puck straining the mesh. It was a goal.

Everything became surreal. The arena exploded but the roar was like a hush. I hardly felt the pounding of my teammates as they poured off the bench and leapt onto me. Inexplicably, I felt myself rising upward out of my body to a place in mid-air above the net, where I floated and looked down the jubilant scene. It was so vivid I was struck by a distinct thought: *I've imagined this moment for years, visualized it a thousand times, and here it is. Am I dreaming?*

The conductor, a stout man in a faded blue uniform, came down the aisle. He scrutinized my ticket, punched it briskly with two holes, then tucked it into a railing above my head. Behind him came the old lady again, this time with hot tea, so I opened my bag and brought out the remains of my lunch.

As I ate and sipped the steaming tea, the hockey memory echoed in my mind. It was a wonderful moment, the pinnacle of seventeen years of hockey, yet afterward I had little time to savor it. The hockey season went so long that it was soon time for football tryouts. I was in far better condition than the previous year and could finally feel confident about my knees. The coaches doubted I could play linebacker because of my size, but thought my agility might be effective on special teams. Again it came down to the final cut, but this time I made it.

By mid-season, I was on all the special teams and at outside linebacker in passing and blitzing situations. With my quickness, I could often squirt into the backfield and chase the quarterback in his backpedal, or be close enough to break up hand-offs and laterals as they occurred. The pitchouts were especially tantalizing, seeing the ball mere feet away and nothing but green grass behind. I still dreamed daily of picking one off and running for a touchdown.

I was picked to start at outside linebacker for the last game of the regular season. It was a proud moment, and I played ferociously to deserve it. I started in every playoff game too, including the provincial final in which we played our oldest rival, the Wildcats, for the right to advance toward the national championship.

At halftime we were losing by three points. My black and gold uniform was dirty and soaked with perspiration. My hands were bound like casts with white tape, stained now with grass, dirt, and blood. Each breath I took sounded loud in my ears. I slowly looked around at the other thirty-nine players in the room, knowing each man for what he truly was, for what he had proven himself to be during the challenges of the season, during the furies of the games. The mood now was somber. Finality loomed large. While some of my teammates would go on to play professionally, this threatened to be, for most of us, the last football game of our lives.

I had a sense of imminence as I donned my helmet and joined the throng at the door. Despite the heat of my body, I felt a shivering over my skin's surface. Blood and adrenaline surged through me as we roared up the ramp and into the sunny tumult, yet at the same time, I felt this strange detachment. Whereas normally I might loosen up with a teammate or stretch my legs, I did nothing. I felt exquisitely ready.

I ran out with the kickoff team and stood without emotion on the line. Out of all the things around me, I noticed how vibrantly green the grass was and how beautiful my teammates looked, standing in formation. The ball was kicked, arcing high and brown against the cloudless October sky, falling into the hands of Emilio Fraietta, their top speedster. The field transformed into a balletic battlefield, the blockers in white moving into position, we like marauders in black, charging toward them. I misdirected my gaze to fool the first blocker, then angled toward the runner. Huge linemen were setting up a sideline return and Fraietta was sprinting into his protective tunnel. At the last instant, I cut sharply and dove through a seam in their ranks, my helmet lowered to knee level. My head snapped savagely with the impact and, as I skidded over the grass, I turned to see the result. Fraietta had soared and bounced and came to rest five yards downfield, and he was now looking back with incredulity to see what hit him. Our eyes met for a brief, satisfying second.

I remained on for defense. They made two first downs, but we forced them to punt from their fifty-yard line. I lined up on the far right, assigned to charge, engage the setback blocker on my side and, if possible, get a hand on the kick. But when the Wildcats came out of the huddle, I noticed something wrong. My man, a gutsy cornerback named Meraw, was lined up to block me, but his partner was missing. There was no one to block Bill Betts, who would duplicate my charge from the other side. Meraw saw this also but too late to call a time-out. As the ball was snapped, he took a half step towards Betts then realized he couldn't stop both of us. The scrappy back turned again to me but was unable set up properly. After all our head-on collisions that year, no quarter asked or given, I finally had him beat. He could barely deflect me off my path to the punter.

As I left him sprawling, I saw that Betts had his arms around LaBrosse, the punter, but in his excitement had overrun him. He barely had hold of the punter's waist from behind, and LaBrosse's hands were free. When I was four yards away, he released the ball and brought his leg up to kick it.

Except that I arrived just then, and saw that football floating there, frozen in space and time. It was new and pebbly brown against the green grass of the empty field behind. I was in full stride, yet again, it felt like slow motion. Although a freak play, there was no question what to do. I had seen it countless times in my dreams. As gently as one might lift a baby, I cradled that football and kept on running.

At first, no one else realized what had happened. The players on both teams were sprinting the other way, waiting for the punt that wouldn't come, and the spectators wondered why a solitary figure in black and gold was racing down the field. As for me, I was all alone, running through the dream I had seen countless times in my imagination. It seemed to happen slowly and the details were vividly clear: the pumping of my arms, the yard lines passing beneath my feet, the end zone just ahead. It was the winning touchdown, the one I had so often foreseen.

The final moment was comical however. As I crossed the goal line and turned back toward the field, I felt a sudden confusion. I had visualized everything in my boyhood daydreams except what to do when I reached the end zone. Spike the ball? No, the coaches didn't like that. What then? Self-conscious, suddenly, of people watching, and having no better idea, I simply dropped the ball. But just then, I remembered from our film sessions how the ball carriers flipped it nonchalantly over their shoulders when they scored. I looked down for the ball and fate played into my hands. The ball bounced right back up, and I dropped it with casual delight over my shoulder, just before my teammates arrived and piled forty deep upon me in the end zone.

I rose from my seat and walked forward through the car, partly to stretch out the stiffness in my knee, but also because the rest of this memory bothered me. I pulled open the end door and positioned myself on the step between the cars where I could look out over the passing landscape. My eyes watered and my cheeks burned with the cold wind, but my mind was still very much in the past, back in those strangely confusing days of youthful triumph.

In one year, against considerable odds, the dreams of my youth had come true, but their sudden absence left me disoriented. I was nearing completion of my undergraduate degree, trying to decide my next step, but in the face of this daunting choice, I realized that I lacked the guiding images that had led me to youthful success. Worse yet, the pleasures of my sporting identity came back incessantly to haunt me, making my daily life and the future seem drab in comparison. In particular, I replayed my touchdown run and breakaway goal, reliving that inexplicable awareness. I tried over and over to analyze this remarkable clarity, even after I realized that incessant thinking served only to amplify my anxiety. It was masochistic but I couldn't help it.

Then one day, in the depths of this unlikely malaise, I began thinking back on the freedom of my European traveling days. I thought again of my friend Ken and the look in his eyes when he said those first simple words: "I've come overland from Asia." With this flash of memory came a rising excitement, for I also recalled the certainty I felt that day that I too would travel through Asia. This seed, long before planted, began now to grow. For three long years I nursed it, reading travel books and studying maps while I finished school and worked to save money. Finally, at age twenty-three, I began this new dream I had envisioned, this trip that would take me around the world toward an entirely new perspective.

Wisps of snow appeared on the neatly furrowed fields. I tightened my coat and leaned my head out the window. Staring into the wind, I could see that the train was rounding a long curve, heading north. To Hokkaido. To Miura. It seemed eerie in retrospect how visualizations had guided my life. I indulged in sporting fantasies as a youth and they came to be. I imagined an Asian journey and it occurred as well. I had a bizarre notion to ski in Japan and there I was, heading north to meet a legendary skier, a descendant of Samurai. Call it a hope fulfilled, a wish granted, or a fantasy realized, but once again, events were unfolding in an uncanny way.

seventeen

By late afternoon, I saw white-capped mountains in the West. The Japan Alps ran due north, roughly parallel to the path of the train. I stared at the peaks, each one so different. Even the same mountain, from varying vantage points, looked totally new.

I had seen this vividly while trekking in the Himalayas, where massive peaks appeared first like jewels on the necklace of the horizon. They grew larger during the long days of hiking, until finally I rose above the world of foliage and wildlife to the barren valleys of glaciers and rock. Higher yet, after countless careful breaths in the thinner, more cherished air, we reached these stone behemoths in their full alpine splendor—the daunting rock faces, the spectacular ice falls, the impossibly high silent peaks. Some Everest hikers fly into Lukla, the tiny, treacherous airfield at 10,000 feet, but I savored these aspects more for having earned them with each upward step.

What about Miura Yuichiro? What did he think while he walked toward Everest, toward his date with destiny? I was awestruck to merely stand at the 19,000 foot base camp and crane my neck upward toward its majestic peak, but Miura was to climb nearly 9,000 feet higher up. How did Everest appear to him on the eve of that climb? Even more incredibly, what did it look like atop the South Col, when he was on skis finally and staring down at the rest of the world? What thoughts could you hold at such a moment? Was he even aware of the natural spectacle around him when imminent death was so likely? Did he feel fear, or was he past that and into the absorbed trance of doing? What kind of man could conceive, and actually perform, such a feat? Was it foolish or brave, or something else entirely?

As the train rolled northward, the windows gathered frost and clouds began to appear. It started to snow. Crystalline whippets danced on the window and wisps of white streaked the landscape. The snow nestled at first in leeward places only, beside trees and buildings, along ditches and roadsides, but gradually, a gray-white carpet rolled out over the land. The dance of flakes became a march as the dark, dense clouds released their legions.

I pulled out *The Japan Times* to check the weather. For Sapporo, the newspaper predicted more heavy snowfall. A small article, commenting on the upcoming Snow Festival there, mentioned that the island of Hokkaido was having its heaviest snowfalls in recent record. While good for skiing and the festival, it said, the snow was hindering farmers and stranding people in rural areas.

I felt a gnawing in my stomach. Heavy snowfalls meant deep powder skiing, my only real weakness as a skier. What little powder experience I had was in the trees, where my fear of hurting or embarrassing myself was debilitating. Besides that, I was haunted by a traumatic experience from my teens, another memory all too willing to return.

I was then sixteen years old. It was late afternoon on a cold February day, and I had been climbing with my friend, Chris, for an hour. We were standing high on an out-of-bounds cliff, resting from the climb and looking out over the valley, when I looked to my right and noticed that the semi-circular cliff was draped with a huge cornice. My eye followed it around until I realized that we were standing right on top of it. Alarmed, I pushed myself backwards and quietly told Chris to do the same.

But just then, a jagged crack appeared in the snow beneath my ski tips. It streaked in both directions, following the contour of the cliff. Chris looked at me for a frozen moment, his face a mask of fear, then he started falling. It was the strangest sight, like a white freight elevator, a hundred yards wide, suddenly dropping away. Chris lunged for the ledge and caught it with his arms, but the snow was too soft. He slipped further, flailing like a drowning man to stay afloat. I watched helplessly, as Chris's horrified face slipped from sight.

A hellish din rose from the rocks below. The bowl became a cauldron of icy fury, an avalanche that spread across the valley and surged mightily down the mountain. Huge snow boulders, weighing 1,000 pounds per cubic yard, were bouncing like pebbles tossed by God. The sliding snow behind them ripped up trees and rocks and pulled everything downward. Then it all disappeared, hidden by billowing crystals of ice.

Uncertainty gripped me. I would likely need patrollers to find Chris, but it would be dark before I could lead them back. If I stayed by myself and searched in the remaining daylight, how would I get him out if I did find him? We would both die of exposure.

The blowing snow receded gradually until I could again see the cliff beside me, shorn now like a poodle. The carnage below was shocking. A huge swath had been cut down the mountain, leaving a rubble-strewn landscape. Without much hope, I looked for signs of life.

But something caught my eye. I scanned the snowfield. Where was it? Was I mistaken? No, there, there it was again, quite high up. I strained to see, but gusts of blowing snow made it difficult. Finally, I got a good look. It was an arm, poking out of the snow, waving. Chris was alive!

By the time I skirted the cliff and skied down through icy aftermath, Chris had used his free arm to clear space around his head. His face was deathly white and he seemed on the verge of shock, but no bones were broken and somehow he still had one ski. I raced to dig him out, knowing that we weren't out of danger yet. We had only three skis and two poles between us, with a mile of hilly backcountry to traverse before dark.

Although we got safely out, I could never shed my fear of powder. I still followed my friends through the trees, but it was macho pride pushing me, not joyousness pulling. I struggled as a result, with fear like a dead weight on my shoulders. Then one afternoon, on a steep slope in a grove of trees, the inevitable happened. In a somersaulting fall, I hit the thick, gray trunk of a dead tree square across my back, hard enough that my breath and senses were snatched away. I lay motionless for a frozen moment, screaming in my lungs and my mind, seeing flashes of life in a wheelchair. Eternity passed until a breath came, longer yet until I could move my legs.

Besides those two traumas, powder mystified me stylistically. I was a mogul masher, capable of cruising and skiing bumps with the best, but deep snow required patience and subtlety, not guts and muscle. Instead of straight-on challenges and clear obstacles, powder offered hidden paths and unfamiliar rhythms. Consequently, I rushed when I needed to relax, bore down when I should have eased up. The harder I tried, the worse I did in the unfamiliar powder snow.

Punctual to the minute after fourteen hours, the train reached the ferry terminal in Aomori. It was long past dark. My car was empty; the entire train was deserted, as far as I knew. It felt eerie. As I donned my coat and hauled my luggage toward the door, I saw the conductor shuffling past toward the station. By the time I stepped out into the cold, he had disappeared. I looked behind me and again toward the terminal. No one. Just that sole set of footprints in the fresh white snow.

I picked up my things and began to walk. The lamps above me were humming and casting pallid light. The illuminated platform stretched out like a tunnel through the darkness. Steam billowed up from the train on my left, engulfing me in drifting clouds. *I'm dreaming,* I thought. *Where is everyone? What am I doing here?* The skis on my shoulder reminded me, but it still seemed unreal. For the first time, I felt truly alone.

The ferry to Hokkaido took two hours. I had taken this same ship on my futile search earlier, but now the sea wind blew colder from Siberia. I looked out over the dark ocean, my eyes tearing against the storm, and tried to foresee what might happen. It couldn't be worse than my first trip, when all I received were blank stares. In a way, that trip made this one easier. I knew the YMCA and a few cheap places to eat. I had even seen some of the ski areas in the distance. One was the site of the Olympics, Mt. Teine. I remembered looking up at the huge ski jump, wondering how I could come so near and yet still be so far away. Now I had a second chance.

At 2:30 in the morning, I staggered with my luggage onto the connecting train. I slept a few short hours until our 6:15 arrival in Sapporo, then climbed down onto another snowy platform. It was cold and dark and I was thankful for my long underwear as I trudged with my skis and bags through the snowy streets to the YMCA. Despite my concerns, I loved the softness of the snow beneath my boots, the wet caress of the falling flakes on my cheeks, the secure feeling of being warmly dressed in a blustery storm. The snow muffled all sound; the air smelled clean and crisp. The storm was gentle on the senses.

I reached the YMCA and within an hour I had checked in, taken a shower, and eaten breakfast. It was light outside by then, time to see how the game would play out. I headed with a handful of coins in my moist palms to the hostel telephone. I inserted the first coin slowly, listening to the metallic jangling of its descent as if the telephone were a slot machine, dispensing fortunes.

Almost in a panic, I heard the phone ring. What was I going to say? A second ring. Maybe no one would answer. Suddenly, I heard a click and a woman's voice, cheerful and expectant: "Moshi, moshi."

I froze for a moment.

"Moshi, moshi," came the standard greeting again, a little hesitant now.

I stammered out a hopeful, "Hello?"

Silence.

I tried again. "Hello?"

After a long pause, the woman burst into Japanese. *Damn,* I thought. *Now what?* There was no one near me to translate.

I apologized and hung down the phone. I would have to find Miura myself. Flush with nervous energy, I pulled on my coat and headed back out on to the street. The city was snowbound and shrouded in a heavy blizzard. It was daytime, yet visibility was near zero and all the streetlamps and car headlights were on. Snowplows roared and people shoveled, but nature paid no heed. Newly cleared sidewalks were covered again in minutes, hidden completely in an hour. Everywhere I looked, the roads and rooftops were perfectly white and softly symmetrical.

Odori-nishi, Sapporo's main boulevard, was transformed also but in a wonderfully different way. Gigantic ice sculptures for the upcoming Snow Festival were nearing readiness. An impressive castle, a towering Brontosaurus, a popular Japanese cartoon character—all had workers swarming over them. While sections were being built and sculpted above, engineers poured over plans and surveyors peered through telescopes below. Other ice statues were less than ten feet high, but they were carved with the precision of ivory miniatures.

I returned to the large sporting goods store and entered with my paper in hand. I found the same squat fellow who had helped me months earlier, and he looked at me strangely, trying to remember. He smiled when I showed him my note, then wrote some numbers down.

"Take the subway three stops," he said, "and go to this address. It's a ski store."

My heart sank. "Miura's not on a mountain?"

"Oh yes, he lives on Mount Teine, but he has a ski store in the city. If you go there, I'm sure they can help you."

I thanked him and headed out into the storm. So it was Mt. Teine after all, the site of the 1972 Olympics. I had seen it in the fall, thought about it all winter, and was heading there finally. This all seemed propitious, like scenes in a movie.

Descending to the subway, I dropped from the featureless fury of the storm into a warm colorful shopping complex, filled with music and merchandise. It was no wonder that the wintry streets were deserted. Further below, at the subway level, a sleek train arrived promptly, whisked me a few quick miles to another spotless platform, then silently disappeared. I rose through a second shopping center, this one smelling of fresh baked bread, and found again, at street level, a wintry scene of monochromatic tonality. There were no colors or shadows, only gradations of dark and light. Even perspective had disappeared—foreground and background merging in a flat, mysterious way.

I trudged on, scarf wrapped tight and eyes squinting at the street numbers, until I found Miura's shop, a small, brightly lit store down a half flight of steps from street level. I peeked in. A stout woman with a round, red face was folding and stacking ski sweaters. She appeared to be alone. I took a deep breath, and another, then went inside. The clerk welcomed me cheerfully, then stopped and squinted. A foreigner.

Surprise sounded in her throat and she pulled out a pair of glasses. "*Oh, sumimasen,*" she said, apologizing.

"*Ei-go, wakarimasuka?*" I said, asking if she understood English. No luck. She gave the negative signal, her hand waved vertically in front of her face. I pulled out my piece of paper. She read it, puzzled and flustered.

"Miura Yuichiro here?" I asked, pointing downward.

"No," she said, with conviction.

"*Doko desuka?*" Where?

She pointed upward, toward the mountains. "Teine," she said.

I pantomimed a telephone and she looked relieved. That was the answer. She dialed the phone and spoke quickly, then handed me the handset. I drew a breath and lifted it into position.

"Hello," I stammered.

"Hello," came a woman's voice. "This is Mrs. Miura. Who is speaking please?"

I gave my name. There was a pause, then the welcome words, "Oh, yes, Rick-san. We're expecting you."

Relief flooded through me. I waited for her next words.

"My husband's not here now."

My heart plummeted, then shot back up on her next sentence. "Can you come to Teine tomorrow?"

"Of course," I said, my breath returning. She gave me the details: "Ten o'clock. Come to the ski school office."

I thanked her and hung up the phone. The clerk, beaming now, bowed repeatedly until I headed out the door. I stood on the sidewalk, staring into the face of the storm. The arrangements were made. I had no place to go, nothing to do—nothing except wait for the morning. I felt like an archer's arrow, drawn back further and further until finally it is released and sent flying through the air. I had no strain, no control, no activity at all. I was soaring through space, waiting for contact.

eighteen

I woke to the tapping of icy snowflakes against the windowpane. This was it, the all-or-nothing morning. I swung down from my bunk, pulled on my sweat suit, and went down for breakfast. The cafeteria was as deserted as my barracks-style room, naturally enough for mid-week in the winter season. An old woman stood alone in the kitchen, cutting vegetables on a wooden board and singing to herself. My Japanese phrasebook came in handy. After a few repetitions, I managed to get eggs, toast, and tea.

My stomach churned while looking outside. The storm was like a torn goose down pillow, smothering the city in soft, white layers. The sidewalk, shoveled clean the previous evening, had two fresh feet of snow. I felt fear's clutch on my throat, squeezing tighter. I had just one chance. I couldn't blow it.

I looked to the clock. The bus left in a half hour. I went upstairs and stretched out on the carpet to loosen the stiffness of the train ride. My knee felt better after the evening's rest, but it was puffy and tight. I massaged the thigh, the calf, and the knee itself, and took extra care to loosen my back and groin. Finally, I stood up and pulled out my ski suit. The sight of it cheered me, iridescent blue with white patches under the arms and on the back of the collar. I laid it over the bed and started dressing. First came the calf-length white socks and my red thermal underwear, snug against the contours of my legs. My white turtleneck slipped reluctantly over my head and allowed my hands through the sleeves. I pulled on my suit and drew the zipper up over my chest, enjoying the sensuous ritual. My blue wool hat fit comfortably over my head and I cinched it with the strap of my goggles. The gloves came last, right then left, pushing each finger fully in. I was ready.

Finding my skis in the locker downstairs, I shouldered them and waded out into the storm. A short walk brought me to the bus depot where I boarded the Mt. Teine shuttle. The bus lurched through the city streets then groaned as it headed up the mountain past roadside snow piles that were level with the windows of the bus. The snow bank had been sliced by the plow like a saw cut through a log, exposing the thin, wavy brown lines that recorded the winter's snowfalls.

We stopped twice on the way up, letting off skiers at smaller resorts. The monstrous Alpine ski jumps of the Olympics, the ones I had seen in the distance back in November, slipped past. Evidently, we were heading higher, into the cloud above. I strained for a glimpse, but visibility here was worse than in the city. Besides the layered snow, all I could see were the trees lining the roadside. Elm, birch, elegant Japanese maple—they were bare of leaves but layered down to their smallest branches in snow and a hoary white frost. There were a few evergreens too, scattered through the forest like dark lint on a white mohair sweater. Stretching, leaning, sagging, their personalities were revealed in wintry relief.

The bus jerked to a halt. I scraped away the frost on the window and saw the five interlocking rings on the eave of the wooden lodge. This was it: Teine Highlands, site of the 1972 Olympic Games, home of Miura Yuichiro. Uphill, to my right, was the loading station of a gondola. Down the mountain, barely visible through the blizzard, were two more large buildings, a cluster of huts, and a large parking lot.

I stepped down from the bus, shifted my skis and poles to a nearby rack, then entered through the rear of the Olympic building. The main floor was a sprawling cafeteria with picnic style benches, a wall of windows, and a full-length balcony facing the ski area. While looking for the Ski School office, I discovered lockers, bathrooms, day-care, and first aid rooms on the basement level, and a second story partitioned into closed, unmarked rooms. Evidently, I was to meet Mrs. Miura in one of the buildings below.

I sat to pull on my ski boots and noticed my hands trembling. The confidence I felt hearing Miura's identity in Tokyo had now faded. I had only enough cash left for four lean days, and no return ticket.

I opened my right boot and worked my foot into position. The fit was friendly, since the soles had long ago molded to my feet. I did the same with the left, wrestling my foot in and getting it situated. I returned to my right boot and began buckling, following a procedure I had established years before in hockey: right skate on, left skate on, tie up right skate, tie up left skate.

Another routine, I thought. *Westerners have them, Japanese have them, everyone has them. To varying degrees, we are all creatures of habit. Although not so intricately as the Japanese, we, too, pattern our social and personal actions to reduce or eliminate the myriad decisions of behavior and motion. . . .*

I caught myself. *Don't start on that. Leave patterns and problems alone for a while. You're not here to think!*

With my goggles pulled down against the driving snow, I hoisted my skis and headed toward the lower buildings. These grew more visible as I neared, two low wooden lodges with facades of glass and huge wavy snowdrifts drooping from their sloping roofs. The structure on the right, disappearing between the rising snow on the ground and the overhang from above, was evidently a second day lodge. The other building, smaller and tan colored, looked like my destination. Stomach bubbling, I climbed the steps and entered.

There were several lithe young Japanese on the far right side of the room, all smartly dressed in red coats and tight black pants. As I entered, they stopped talking and looked over. The silence was thick.

A trim, middle-aged woman looked up from the counter and came hurrying over, smiling widely. "I am Mrs. Miura," she said. "You must be Rick-san."

I nodded, returning her short and friendly bow. Before I could speak, she went on. "I'm sorry we have such awful weather."

"It's beautiful."

She smiled and turned toward two men at the reception desk. "I would like you to meet Daichiro, my husband's senior instructor," she said, indicating a tall fellow with elegant features and erect posture.

Evidently accustomed to foreigners, he immediately stuck out his hand. "Nice to meet you," he said perfectly.

I shook it and bowed slightly as well, then turned to the smaller man. With narrow eyes and lips and a round red face, he looked like an elf or a leprechaun. "And this is Ozaki," she said. "He's a photographer and a writer who has just come back from Europe. He speaks English also."

This fellow was evidently comfortable with foreigners. I guessed that a bow wasn't necessary but gave one anyway. "Nice to meet you," I said. He nodded, smiling nonchalantly.

Mrs. Miura spoke again. "We have another Canadian here. Mr. Tom. He's out skiing right now."

I tried not to show surprise, but my mind was racing. This must be the Canadian that Brian had heard about in Tokyo. *What was his role on the mountain? Would another foreigner help or hinder my chances?*

Mrs. Miura looked outside to the racks, hoping to spot him, but gave up. "Why don't you ski with Daichiro and Ozaki this morning?" she asked. "When Tom-san comes in, I'll have him wait for you here."

"Fine," I said, wondering where Miura was.

As if reading my mind, she went on, "If you'll join us later for lunch, you can meet my husband."

I nodded and bowed to Mrs. Miura, then looked over at the group watching me. These must be the instructors. There were no smiles in evidence, only impassive faces and curious looks. I gave a slight bow of my head, then lowered my goggles and followed Daichiro and Ozaki out the door.

As I put on my skis, I realized that this was to be a test. Both men spoke English well and they would probe me as directly as propriety allowed. After we had skied the morning together, Miura would hear their opinions before I met him. Nonetheless, I felt better. Like the first collision of a hockey game, I was finally involved. There was no more idle speculation, no thought of alternatives. I was on skis and ready for the challenge.

Daichiro described the landmarks as we shuffled into the lift line. The building where I arrived was the Olympic Center. A cafeteria occupied the main floor and the closed upstairs rooms I had seen were formerly press facilities, converted now into dormitories for the instructors. In the lower area, the ski school co-existed with a Japan Air Lines tour office in the smaller lodge, while the larger building housed a second cafeteria, the ski rental shop, and Miura's private residence underneath.

There were five main lifts, he explained, four of them originating at the bottom. There was the high-speed gondola, which I had seen already, three chairlifts fanning outward from the base lodge, and a T-bar up on top. Squinting through the storm, I noticed something odd about the chairlift we were approaching. There was only one chair rising at a time instead of the two, three, or four seat chairlifts I was accustomed to.

Noticing the direction of my gaze, Ozaki scoffed. "We still have single chairs. Until recently, old men in the government thought double chairlifts were unsafe."

I tried to read Ozaki. He had traveled extensively. Was he frustrated now in Japan? But his eyes revealed nothing.

I slid into position as the single chair clanged around. The attendant swept the seat quickly, then I was off, borne upward on the "conservative" apparatus. Within seconds, I was alone in a wintry silence, floating through white space, watching snowflakes collect in the folds of my suit. My breath was steady and deep, and the relentless snowfall muffled all other sound. The lift cables arched upward and disappeared into the whiteness. Every few seconds, like a guard post on a frozen frontier, a steel lift tower would pass. I could see nothing else, neither the ground below nor the trees on either side. Time seemed suspended, frozen in the icy mist.

Suddenly, like an apparition, the upper lift station emerged out of the cloud. It was a square, sheet metal hut with large windows and steam wafting from a thin chimney. Inside sat a wizened sentinel, staring out through round spectacles into the blustery void. Hanging beside the door was a large circular thermometer reading -10º centigrade.

This fact invaded my brain: *Minus ten degrees—perfect temperature, just cold enough to keep the snow light. Thank God for that. It looks three feet deep.*

Alert now, I looked around. Snow was everywhere, smothering trees, buildings, and equipment in a fluffy quilt. A gentle breeze pushed across the mountaintop, angling the descent of yet more snow to the earth, sculpting that which lay already. Through the storm, I saw Daichiro waiting for me.

I slid down the unloading ramp toward the Japanese leader. He was poised, almost aloof on his own ground. In a polite tone, he continued his tour by drawing with his pole on the snow.

"The mountain curves like a big question mark," he said. "And this lift, and the gondola over there," he pointed left into the blizzard, where I could just discern a large building, "come right up the middle."

As I nodded, he continued. "Beginning over there," he pointed further left into the whiteness beyond the gondola station, "is the Men's Giant Slalom course, but it is closed now."

The silence begged the question. "Why?"

"Avalanches," he said simply. "That area is dangerous in these conditions."

Great. Just what I needed to hear.

"Down there, Rick-san," he said, pointing to a narrow curving gully on our right, "is the trail to the Ladies' Giant Slalom."

"From the Olympics?"

He nodded. "Over there," he said, pointing much further right, "are easier slopes for recreation skiers."

I had to take his word for it, since anything beyond thirty yards was completely obscured. Daichiro returned to his question mark in the snow. "This part below us is where the area curves around. Later, when we get down and around the mountain, we will find the Men's and Ladies' Slalom courses on the other side."

He was now pointing horizontally into the fog, which could have indicated Siberia for all I could see. "Where was the downhill held?" I asked.

He tilted his head and sucked air back softly through his teeth, as Japanese often do when an awkward subject came up. "There are no downhill courses, Rick-san. That event was held at another mountain. Mt. Teine was . . . too small."

He struggled with this admission as if he was responsible somehow. I tried to ease the silence. "What's down here?" I asked, pointing to the precipitous drop beneath the chairlift.

"That is *Kitakabe*."

When I stared at him blankly, he went on, "What do you call it, in mountain climbing, when the rock goes almost straight up?"

"A headwall."

"That's right. That is our 'Headwall.' In Japanese, we say 'Kitakabe.'"

I mouthed it to myself as Ozaki slid up, then off we went. Daichiro headed toward the "recreational" slopes first, apparently to give me an easy start. Squinting uphill through the storm, I saw the indistinct shapes of an Alpine-style upper lodge, a maintenance shed, and a weather station behind a perfectly frosted wire fence. As far as I could see, that was the upper extent of Mount Teine.

Daichiro dropped suddenly out of sight and I soon knew why. He had led me off a small bluff, though a gentler approach was only feet away. It didn't matter, since the landing was clear and smooth, but I skied more warily onto the main run where the snow tractor was at work. I couldn't see it but I recognized the smooth, buttery feel of freshly groomed snow. I was glad. My skis found an easy rhythm behind Daichiro, one turn flowing silkily to the next. When he slowed and stopped and I pulled directly in beside him, he seemed surprised to see me so close behind.

Daichiro's technique was graceful and flawless, but Ozaki's primary skill was surely as a journalist. He skied boldly, but errant arms and straying tips were often evident. My stomach churned, knowing that their judgment of me was imminent.

We cut back through the trees to the steeper central run, the Ladies' Giant Slalom. Soon we stood atop a mogul field, how long or wide I couldn't tell. Daichiro pointed down the fall line, then pushed off. I moved to follow but Ozaki touched my arm. "Wait," he said.

Half a minute passed.

He shuffled forward. "My turn," he said. "We'll wait down there."

Ozaki dropped from his perch, the storm swallowing him instantly. I was alone, waiting to ski. They were below, waiting to watch.

This is it.

I drew a deep breath and expelled it from as low as possible in my abdomen. I shuffled my skis and fingered the handles of my poles. I crouched, stood, and stomped my feet. Another breath. Another.

Go.

I tried to absorb the first mogul and come bobbing up over the crest, but instead, it collapsed and curled around me like smoke. I met another, just as soft. Instead of rapid jarring, these quilted bumps gave me a flowing, molten sensation.

A half swivel led to a pair of pillowy turns. I burst off a crest, sucking my legs up beneath me. Into the air I went, skipping the trough, landing with my skis already turned. I reversed directions, blew through a huge mound, then gathered speed off some firmer bumps in a soft staccato flurry. Ahead, through the blizzard, I saw the dark forms of Daichiro and Ozaki. I was in visual range.

But pleasure had overcome nervousness. Skiing these snow-laden moguls felt like hopping down a mountain of cushions. I bounced or blew through them in rapid succession yet it seemed to occur slowly. Snow was everywhere, in my face, pinned to my suit, boiling up around me. I skied past my two observers—not far, but enough to complete three tidy turns on a glassy smooth knoll.

When I stopped, Daichiro skied down with the aplomb of a top dollar tax lawyer, Ozaki swooping behind like a circus entertainer, pretending he could fly. It was apparent, when they skied up, that I was doing well so far. There was new respect in their eyes and tone of voice.

"Mr. Tom" was watching from the ski school window when we reached the bottom. He came out immediately, wearing a wide grin. "Sorry I missed you earlier," he said, "but the first run on a morning like this is hard to pass up." He held his hand just below his chest and hooted, "This deep."

I laughed, introduced myself, and soon learned that this was indeed the Canadian I had followed to Sapporo. Tom Wright. He seemed friendly and even-tempered. His face was wide and deeply tanned, including a bit extra exposed by a retreating blonde hairline. He had rocky blue eyes that were riveted upon mine when we spoke. A thick red jacket made him seem huge, but his blue stretch ski pants revealed the slenderness of his physique.

When Tom was ready, we slid to the chairlift. The four of us talked as we neared the loading platform, mostly about the snowstorms. "It's been snowing like this for three days already," Tom chortled. "And they expect more. Lots more."

Tom laughed out loud yet the Japanese were impassive. As for me, I was more interested in Tom's arrangement. *Where was he was staying? How much was he paid?*

We had time for one more run before our lunch with Miura. Ozaki suggested we ski Kitakabe, the Headwall. Tom again held his palm up to his stomach and gleefully gave approval, "Powder . . . this deep."

My stomach began bubbling. The voice in my head started in: *Just relax, Rick. Take it easy.*

Within minutes, we were standing above the aptly named run, which dropped like a waterfall through a narrow grove of trees. Daichiro skied straight into them, cutting an effortless swath about ten feet wide. After a half dozen turns, he stopped and looked up, close enough that we could just see each other. Ozaki took off into his bird-like motion, swooping down the mountain, banking rather than turning and somehow coming to rest upright.

I asked Tom, "Do they always ski like this? One at a time?"

He nodded. "Pretty much. They watch each other."

I pointed downward. "OK. After you then."

He laughed and pushed off, also attacking the hill head on. Tom wasn't a tremendous skier, but he was steady and game. And he enjoyed it, which was more than I could say at that moment.

Forget it, I thought. *Just ski.*

Now.

The first turn in steep, deep powder feels like jumping off a fence and waiting to land. Except that you never land, not really. It's all curving and careening. Powder skiing is soft, flowing, and devoid of hard sensations, much like scuba diving. You sink slowly into the whiteness, feel it surround you and tug so very gently. It's delicious and sexy and remarkably sensual, except for one thing. You gather speed.

If you think about it, there's a lot to remember and do all at once. You must instantly find and adjust your balance, not only to the angle of the slope, but also to the varying depth and texture of the snow. You must start your turn and then, in the moment of weightlessness, reverse your body position. You must be aware of your next turn also and of your planned route down the mountain, particularly if there are trees or rocks looming. You must time your next breath for when you emerge from the smothering snow. Most of all, you must keep your cool.

It was all too much. I was on mental overload.

In my very first turn, I panicked and pulled up on my skis, trying to force them around, but the natural forces—gravity, resistance, momentum—were too strong. Gently but firmly, as if by a huge feather duster, I was lifted and pushed over on top of myself. I started tumbling slowly, somersaulting forward through the snow. There was a brief fear of injury, then cushioning reassurance. Though then a small consolation, falling in powder snow is the gentlest rebuke in sports.

My first thought, when I stopped, was of my audience. Bad enough to fall, I couldn't keep them waiting too. I moved my legs and thankfully found both skis still attached. *God, don't let me lose one.*

I stood and shook off the snowy evidence, trying desperately to visualize the proper rhythm—that bounce to begin, then the flowing motion back and forth. It worked, sort of. I wrenched through a few turns then took another silly fall. Embarrassed and flustered, I started again immediately, not even brushing myself off. I joined the others and saw their surprise. I bit my lip. Excuses were useless.

Once in the lodge, Daichiro and Ozaki went to Miura's house to check on lunch. Tom and I had a moment alone and I couldn't resist asking, "So, what have you got worked out here?"

"A pretty good deal," he said. "We live right here on the mountain, in the Olympic Center."

"Are you paid?"

"No, but I don't pay for anything either, except the odd coffee in the lodge."

A good deal? It sounded perfect.

"And in return?" I asked.

"I teach English to Miura's son twice a week and to the instructors every evening."

I thought awhile. No money, but no expenses. That could work. "They all live with you in the Olympic Center?"

He nodded. "Except Takao."

"Takao?"

"Yeah, you'll meet him. A strange guy, for a Japanese. Miura likes him because he's so wacko."

We fell silent. Tom had what I had dreamed of, a live-in position at Japan's most famous ski area. Was there any need, I wondered, or any room, for another foreigner? Neither Mrs. Miura nor Daichiro had given any hint. I tried to let these thoughts settle. *Just trust yourself, Rick. Trust the moment.*

Slightly after noon, we went through the basement of the main lodge into Miura's attached home. It was an open design, with the foyer and kitchen blending into the living room. There were stained wood walls and exposed beams and an aura of warmth and activity throughout.

I was greeted cheerfully by his wife, Tomoko, and introduced to his mother, a frail, elderly woman, slightly stooped, but with clear, liquid eyes. Daichiro and Ozaki disappeared again, leaving Tom and me with Tomoko. Not at all shy, she served steaming green tea and talked about her daughter, Emi, attending university in Canada, and her oldest son, Yuta, studying at an American college and practicing with the American National Ski Team. Her second son, Gota, still lived at home, but he had already begun international competition.

Tom looked at me. "Gota finished fifth in the Canadian Men's Mogul competition," he said admiringly. "He's only twelve years old."

I was taken aback, more so as Tomoko went on. The previous summer the entire family, Miura's seventy-eight-year-old father included, traveled to Africa and skied Mount Kilimanjaro. They filmed it all for Japanese television and were now known as the "The Miura Action Family."

Judging from their home, they were more practical than fastidi-ous. A dozen pairs of skis stood in the corner of the entranceway, and ski boots stretched in an uneven row along the wall. A large metal shelving unit had stacks of gloves, goggles, hats, scarves, sweaters, vests, and jackets. But for a few woodblock prints hanging on the walls, and some Japanese magazines on the table, it could have been a ski home anywhere in the world.

Tomoko chatted gaily as she worked, darting back and forth from the counter to the table with laden dishes. She set out food for nine people—soup, rice, pickles, grilled fish, and seaweed—without once showing concern that her husband might be late. Her confidence was justified, for within moments the rear entrance reopened and a handsome, powerful man appeared.

This was Miura Yuichiro. It was obvious from his bearing. I stood as he approached, facing him. When Tomoko introduced us, I resisted the urge to shake hands and bowed low instead. Miura returned an abbreviated bow, then turned to introduce the three men who had come in behind him. "These are my senior instructors," he said. "This is Hiro, Daichiro's brother, and Makoto, and Saito."

He spoke to them in rapid Japanese. I heard my name, followed by the English words "Canadian ski instructor."

Miura's eyes were deep and dark, widely set in a chiseled, weathered face. He had thick, black, longish hair, brushed casually back, and perfect white teeth. He seemed to have no neck, his head merging directly with the upward swell of his shoulders. He wore street clothes, including a loose-fitting sweater, but there was no hiding his bullish torso and massive thighs. As strong as he appeared, I was more impressed by his sureness and grace. There was no pretense or boast about him. He radiated an aura, a blend of confidence, humility, and compassion.

When he concluded, we exchanged short bows and sat for lunch. Daichiro and Ozaki, trailing behind, joined us at the table, along with a spry older man carrying an elaborate camera. Miura introduced his father, who nodded from the far end of the table, then ate without speaking. The women, too, were unobtrusive, disappearing once the food was served.

There was a dignified kindness about Miura. He inquired gently about my travels and life in Canada and asked how I had ended up in Japan. When I, in turn, asked about Everest, he deflected my questions softly, "You can better understand from my book. I'll give you a copy."

Miura spoke usually to ask questions, I realized, preferring to let others do the talking. Conversation around his table was lighthearted and simple. His instructors acted naturally, without the hesitation I had often seen among other Japanese subordinates. Despite my nervousness, I also felt comfortable.

Miura spoke finally. "I understand that you are a good skier, Rick-san. A Canadian ski instructor."

I nodded.

"Having a little trouble in the powder?"

I blushed and nodded again.

"Powder is actually easiest once you know it."

"I hope so," I replied.

"Perhaps you will learn," he said, looking directly at me now. "I understand you wish to spend time with us?"

I nodded, meeting his gaze. I saw strength, tenderness, and openness there. For a long moment, it seemed I was swimming in his eyes, sinking deep into their liquid recesses. My own eyes felt as clear, as permeable to his perception.

Miura smiled faintly, then turned to Daichiro and asked in English, "Is there a bed available?"

Daichiro nodded.

Miura looked back to me. "Fine. I suggest that you stay at Teine a few weeks on a trial basis. If it works out, you can stay longer. How does that sound?"

The offer hung a moment in the air.

"Like a dream, Miura-san."

nineteen

After lunch, Daichiro showed me around and made more introductions. The other instructors were polite but distant. From Daichiro's descriptions, I realized that these were some of the best young skiers in Japan. The national mogul champion, Igarashi, was a small, sprightly fellow who competed on the international freestyle circuit. Ogata was a muscular, hawk-eyed racer who specialized in the slalom. The others—Sasaki, Naomi, Yasu, Miya, Yoko, Hide—whose names I immediately got confused, were each distinguished in some way.

Similar to my students in Tokyo, all the instructors had trouble pronouncing my name. The single syllable sounded strange to their ears. Invariably, they rounded Rick off to something like, "Reek-uh." When the added the honorific suffix, it came out as "Reek-uh-san." That was me. Mr. Reek. Of course, I wondered how badly I was pronouncing their names.

An attractive young woman in an instructor's uniform entered. Daichiro motioned her over. "Rick-san, this is my fiancée, Emiko."

"Nice to meet you," I said.

Coyly, with a hybrid curtsy-bow, she said, "The pleasure is mine."

Emiko had the studied charm of a southern schoolgirl, conversing carefully, laughing lightly. Daichiro's brother, Hiro, one of the senior instructors I had met at lunch, sauntered over to join us. He wore his hair long, the only one to do so, and had an aloof manner. He began telling me of his previous summer in Threadbo, an Australian ski resort, but fell silent when he noticed the other instructors watching him.

Daichiro took a large chest pin from his pocket and gave it to me, saying "It's an instructor's badge."

Over his shoulder, I saw Tom wince. Later, when we got outside, he explained. "I can't believe they just gave you a badge, automatically."

"Why not?"

"I didn't get one for weeks. I had to ask Daichiro finally because I had trouble getting on the lifts."

"Why'd they wait?"

"I'm not an instructor like you. I don't have a pin on my chest."

He referred to my Canadian Ski Instructor pin, which had attracted admiration from the Japanese.

"It's an elite group here," he said. "They were disappointed when they realized that I wasn't an expert. I think that's why you were invited—you ski as well as they do. They want to compare themselves to Western skiers."

Tom's outburst caught me off guard. I hadn't envisioned myself as the representative of Western skiers. Even if only symbolic, this was a little more pressure than I needed right off. These were Japan's top skiers, in mid-season form, and I had skied just three days that winter.

"See this coat?" Tom indicated the new red jacket he wore. "This isn't mine. They gave it to me a few days ago. Emiko politely suggested that I might like this better than my old yellow one. I did, in fact, but it was the timing—just after they'd given me their badge—that got me. It was like saying: To associate with their school, I had to dress the part."

"Attention to form," I said.

Tom raised a finger. "Yeah, well, there's an exception to that too."

"What do you mean?"

"Takao, that guy I was telling you about. He's the black sheep here. Miura picked him out of a special camp at the beginning of the year, but the instructors consider him an outsider."

"Did they give him a lift pass?"

"Yeah, and an old uniform too. When Takao got here, he wore all secondhand gear. Real grungy. Drove the instructors crazy."

"Sounds like a character."

"You don't know half of it. He's the oldest son of a famous *Aikido* master but he gave it up and became a ski bum." He paused for effect. "You know what that means?"

"What? Foregoing his responsibility as the eldest son?"

Tom nodded. "Even though family law was abolished after WW II, the oldest boy in a Japanese family is still bound by tradition to inherit his father's responsibilities."

"Really?"

"That's right. Out of an entire family, the oldest son inherits the obligation to take care of brothers, sisters, grandparents, grandchildren, family business, family honor, etc. The whole works, just like that."

"No choice?"

Tom shook his head, "Not in theory, at least. But Takao chucked all that. He was always an oddball apparently, even when he taught *Aikido* in his father's *dojo*. Then he met Nancy, his American wife, about five years ago, and she introduced him to surfing and skiing. Forget about it. He quit *Aikido* cold and they got married. Now Takao's a fanatic, skiing all winter, surfing all summer."

"How do they live?"

"Meagerly. With money from his odd jobs between seasons and help from his father, who's furious with Takao but helps him anyway because of his granddaughter, Yuuki."

"What does Miura say about all this?"

"He doesn't handle the day-to-day affairs of the instructors. That's Daichiro's job and, to a lesser extent, the three senior instructors beneath him."

"Makoto, Saito, and Hiro."

"Right. And some are more equal than others, if you know what I mean."

"I'm starting to."

"Hiro is in the inner circle by virtue of being Daichiro's brother, but he's a troubled prince."

"Yeah, I picked up on that. What's the story there?"

"I can't figure it out exactly, but they have a third in Emiko, Daichiro's fiancée, who ascends officially in June into the ranks of Miura. They form a triangular power faction on the mountain."

"You got a quick handle on this, Tom."

"Not really. I'm echoing Takao's wife, Nancy. She knows what going on better than anyone."

"How come?"

Tom shrugged. "You'll have to meet her. She's lived in Japan for years. First she learned Japanese at some Tokyo university. Then she studied *Aikido*—that's how she met Takao."

I mouthed his name. It sounded like "Tah-Cow."

I looked at my watch, and said. "Speaking of Takao, where is he? It's almost time to start." We were standing in front of the main lodge waiting for the ski school to begin. The other instructors and the students were climbing up into position.

Tom laughed. "Don't worry. He'll be here."

When Miura appeared in a dark blue jacket, carrying his skis, I checked my watch again. It was nearly 1:30.

"Here he comes," Tom said.

I looked up and saw a dark form, hurtling through the blizzard. At the last second, he opened up into a wide smooth turn and stopped in front of us with an impish grin. He appeared entirely ordinary, a slim fellow, with a sparse mustache and dark eyes behind wire-rimmed glasses and goggles. He wore a faded blue and white uniform with some Japanese characters stitched onto the chest logo. Had Tom not intrigued me with his description, I would certainly have passed Takao by on the fast track of snap judgments.

As Tom introduced us, Takao asked, in a simple, almost childlike tone, "How're ya doin', Rick?"

I paused. The casualness of his speech threw me off. He sounded like a Californian. He repeated my name, "Rick, right?"

"That's right," I said.

"You ski in Canada. That's great." He beamed at the thought and announced, "I like Canada." Again I noticed the phrasing.

We bantered a little about ski areas, Takao describing the areas near Seattle where he worked on the pro patrol. I liked them both already. Their unguarded friendliness was refreshing.

When the ski school was ready, Miura welcomed the students, fifty or so in a line stretching up the mountain, then began separating them according to skill level. As the students skied one at a time toward him, Miura directed each to the appropriate instructor. Once divided into groups, they swooped off like ungainly flocks of colorful birds.

There was no class for the three of us, or for the freestyle specialist Igarashi, the racer Ogata, or Daichiro. Tom leaned over and said quietly, "There's a pattern to this. The young instructors work all the time, usually with the beginners. The senior instructors take the better students or get the shift off. Ogata and Igarashi practice their specialty unless it's very busy."

Miura slid over to us. "Shall we ski together?"

We nodded and followed like three schoolboys. Miura had that effect on people, his aura intimidating in the gentlest way. He led us to the last of the three chairlifts, also with single seats, which serviced the front side of the curving mountain. This was the site of the Men's and Ladies' Olympic Slalom course.

Just before loading, I looked over to the other chairlift where the classes were shuffling through the line-up. A few instructors watched us skiing with Miura. Hiro, in particular, did not appear pleased.

Miura went first onto the lift. Although directly ahead, he was barely visible through the storm. He shifted positions in his chair, striking a pose with his skis, holding it a few seconds, then trying another. He did a dozen or more, each an imitation of a skiing posture. I tried it myself, copying him as closely as I could. As much as with the drill itself, I was impressed that Miura took the time and trouble to do it. Nearly fifty years old, legendary already for his exploits on skis, yet he still used spare minutes for practice.

At the top, I came down the ramp and around to where Miura stood at the crest. The wind gusted briskly, shooting icy needles up the narrow funnel toward us. Visibility was near zero, like standing in a cloud with a chairlift going past to heaven. I was conscious of Miura, and nervous about skiing in front of him, but his gentle demeanor set me at ease. Even as the others skied up, we stood still, bathing in the quiet fury of the storm.

Finally, Miura pushed off. He skied unhurriedly, bobbing and weaving with measured evenness, his body a quiet jockey on a pair of thoroughbred legs. As he disappeared, Takao took off. Literally. Within seconds, he was flying, bouncing, and recovering, arms extended. He was a challenger, a thrill-seeker. I knew the type. Tom went next, picking his way gamely through the deep troughs. My turn.

I dropped rapidly, aiming for a quick deflection off the first mogul, but instead got a soft surprise. Instead of a passing greeting, the large mound embraced me, wrapped itself around me like an icy friend. Thrown forward and stopped short, I had just enough speed to shed its snowy grasp and draw a steeper bead yet on the next mogul.

Whoomph!! . . .

It exploded under the pile-driving pressure of my thighs, blasting snow outward that billowed silky soft over my chest and face. The absorption was incredible. Down again, whoomph, and again, whoomph—on mogul after mogul, I slowed and surged in a gentle rhythm, like a wader in the undertow of waist-deep surf. Dropping felt like the push of the wave, the resistance of the snow was like the water rushing back out against my thighs.

Three dark forms emerged. I slowed and stopped beside them. Tom's grin covered his entire face as he slipped into a brogue, "Aye, an' you've got to admit lads, it's a fine day we'd be havin'."

Miura laughed with us. He was good that way, questioning and listening pleasantly, watching without apparent judgment. We skied for a couple of hours, always one at a time, always with Miura in the lead. Thankfully, he kept us on the main runs and out of the bottomless powder in the trees.

He must have noticed something about my skiing, for when we stopped at the lodge in late afternoon, Miura asked me, "Why do you use such long skis?"

I looked at them, a year-old pair of Hart 207 cm Giant Slalom skis. In Canada, especially for skiers that prefer to cruise at high speeds, such long skis were common. Stuck for an answer, I shrugged.

"Perhaps they're too long for these conditions. Would you try a shorter pair?"

"I'd love to," I said, thinking fast. Although flattered by his thoughtfulness, I sensed something in his suggestion besides largesse. What was it?

"Fine," Miura went on. "I am going to Alaska tomorrow, so Daichiro will take care of it." With that he departed, skis over his shoulder, to his home. Everest, Kilimanjaro, Fuji, now Alaska—was there anywhere Miura hadn't skied?

The lessons were over when we finished our break, and Naomi and Miya, two of the young male instructors, decided to join us. Once up the chairlift, we discussed our options. Naomi and Miya were agreeable to anything, and I stayed silent, my nerves tingling, but for Tom and Takao it was only a question of where to ski powder.

With them in the lead, we traversed beyond the gondola to the closed Men's Giant Slalom course. I stared down into the blizzard. It was wide and clear of tracks at the top, and steep enough certainly to suffer avalanches.

Tom pointed downward with his pole and said, "This funnels into a creek bed a couple of hundred yards down, then we veer right and link up with a trail back to the lodge."

I nodded. The others disappeared in turn, one, two, three, four, weaving down through the powder. I swallowed hard and breathed deeply. I tried to imagine the oxygen entering and leaving my lungs, but instead saw wisps of images: harried turns, rocks and trees too near, others watching me.

Don't think.

Just relax.

Be natural.

Just flow, you can do it.

Come on now.

Relax.

Relax

Don't think.

I had the initial turns all planned out, but the first took too long and I rushed the second. Suddenly, I was going down. I knew it for a long second before it happened. Aaaaarrrggghhh!

The fall was embarrassing enough, but halfway through my second somersault, I felt my right ski release. I came to rest finally and looked uphill. No sign of it. The others were well below, too far down to help. They waited as I climbed and probed. No luck.

Within minutes, I was sweating and dizzy from floundering in the waist deep snow, and feeling bad that Naomi and Miya, who had been teaching all day, would miss their last run because of me. The seconds ticked past and still they waited. Finally, when I was exasperated and exhausted and it was painfully obvious that we wouldn't get another run, I felt the telltale *thunk* of metal on metal.

But the afternoon wasn't over. Back at the lodge, where I sat stupefied with fatigue, a few of the male instructors began arm wrestling. Well, it wasn't long before someone had the bright idea of challenging me, the Canadian ski instructor. For an instant I hoped the idea would die but, judging from the excited roar and the ensuing debate about who should go wrestle me first, I knew I couldn't say no. Despite my exhaustion, I could hardly balk at the first friendly interaction I'd had with the Japanese skiers.

A table was readied while they decided on my opponent, but Hiro had his own idea. He simply walked across the room and sat down, ignoring everyone except me. The group fell silent. This was a sullen Hiro now, not the man who chatted nonchalantly earlier. There was leaden certainty in his eyes. He was challenging me, or making a show, or both.

We started evenly, but I knew that I couldn't win a prolonged struggle. I was good at arm wrestling once, but my overall strength, regardless of the lost ski fiasco, was greatly reduced from my pre-Asia days. The body that propelled and protected me as a middle line-backer and hockey defenseman was gone, melted by the heat of an Asian summer.

Amidst cries of delight and encouragement, Hiro slowly gained the upper hand. Like soup leaving a ladle, my energy was disappearing. Realizing this, I tried to surprise him with a last burst. It nearly worked. I got him back past halfway and raised an uproar in the room. Many men would have quit, but Hiro's face grew yet more impassive and his grip gained new vigor. He slowed my momentum and returned me gradually to the defensive. It was over. I had nothing left. Hiro looked up, smirking as my knuckles touched the table, and I sensed that this wasn't the end of our struggle.

twenty

As the excitement died down, we made our way back to the Olympic Center. Everyone changed into casual clothes—ski team sweat suits and sandals were the outfit of choice—then either worked on their skis, did laundry, or sat around the kitchen watching TV. Naomi offered to help me get my things, so we dug his orange Beetle out of a snowdrift and wound down through the blizzard to the YMCA.

Naomi was a slim, handsome, first-year instructor in his mid-twenties, one noticeably more relaxed away from the others. As we talked, alternating his English with my feeble efforts at Japanese, he said how proud he was to be on Miura's team, the Snow Dolphins. He even described how he had fallen one day and immediately covered his instructor's badge so that no one would see that he was one of Miura's instructors. His concern was striking, as was his confessional manner in telling me this.

It was dark when we started back up the mountain. The snow banks, which seemed high from the bus earlier, now loomed huge. They towered above the car, making the winding road look like a mammoth bobsled run.

How different from the morning ride, I thought. Barely eight hours had elapsed, yet everything had changed completely. No longer was my dream of a ski adventure just wishful thinking. It was happening. I had a few friends; it seemed that I even had an adversary, although I didn't know why.

We arrived back in time for dinner. The kitchen was square and drab, tucked into the corner of the Olympic Center. A sink and a stove were on the left side as we entered, and an L-shaped table arrangement and metal chairs filled the room. A television, the room's sole adornment, was mounted high in the far corner. The right-hand wall had been cut away, linking the kitchen to an adjacent lounge with *tatami* mats and pillows for relaxing. A clothesline stretched above it, laden neatly with white socks and turtlenecks.

The others were already eating. A few glanced up as we entered, but most eyes remained on their plates or the screen overhead. Tom passed me a plate from a stack on the table. "Serve yourself," he said, pointing to the stove.

Dinner was curried stew over white rice, with pickled radish on the side. Chopsticks stood in a jar at mid-table but everyone used spoons. They ate silently, eyes upturned to a Samurai program, a genre as familiar to the Japanese as Westerns are to Americans.

The swordsman and the gunslinger, I thought, two fitting archetypes. Both were famed for their poise in duels to the death, yet one was born to his position and groomed for a unique role in a stratified society, while the other was the product or epitome of unleashed free will. While Japan respected the precision and unwavering loyalty of the Samurai, America embraced the maverick, free-spirited ways of the gunslinger.

When this gave way to a news broadcast, Tom stood up and began his English lesson. He asked generally for approval, then turned the TV down. About half the group turned to him and listened in; the rest simply drifted out. The moment felt awkward. The idea of English lessons was good, but the timing and the location didn't feel right.

On average, the instructors could read and write English well, having completed compulsory courses in school, but most of them had trouble speaking. It was partly timidity, partly lack of practice, and partly poor pronunciation. The reason for this last difficulty had been sadly, if humorously, demonstrated for me in Tokyo. After a labored five-minute conversation at the ESS, I asked a new customer what his occupation was. "I am an English teacher," he bragged.

I had struggled myself with French during high school, and I was wrestling even then with Japanese. As often as I told them to relax and let it happen, I could not do so myself. My mind raced whenever someone spoke Japanese to me. If I thought about the first few words, I missed the rest of the sentence. Because of my fear that I would not understand, I suffered a blizzard of negativity that ensured it. When I tried to speak, I was numbed by the vastness of what I didn't know and by self-consciousness that I might sound foolish.

Tom's lesson whimpered out after an hour. Almost uncannily, the missing instructors began reappearing. Igarashi produced a bottle of the vodka-like liquid, *shochu*. I wanted to stay awake, to get to know the guys, but I couldn't. The twenty-four hour train ride, the skiing, the anticipation, it all caught up with me. My eyelids drooped.

Daichiro noticed and said, "Come on, Rick. I'll show you to your bed."

I nodded groggily and followed him up the wide stairs. We went to the end of the dim hallway and into a large darkened room. By the light of the parking lot through the window, I could see four double bunk beds, a few already occupied. Daichiro steered me to an upper berth, where something lay on the mattress. He handed it to me, saying, "A gift from Miura-san."

I held it up. It was Miura's book, *The Man Who Skied Down Everest* (Harper and Row, 1978). I turned to thank Daichiro but he had already slipped out. Rummaging in my bag, I pulled out a candle and lit it. I positioned the flame on a ledge near my head and climbed up into bed. The photograph on the jacket cover showed a tiny skier, a billowing parachute, and a massive, spectacular mountain. This, of course, was Miura on Everest.

I turned to the preface, to Miura's account of his early years. It began with speed skiing trials in Cervinia, Italy, then shifted to his historic descent of the revered Mount Fuji:

Standing on the rim of Fuji's crown, staring at the straight and deadly run below, I experienced a momentary clarity of spirit. Everything inside me gathered to fullness. I was convinced of the possibility, but not the inevitability, of success. Other than that warm and guiding hope, my mind was utterly empty and therefore, infinitely adjustable to the unforeseen. If it were filled with thoughts and predeterminations, it could never respond in time to necessity.

And when I launched myself into the accelerating rush of cold, white speed, I discovered a peculiarity, a pattern in my nature. Perched at the point of life and death, I like to look straight into the eye of destiny. . . . Only when I'm poised on the edge of life and death do I fully appreciate the wonder of the human experience, the beauty of humanity and the spontaneous pleasure of my inner self. Only at the threat of loss do I fully cherish what I have.

I put the book down, struck by Miura's simple yet succinct description of an absolutely incredible moment, and by the realization that he had gone to that moment entirely by choice. With months of planning and each upward step, he had taken himself willingly to his rendezvous with destiny. Finally, he experienced the most rare and refined type of awareness, what I had come to call the "clarity of consequence."

I tasted first of this nectar when only eight years old. I was standing on a pedestrian bridge near my home, staring down into the dark, cool forest, when I had the sudden urge to climb over the guardrail. In the precise middle of the bridge, above a 200-foot chasm, I lowered myself down until I hung by my arms. I heard my breath, loud in my ears, and felt the warmth of the sun on my back. Then I let go of one hand and hung by the other, looking down all the while into mysterious forest below. I wasn't angry, upset, or frightened but rather, more lucid than ever before in my life.

Although I could never explain it, this clarity touched me repeatedly during my life. Contests, conflicts, dangers—I seemed to seek out activities that increased the stakes of the moment. Even if the challenges were temporary or contrived, I sensed in those threatened moments the same inexplicable awareness, the same universal empathy, referred to by Miura. In fact, it seemed to come in direct proportion to the significance of the moment; a huge bet being more memorable than a small one, a playoff game more vivid than those in the regular season.

But risk brings with it a corresponding surge of energy and adjusting to this pressure is critical. I learned that if I was afraid, the flood of adrenaline and panicked thoughts would spill over the grooves of my training, swamp my control centers, and drown out my guidance signals. If I was calm however, this heightened energy remained channeled. It ran swiftly and surely through my body, elevating my normal abilities. Instead of debilitating distraction, I gained incredible lucidity. In facing death, as Miura had, the ultimate significance triggered the ultimate response: a pure focus of body and mind.

I read on into Miura's book. After Fuji, he tackled Everest, the highest mountain in the world. After years of preparation, he was finally standing atop the South Col, looking down at the world and the yawning Bergschrund, the awesome crevasse straight below him. With only his skis, "sharpened like twin samurai swords," Miura attacked. He accelerated quickly, like "a rocket streaking through vacuous space." The parachute opened but scarcely slowed him down. Within seconds he was skiing much too fast, directly toward the Bergschrund and certain death. Somehow he kept his balance but, after skiing 6,000 feet, more than a mile down a rock-strewn wall of steel blue ice, the inevitable occurred: He fell.

> Then I feel my spine turn cold. My legs flip from under me and begin scraping the slope. A great sense of resignation comes over me, as though I were drowning in a hopeless sea.
>
> There's nothing I can do. Up to this point, I had been trying to fight with legs and skis against the waves of ice, snow, and rock. Now, I have nothing left with which to fight. As my body slides swiftly down the slope, I feel I am being

held by a pair of great hands. There is a sense of relief, and I feel I am entering something gigantic with my whole soul . . . .

. . . I wonder what it feels like at the moment of death. I am only mildly curious and slightly interested now. My experience of myself balloons into a slow and vacuous ballet. I am saying good-bye to my life. I am saying good-bye to being a human.

I wonder what happens at the moment of cutting away, but even more, I feel a tremendous emptiness. Was life nothing but a dream? The word keeps rolling in my head. I wonder if this is the instinct of all living things—to disbelieve life when faced with its end . . . .

. . . Then I realize that the rock—the very one about which I had decided long before I started, "It will be the end if I ever hit that rock"—is looming closer and closer. It looks like a house, doors flung open, bearing down. There is no escape. Time has stopped—now.

But that rock saved Miura's life. It broke his momentum and he landed in a patch of snow beneath it, a hundred yards from the crevasse.

I am alive and safe! But what does that mean? And what does it matter that I continue to struggle in this world and not some other?

Since the magnetic darkness of death has drawn back—for a while—the bright play of living reclaims my best efforts.

I lay back in my bunk and stared at the ceiling. I thought of Miura description of "best efforts" in the modern world and, as well, of the Bushido code of his ancestors—the dictums of sacrifice, loyalty, and effort over time—but now I was thinking differently. Quite suddenly, I could give voice to questions that had long troubled me. What is the equivalent of Miura's "best efforts" in the Western world? What heritage, what historical examples can be used by those who would attempt to live a nobler way?

The guide I had followed so far was an odd spiritual amalgam. First, there was the simple maxim given me by my mother: "Do your best." This notion was galvanized when I read Carlos Castaneda's explanations of the Yaqui Way of Power. The premise was that a warrior must always strive to act *impeccably*, that is, with the sum total of his or her faculties. Why? Because then you need not fear the future or worry about the past. You did your best; you will do your best; nothing more is possible.

Suddenly, I felt closer to Miura. I related to him as a sportsman and a traveler, but also as a human being. I empathized especially with his mystic vision:

> For the medieval samurai, to cut yourself free from your family and home was thought to be the most difficult decision, next to the final sacrifice. One of the last things an adventurer could bring himself to say was: "I have left my home. I have left everything that I love behind. Now, what is my future?" The word adventure sounds a little cheap to describe a commitment like this. But then, nature itself is an adventure in survival. That is the way of life.
>
> People who understand this can live bravely and die with confidence, knowing that they remained true to themselves, as did the ancient samurai. I made up my mind to live that way. It is a feeling somewhat different from being a hero, or a showoff, or merely courageous. It's a question of spirit— like following an order from a different world or fulfilling an oath, unspoken but binding. I cannot pinpoint the reason for my actions, but I have begun to realize that there is validity in everything one does. It is not on the same plane as being good or bad. Maybe it is love? When, after everything is over, I look back, there is this something which I cannot put into words,

something very gentle and sweet. I feel totally alive. I am alive as a person. The things that I wanted to say in this book all boils down to this: in going to Everest, we were trying to repeat the dreams of the samurai—dreams of glory and transient beauty. If life is a dream, let's dream a great dream, until life disappears into eternity, and nothingness.

The sputtering of the candle brought my attention back. I blew out the flame and lay back on the soft pillow. The lights from the parking lot cast shadows across the ceiling and blowing snow tapped softly on the glass. The others lay asleep in their bunks.

I thought about Nobu in the monastery, saying: "There are many paths and different Masters. I'm sure you will find both." Now Fate or Karma or Kismet or Synchronicity or Luck—whatever it was called—some force had brought me to Yuichiro Miura, Japan's Ski Master and undoubted spiritual skier. I thought again of his last line, at once challenging and inspirational: *"If life is a dream, let's dream a great dream."*

twenty-one

My muscles stiffened overnight, working only under protest the next morning. I struggled to sit upright then squinted to focus my eyes on the large room around me. On one side near the window were four double bunks with *tatami* mats between them; on the other was a forest of skis and a long table strewn with ski paraphernalia. Lockers covered the far wall, half of them open and spewing clothes. A glance out the window confirmed that it was still snowing.

Climbing down gingerly, I grabbed my towel and toilet kit and hobbled down the hall to wash up. A few minutes later, shaved and feeling better, I shuffled into the kitchen. Tom, sitting with Naomi and Igarashi at the table, saw me limping and smiled sympathetically.

"I can hardly walk," I muttered.

He laughed and said, "I'll show you some stretches I learned in India."

We stepped into the *tatami* area off the kitchen and spread out on the floor. Inch by inch, joint by joint, I felt the blood and energy start flowing. There was a familiar, almost pleasurable pain. *Just a little more*, I thought, *just a little more each time*.

Stretching is like a territorial feud where you reclaim territory every day, forcing your will against a dark perimeter of pain. Willpower isn't the secret, quite the opposite. You have to give up, to release, to breathe deeply, and let your increasing relaxation simply melt the tension and stiffness away.

Tom talked as we stretched. An inveterate traveler, in Japan for five years and Asia for ten, the stories poured out of him: ashrams, elephant safaris, scuba havens—he described them with flourish and laughed easily, at least until Hiro came into the kitchen. The tall instructor looked over at us stretching, and fleetingly to the others who glanced up, then turned abruptly to get his breakfast. He was totally removed, as if no one in the room held the slightest interest for him. The others displayed no overt reaction but there was a new tension in the air.

"Try this," Tom said quietly, kneading and pounding the muscle tissue of his neck, shoulders, and arms.

I followed his example, enjoying the glow that the attention brought to each muscle and joint. I seemed to be reawakening my body, pampering and preparing it at once. We focused next on our hands and feet, twisting and pinching each toe and finger separately.

I knew the reasoning here, having learned from an acupuncture student in Hong Kong that the internal organs are each linked with one of the fingers and toes on the body's five energy pathways. By massaging different parts of my hands and feet, I stimulated my heart, lungs, liver, kidneys, and intestines as well. As I learned more about acupuncture, acupressure, shiatsu, reflexology and iridology, the Eastern emphasis on preventing illness with diet and exercise seemed wiser than the Western practice of curing ailments after the fact.

Which is not to speak ill of modern medicine. Radical solutions are possible and I had the scars to prove it. My eyes followed the downward path of the scalpel from a point three inches above my right knee on the inside of my thigh, angling across below my kneecap, then three inches further down my shin. As bad as it looked however, my other knee, which had sacrificed cartilage on the altar of football, was actually more prone to problems.

It was stiff even then, but after suffering numerous fractures, concussions, cuts, and separations over the years, I had learned that pain is usually tolerable. I'd learned, in fact, in my college physiology courses, that the electrical impulse sent to the brain does not differentiate between pleasure and pain. Our mind makes the distinction. This process can be suppressed, controlled, or distorted—as in overcoming pain, transcending pain, or succumbing to imagined pain. Again, I had firsthand knowledge, having experienced all three states. Often I hobbled from the trainer's room onto the field and then found myself, minutes later, playing with abandon. But I had also fallen victim also to my own imagination, dwelling on symptoms or taking minor injuries too seriously.

Feeling better, Tom and I moved from the mats to the table, talking quietly about the prospects of the day. He pointed to the snow scrapers at work in the parking lot, yellow behemoths with stainless steel smiles, slicing swaths through the undulating mantle. They had scraped the parking lot the night before and another thirty inches had fallen since. I felt my fear rising; I didn't want to flounder again in front of the others.

After we finished breakfast and went upstairs to change, Tom explained the morning procedure. "Normally we free ski between 9:00 and 9:30, then line up to arrange the morning's lessons. If you don't have to teach, you free-ski again until lunch."

I nodded. A fairly standard ski school itinerary.

"On days like today, however," he gestured to the storm outside, "we start earlier to help the resort staff get the chairlifts and the area ready."

"Really?"

He nodded. "It's interesting. The lift operators and the ski instructors are distinct groups on the mountain, each with its own function and hierarchy, but when it comes to getting the ski area open each morning, that all seems to be forgotten."

"Forgotten or suspended?"

"That's closer, I suppose. There is a rivalry. The lift operators are employed by the Obi Paper Company and the instructors work for Miura."

"What has Obi Paper got to do with the ski area?"

"They own the land."

"Oh, I see." The notion that a mountain could be owned by a private company struck me as odd, like an ocean beachfront being fenced off as private property. Certain things seem inherently communal.

Tom went on. "There's going to be race later in the winter. Obi puts up prizes each year for a 'friendly' competition between the operators and the instructors."

As we entered our dorm and began dressing, I thought about the instructors and their perception of me. I had grown accustomed to overwhelming hospitality in Tokyo, and now it seemed the opposite, almost a void. Hiro acted particularly distant, but they all seemed insular. A small fear crept in. I tried to shake it off, to imagine myself skiing instead, bouncing and swiveling smoothly, but in this too I saw myself struggling, wrenching turns, ducking trees. Fear grew in the pit of my stomach, constricting my breath. I tried to breathe deeply, to quiet and guide my mind, but this required patience and discipline and my mind, like my body, was out of shape.

I drew another breath, more deeply this time, down into the depths of my abdomen. The secret was there, I knew, in the region that holistic healers, spiritual leaders, and martial artists know as the source of *chi*, of *ki*, of *pranha*, of *élan vital*—of life force by whatever name.

Relax into it. Let it flow.

We finished dressing and headed out, plowing through the thigh-deep drifts to the lodge. The air was crisp but not cold, utterly still. The instructors were gathered before the lodge, goggles drawn down against the storm. I could scarcely tell them apart in their black stretch ski pants and bright red coats. Only their hats were distinct.

We set to work clearing the lift platforms, sundecks, and sidewalks. Tom and I waded with shovels over our shoulders toward a huge drift on the steps of the restaurant. The snow had been so beautifully sculpted by the wind, it seemed a shame to spoil it.

"Allow me," Tom cackled, plunging his shovel into the flank. Once begun, we hacked and heaved and forged anew a sense of order.

As we worked, I thought about the night before. Finally, I shared an opinion with Tom, "I don't know if the English lessons are unanimously popular."

"I sensed that," Tom said, "but no one says anything."

"I think there's an undercurrent we should watch out for."

He nodded. "It's too bad. Those lessons are the only thing that make me feel useful here."

"Perhaps if you moved them upstairs to the lounge, we could make them casual, drop-in affairs."

"Might work," he said. "Let's try it."

I enjoyed cleaving the snow, balancing it on my shovel, then tossing it through the air. Satisfaction filled me as the steps slowly emerged. We did extra things too, like squaring the corners and shaking the mats, until finally, the job was complete. Looking around, I saw the others finishing their tasks also, and moving to the racks to get their skis. Time for the reward.

One at a time, on the single chairs, we got the first rides of the morning. Led by Daichiro, Hiro, Saito, and Makoto, the four senior instructors, we rose through the blizzard. My stomach was percolating. The roof of my mouth and my tongue threatened to bond in cottony union. I tried deep breathing but it didn't work. I tried to visualize positive skiing episodes but couldn't sustain them. When it came to deep powder, I had no storehouse of calm imagery to draw upon.

My perspective had changed dramatically from the morning before. With my status still uncertain and Daichiro and Ozaki escorting me to my trial runs, I had been psyched to win. Now, amongst my new peers, with a visit to Kitakabe imminent, I was more worried about embarrassing myself.

This thought snapped me awake and I chided myself. *It's stupid to worry. I'm skiing after all, doing what I had hoped for.*

I realized suddenly how peaceful it was. I could see nothing, hear nothing except my breath, loud in my ears. Within my suit, behind my goggles, the blizzard seemed a wondrous thing. It was furious yet quiet, relentless yet unhurried, exquisite in its gentle energy. For that moment, I was beyond fear, beyond thought. I was there with the mountain, inside time.

Two groups were forming when I reached the top. Hiro, Makoto, and Saito were traversing back under the lift toward Kitakabe, while Daichiro, Ogata, and Igarashi were headed for the Ladies' Giant Slalom. The choice was mine. Swallowing hard, I took the more difficult route.

"Wait up," came a voice from overhead. I looked to see Tom on the chairlift above me. He was off and around and beside me in a minute, telling me what to expect. "We're going further over. To the cutline."

"The cutline?"

"Yeah, past Kitakabe, under the gondola. Just keep bearing left and don't go below the other tracks. They'll be waiting." He adjusted his goggles, dug in the heels of his skis, and gave me a parting bit of news. "It's steep as hell."

Then he was gone. The storm alone could have easily hidden him, but his disrupted snow boiled up instantly to do the trick. I was alone again, alone with the mountain, alone with my breath and my beating heart. The huge flakes sank resolutely down. The frosted trees sang hypnotically, like sirens on the rocks. I looked down into nothingness. No other choice remained.

I leaned forward. Gravity pulled me down, the snow pushed me up—it was momentum versus resistance with me as the mediating force. I twisted, turned, ducked, whatever would work, straining to see and ski at the same time. There was no rhythm or balance, only effort without grace, but somehow I avoided the trees and stayed upright.

I found the others staring down a steep white slash in the forest. A hundred feet below, a gray metal lift tower stood barely discernible, but beyond that the run dropped like a roller coaster in heaven. I heard a hum overhead and looked up to see the gondola and a few onlookers hoping for a show. But no one moved. We waited, silent in the storm, like sentinels on high, misty ground or ghosts suspended in a haze. It seemed sacriligious to disrupt the trance or the beauty of the unbroken snow.

Not for long. In a silent, swooping turn, the first skier passed me like a phantasm in a snowy vision. A second specter followed, as smooth as the first, then a third and a fourth in turn, each identical in black and red, each with a huge V of snow splitting from their skis, boiling up over their shoulders into the whiteness of the sky. They disappeared, one after another, as magically quiet as they had come.

"Loooooooking good," came Tom's voice suddenly. He stood snow-laden above me, his hat, goggles, and clothes holding evidence of a fall. Gleefully, he pushed off and swept past, disappearing into the cloud.

No point in waiting, I thought. I pushed off, dropped quickly into the fall line, and struggled myself into a jerky rhythm down the untracked right side. Ten turns, fifteen, twenty. The huge lift towers came and went; my thighs burned with the strain. Finally, seeing the group clustered near the bottom, I skied toward them through the storm, as grateful as a blushing bride for the veil nature hung.

The ski school was gathering as we arrived. Miura had left already for Alaska, so Daichiro stepped up in his absence, welcoming the students and dividing them into classes according to their skill. Within minutes, the groups were assembled and heading off with their instructors to the chairlift. As they flocked away, Ogata immediately threw some plastic slalom poles over his shoulder and started a herringbone trudge up the mountain. Igarashi, who had worn his short ballet skis in anticipation of free time, began immediately to practice a slow-motion tip roll. Daichiro took off his skis and headed into the ski school. Tom, Takao, and I seemed like special case instructors, that is, we were but we weren't. Standing alone in the wake of the student exodus, we looked at each other and said, "Let's go."

Off we went, up the mountain, down, then up again—over and over again all morning. Powder snow lay everywhere, way more than the grooming machines could possibly handle. It didn't matter where we skied; there was two feet of untracked snow on every run. Even if we went back to the exact same line, our tracks would be already hidden by the relentless blizzard.

We skied the gondola cutline and the wide bowl, Bougisawa, then wove through the trees between Kitakabe and the Ladies' Giant Slalom. The steeper and tighter it got, the more Takao liked it. Tom, more cheerful than graceful, seemed able to follow anywhere. As for me, I found it much easier to ski with these two. Although tackling difficult terrain, we skied together, not one at a time, and often gave "yips" and "yahoos" and shouts of encouragement. Despite my butterflies and interior dialogue atop each run, I was gaining confidence. The more I relaxed, the more familiar I became with the sensations and timing, with the causes and effects and various subtleties of powder.

Takao's role, or non-role, on the mountain was evident at lunchtime. We went together to the kitchen where, amid the din of clanking cutlery, shuffling ski boots, sliding chairs, and the television above, we found seats along the back wall. Tom and I had a plate of food waiting for us, but Takao reached into his pack for a sandwich. Being excluded didn't seem to concern him. He ate staring off into space, his face curiously blank.

Outside after lunch, I asked Tom about it. He shook his head. "They're telling him something, but Takao's just not listening. He wants to ski here with Miura, and he's willing to put up with anything. The instructors can't be too hard on him because Miura might hear of it."

"He doesn't know?"

"Miura sees the big picture. He knows that Takao is not a typical Japanese and likely suffers certain consequences, but he won't force him, or you or me for that matter, onto the group. That would be unfair to them."

"Sounds reasonable . . . I guess."

"I don't know if it's reasonable, but . . . "

I knew exactly. It was the Japanese way. It was one thing to observe or visit small groups in Tokyo, and to read about them abstractly, but quite another to actually live with a dozen Japanese. This wasn't the type of team I was used to. Often it wasn't what you said that mattered but what you didn't say; not what you heard but what you sensed; not what you did but how you did it.

My situation on Mt. Teine had seemed simple but that illusion was fading. As badly as I wanted to fit in, I simply wasn't sure how. Even before the glow of acceptance had faded, I was already aware that the group could reject me like a transplanted organ. *What if my trial period is politely termed a failure? What if my dream becomes a nightmare?*

After lunch, the afternoon ski school gathered, sorted, and dispersed, and again the three of us were left standing alone. Takao and Tom were unfazed, heading straight for the lift, and I had little choice but to follow. Once again, we skied and skied, through glades and gullies, down startling steeps, along silky trails. Since it was a weekday and there were no lift lines, we could ski until our legs gave out. Up, down, up, down—I was going to master powder or die trying.

But in the late afternoon I felt a familiar tightness in my left knee. I knew without looking that the swelling had worsened, that the toll for the relentless pace was now to be paid. Later, back in the room, I checked the damage. Fluid had entered the joint, swelling the skin enough to obscure my kneecap. This was not good. A bag of ice, double-bagged and wrapped in a towel, would stop the swelling, but nothing, except time or a hypodermic needle, would remove the fluid already accumulated.

The problem was worsened, unwittingly, by a gesture of friendship from two of the younger instructors, Naomi and Miya, and our cook, Chie, who invited me that night to see the Snow Festival in downtown Sapporo. Pleased to be included, I ignored good sense and piled into Naomi's VW Beetle with the rest of them. My knee grew worse as the night wore on, but the sculptures were remarkable, astounding really, in their size and complexity. Glowing white against the black, blustery sky, complete to the smallest detail, they occupied five blocks of the central boulevard. Some were huge, bigger even than the actual buildings nearby; others were tiny but intricately detailed. Although the evening was cold, at least ten degrees less than in the day, and it was still snowing heavily, we walked for over an hour.

Afterwards, we followed Naomi to a second story cafe overlooking the boulevard. It looked Parisian, with marble tabletops, wire bistro chairs, and various prints of Impressionist paintings on the walls. We clustered around a window table, laughing and talking as much as our language limitations allowed.

Naomi, I learned, lived in a nearby city, while both Chie and Miya came from Tokyo. They were all in their early twenties and in their first year with Miura, whom they referred to as *Sensei*, or Teacher. It was clear that to be on his ski team, the Snow Dolphins, was a matter of great pride for them.

When I asked about the race with the lift operators, they all leaned forward, as if it were indeed an important matter. "Of course it's for fun," Naomi said. "But it's also a big . . . " He stopped and asked the others for the right word.

"Pride," Miya said.

"Right," said Naomi. "It's a big pride for us. We must win."

"That shouldn't be too hard. We have lots of great skiers. Ogata, Igarashi . . . "

"Yes, Rick-san, but the lift operators get a handicap."

"A handicap? How much?"

"I'm sorry. I don't know."

"Enough to help them considerably, I'm sure." Everyone nodded. The race would be held the following month, about four weeks away. *Will I be included? Will I even be on the mountain?*

Our chatter continued as we drove through the snowy city streets, but dropped off noticeably as we climbed the mountain. We had a last laugh comparing Naomi's gleaming car to the others in the parking lot, buried like mounds in a snowy graveyard, but the warmth of this moment evaporated as we entered the Olympic Center. Everyone grew quiet, Chie and Naomi heading upstairs, Miya and I entering the kitchen. I only wanted ice for my knee but Igarashi, Ogata, and Hiro, who were up drinking shochu, insisted that Miya and I join them. We agreed on one, a dangerous concession, and sat down.

When I told them about the Snow Festival and got bogged down in the description, I looked to Miya for help. But his eyes went wide and his posture grew defensive. Something about these three, particularly Hiro, bothered him. He stammered out a few weak sentences and shrugged nervously. There was an awkward silence.

Igarashi changed the subject. "Rick-san," he said, refilling my glass, "Canadian skiers are crazy, right?" he said, eyes twinkling. He launched into a rapid anecdote in Japanese that earned laughter.

I tried to joke along. "We're not ALL crazy. Only most of us."

Igarashi and Ogata laughed but Hiro barely sniffed. *What's with this guy?* I wondered.

Speaking rapidly, Igarashi told another story in Japanese, then lifted his glass toward me, "Canadians are big drinkers. You too?"

I shook my head. "Lots in university. Not so much anymore."

"Maybe you change," he predicted slyly. "It's a long winter."

Tom stuck his head in, towel over shoulder and hair wet, to announce that the bath was free. I seized the chance to slip away, downing my glass in a single long gulp that met with general approval. They watched as I left, then returned their gaze to the TV screen.

My mind whirled as I entered the bathroom and undressed. *Why did Miya grow so timid? Why did the others become quiet so suddenly?* I scrubbed myself, rinsing with a bucket poured over my head, then dipped my toe into the water. Hot. I slipped in slowly, carrying on my interior dialogue, but the scalding water soon evaporated all thought. As I sank to my neck, I felt the stiffness and worry melt away. I soaked for ten long minutes, then climbed out and toweled off. My body was pink and steaming, clean of sweat and tension. My mind could hold fear no longer.

As I walked through the darkened cafeteria on my way upstairs, a noise caught my attention. The windows facing the mountain were vibrating with the storm. I moved through the aisles for a closer look. Drifts were piling high on the porch and railings, sculpted by gusts and gravity. I looked up past the frenzied wisps into the darkness and imagined my tracks of the day filling in, disappearing slowly. *Somewhere out there,* I thought, *is a mountain I have yet to see. How long can it keep snowing?*

I headed upstairs and climbed—tired, sore, and a little light-headed—into my bunk. I wrapped the ice in my towel, fixed it in place on my knee, and fell back. Exhaustion overcame me. Neither the day's tempest of images, nor the cold on my knee, could keep me awake. Like the swirling snow settling on the ground outside, my mind came finally to rest.

twenty-two

I slept fitfully and woke early, troubled by my knee. It felt heavy and stiff. Climbing carefully from my bunk, I limped down to the kitchen where Chie worked alone preparing breakfast. The television displayed a satellite view of the storm, circling over the region as far as Russia. It seemed impossible, but that meant snow for several more days.

I called out the morning greeting, "*Ohayo gozaimasu.*"

Chie looked up and smiled. "*Ohayo*, Rick-san."

I moved onto the *tatami* mats near the kitchen and examined my leg. The ice had stopped the swelling, but the knee puffed out badly. I stretched my other muscles as best I could, then focused on the injury. The leg would bend, but only reluctantly. There was increasing pressure when the lower limb passed ninety degrees. I decided it was possible to ski, so long as I didn't aggravate the condition any further. Too often, I knew, a small injury becomes serious through abuse.

Without any medical staff on the mountain, I had only one treatment available. I placed my hands over my knee and closed my eyes. Breathing deeply, I tried to empty my mind, to replace my thoughts with an image of golden healing, of energy flowing out of one hand, through my knee, and into my other hand. I imagined my knee getting stronger, healthier by the moment. I visualized the joint pulsing with energy, fresh each instant from my hand and the replenishing cycle of my body.

This technique, called *Reiki*, promotes the concept that illness or injury resulted in a blockage of one's life force. The laying on of hands helped to restore the natural healing flow of the body. The old woman who taught me, a Japanese-Canadian with gentle hands and manner, spoke of illness as a detour from health.

Tom came in and sat down. "How was the Snow Festival?" he asked.

"Great, you should have come."

"I tried to," he said quietly, so that Chie wouldn't hear.

"What do you mean?" I whispered.

"When I heard you were going, I suggested we all go together."

"Right."

"Chie hinted that the car was full." He sounded hurt.

"There were four in a Volkswagen, but we could have squeezed you in."

"That's what I thought, but I didn't push it."

"Sorry to hear that."

"It gets worse. As soon as you left, Hiro turns to me, with that assassin cool of his, and says, 'There was room.'"

"Really?"

He nodded. I was stunned at Hiro's attitude. And the others, why would they invite me only?

Tom had a guess. "Maybe they want to separate us. That way they can get to know us at their own speed."

"That might be it. When we're together, we tend to speak to each other."

"Maybe we should sit apart at the dinner table. Be more accessible."

I agreed. As the instructors slowly filed in, we shifted to opposite ends of the kitchen. Tom's news sent me off on new tangents of speculation. *What was expected of us on the mountain? How did they expect us to act?* It was a puzzle with strange clues.

We finished breakfast and went upstairs to our room to dress. Daichiro came in carrying a pair of skis.

"Miura-sensei asked me to give you these."

I took them, a little sheepish, and mumbled thanks. They were K-2s, nearly new, much shorter at 190 centimeters than my own. The bases were perfect, a far cry from the battle scars on the bottoms of my own skis. Daichiro watched me strangely.

"Wait a minute. Are these your skis, Daichiro?" When he nodded, I handed them back. "I can't take your skis."

"It's all right," he said. "I have other pairs."

Tom, who was watching from across the room, gestured emphatically toward the skis. I looked back to Daichiro, who was serenely expressionless, as always. He offered the skis again. A little uncertain, I accepted them.

After Daichiro left, Tom explained. "Miura is sponsored by K2."

"He gets them for free?"

"Right. So naturally he wants his ski team to wear them."

I felt better hearing this and began adjusting the bindings. I set them to the proper size and tension, then cranked them down a half-turn further. I didn't want to get hurt, but I couldn't stand losing another one in powder.

After fifteen minutes, I was done, changed, and out again into the storm, excited about my new skis. But the first few steps brought me back to reality. My knee felt like a grapefruit, and I struggled just to wade through the waist high drifts.

Once at the lodge, we picked up our shovels and began digging. The snow lay as deep again as the two previous mornings. However thoroughly we had shoveled, however beautiful our ski tracks had been, nature had restored its finer sense of order. My knee would heal the same way, I knew. I simply had to wait. I had been hurt many times but each cut, bruise, or bone repaired itself with miraculous efficiency. For some reason I trusted this, but was less faithful in my skiing or in my relations with the Japanese.

What about the young instructors? I relaxed with them in Sapporo, but we had all tightened up back at the mountain. Why? What was it about the older instructors that caused this unspoken tension? I thought of Randy's hockey team and the problems they had with seniority. I thought of Randy too, and his role as foreigner in residence. Now it was me in the fishbowl, struggling to adapt. Would I enhance or disrupt this group? I resolved to try harder, to double my efforts to learn Japanese and to begin running in the evenings once my leg had healed.

Our shoveling complete, we were off again soon, rising up the chairlift cable like birds perched on a wintry wire. The trees on either side were exquisitely beautiful. Strange to say in their dormancy, but I had never seen trees more vital, more distinctive in character: the tall oak reaching proud, the gnarled elm eking out a contorted existence, the drooping pine with its mournful branches. The frost accentuated this effect, rendered it magical. Each tree was coated in a crystalline sheath, from the coarse bark on the trunks to the glazed twigs on the expressive branches. No color could be seen, only perfect chiaroscuro. I tried to pick out one detail and study it but could not. The scene was an entity, a sublime and indivisible sum total.

I disembarked and followed the others across the dizzying traverse to the gondola cutline. Yesterday's tracks had vanished. Straight, steep, deep—it had returned to perfection. I looked up at the other instructors, to their poised bodies and dark eyes behind goggles, and saw hawks peering down from high perches. Predators.

They looked identical yesterday, I thought. *Had a day really passed?*

In the snowy silence, amidst the spectral forms of snow and ice, I couldn't be sure. Down swooped the first skier, arcing with the same rhythm from side to side, the same cleaving of snow, the same disappearance into the gauzy distance. Another skier and another, it was happening again.

Suddenly, they were all past and I was alone, looking down into the empty whiteness. Despite my accomplishments with Tom and Takao the day before, I found my fears welling up bigger than ever. Back with the group again I was utterly frozen by my fear of embarrassment. Ten seconds passed . . . twenty . . . maybe more. I couldn't bring myself to face those eyes, silently judging me, but I couldn't stay there either, gripped by the moment. Life, the others, everything waited below.

I pushed off and quickly felt the cold rush of speed. A choppy first turn forced me to rush the second. My breath came too fast and sounded too loud in my ears, but it was all drowned out by the urgency of my thoughts:

What's the matter? No one is watching, except me.

That's the problem.

I'm too conscious. I'm trying too hard.

Relax now, let it happen.

Come on now, you can do it. You felt it yesterday.

But I fought the mountain instead of flowing with its natural rhythm. I talked to myself in the second person, saying *"You can do it,"* as if my mind were encouraging someone else.

What's happening?

I was comfortable with Tom and Takao yesterday. Where's that feeling now?

I spotted the others and skied raggedly toward them. As usual, they were silent when I arrived, withholding whatever judgments they had made. Instead, they turned *en masse* and headed toward the lodge. As we merged with the main run, I noticed with pleasure the groomed swath down the left side. Quick, exquisitely soft turns came easily now, and I remembered for the first time that I was on new skis. The realization was unnerving. *How could fear have captured me so completely?*

Takao joined Tom and me in the ski school lineup, muttering about delays on the mountain road. Since so few skiers made it up, the ski school turnout was extremely light. Only Miya and Yoko, the two youngest, got classes; the rest of us hustled to the chairlift for more free skiing. When I reached the top, I saw that Takao and the rest of group were already heading up toward the upper gondola station. The runs beyond required a climb to get there and a snowy traverse back. Considering my knee, it did not seem wise.

As Tom started after them I called out to him, "You guys go ahead. I'm taking it easy today.

He nodded and set off in a herringbone climb. I watched them disappear into the blizzard, then headed the other way alone. I took the intermediate chair for a couple of runs, followed by three more on the T-Bar. Takao considered these runs too easy, but they were just what I needed. Besides favoring my knee, I was desperate to find my rhythm, to get centered again.

The tractors were chewing up the powder and leaving a delightfully smooth surface. Here, where I was familiar with the sensations, my new skis performed perfectly, sliding like a putty knife over the snow. Long, lean turns took me down the mountain, opening into staccato combinations and sweeping caresses.

But this joyful skiing ended too soon. When I came down to the main lodge, Hiro was standing alone out front. Seeing me slide up, he said, "Rick-san, I have a special run to show you."

It seemed more like a challenge than an invitation, but I couldn't refuse. I had to make contact with Hiro, find out more about him. Besides, if I declined I would lose face. I nodded and said, "Let's go."

As we rode up, I tried to imagine what motivated Hiro. Did it frustrate him to be in his older brother's entourage? Was he chafing under the collar of tradition? Was he jealous of Tom and me and the attention Miura gave us?

When the chairlift dropped us at the top, Hiro headed at an unusual angle into the trees above the Headwall. I fell in behind, churning in his track. My knee didn't hurt, but it felt tight and I couldn't keep the thought of it from my mind. This was bad, I knew, simply inviting further injury.

Hiro stopped above a steep, funneling chute, bordered on both sides by walls of rock leading to a narrow bottleneck exit. Squinting through the storm, I saw enough room for two, maybe three turns, but no mistakes. Complicating matters was the initial drop, which I guessed to be six-foot leap from where we stood on the ledge. My knee and the lump in my throat were competing for attention. I felt Hiro's gaze on me, searching for a reaction, but I stared downward through the snowy haze. If he was trying to torment me, I would give him no satisfaction.

Without speaking, Hiro jumped off the ledge into the gully. His landing cast up snow on either side as he plunged into the snowy depths. For a moment, he seemed stopped, frozen at the kinetic frontier between momentum and resistance, but slowly, inexorably, the balance tipped. His downward motion prevailed, and he burst forward into space, snow laden and poised, waiting for gravity. It came, quickly now, drawing him down again into the white inertia, into the equation where he was the variable between two constants. I saw just one more turn before he disappeared through the gap, obscured by his own frothy wake. The gully was chewed up now like a tight corner in a freshly plowed field.

Time to go, I thought. *For better or worse.*

It was worse. Landing stiffly, and with my weight too far forward, I struggled to remain upright, fighting the immense pressure like a water skier being yanked out of the depths by a powerful motorboat. No chance. Over I went, head over ski tips, fear flooding though me. *Where are the rocks?*

I tucked my head and tried to somersault out of the fall. Miraculously, it worked. My skis stayed on, passing like rototiller blades through the snow and coming back up under me. I kept on skiing. My goggles were full of snow and useless, so I wrenched them down and contorted through a desperate turn. Adrenaline, like an elixir, washed through me, steadying me, readying me, taking me closer to the thin rocky exit.

I forgot my knee, forgot Hiro, forgot Miura, and just focused in on the moment, big and round and real. My hands came forward, my breath evened, my mind stopped. I waited . . . waited . . . waited until my inner guidance took over. At the last second, I curved around and down, inches from disaster, as smooth as a dream.

I cruised into a beautiful new scene, ducking a low-hanging branch and weaving into my own patch of perfect, unbroken snow. For a few brief seconds, I was dancing, cavorting, floating semi-suspended through this miraculous substance. I swept through a glade of frozen birch, between two snowy spruces, and around some fallen logs. Scene after wondrous scene appeared, each giving way naturally to the next.

But it couldn't last. I crossed a ski track eventually, then another, and another until finally, through the blizzard as I skied, I saw Hiro waiting. Almost instantly, I felt my dispassionate fluidity disappearing. In its place came thoughts and a renewed awareness of my *self.*

Hiro appeared to scowl before he turned and skied on ahead. I followed, my mind remaining active. I had zoomed from fear and embarrassment to utter concentration, then as quickly returned to self-consciousness. *Why? Why does the clarity of self-preservation suddenly take over my body then leave just as quickly?*

It was so frustrating! When I sensed that delicious awareness, and wanted more than anything to hold and savor it, it would fade instead, leaving me confused and wanting more.

It was doubly exasperating that I had thought so very clearly about these things in Tokyo but couldn't any longer. It wasn't that the ideas were no longer relevant; my concerns about skiing and the group had simply assumed priority. Perhaps I felt like a fake too, supposedly there with Miura to learn about meditative awareness, but being fearful in actuality. Maslow was right, and I was tumbling fast down his "pyramid of needs."[4]

Was this linked to my knee? Physical ailments often develop when one is struggling with problems, as if the body seeks to represent the state of mind. Who was it that said, "What are our bodies but our thoughts in a form we can see?" Whether manifest in the pimples of

---

4   Abraham Maslow, a noted behavioral scientist, theorized that we attend to our needs in a hierarchical order. We seek, obtain, and maintain safety, food and shelter, love and respect, before we search for our highest wish, which he termed self-actualization, or the connection with God.

an adolescent, the weight disorders of the insecure, or the physical vitality, or lack thereof, of the depressed, these symptoms indicate that we unconsciously adapt ourselves physically to match our mental image. This supports the precognition ability. People's conditioning, posture, bearing, skin, and hair appearance all speak tellingly about their character. We become as we imagine ourselves to be.

It was time for lunch when we reached the bottom. I ate quickly, and then went upstairs to check my knee. It had swollen more since morning and would likely get worse. Rest was necessary. That would mean missing the ski school line-up, but since I had yet to be assigned a class, I doubted if my absence would matter.

I was wrong. No sooner had I changed out of my ski clothes and propped up my leg on pillows, then Naomi came looking for something on his shelves. Although he remarked on the size of my knee and pretended to understand my decision, I saw his surprise.

It was worse when Daichiro appeared moments later. He, too, masked his surprise behind a show of concern, but I got the idea. Unless deathly ill, and even then sometimes, Japanese were expected to join the group. I recalled stories of pitchers in Japanese baseball, forced by opinion to pitch through injuries, often ruining their arms to show "fighting spirit."

After Daichiro left, my guilt, though unreasonable, bothered me more than my knee. Now I would have crawled out to join the ski school lineup, but it was too late. By the time I dressed and made it across to the lodge, it would be over. I had missed it. It pained me to imagine everyone standing there, silently noticing my absence.

I didn't like to let my teammates down. I had played an entire football game once with a concussion and a jaw broken in three places, and another with a newly broken bone in my hand. I played while injured countless times, delaying stitches or operations until after games or seasons. Although foolhardy, in retrospect, it was fueled by the desire to play, the urge to contribute, and the need for respect and acceptance.

It was strange to face these conflicts again, to find my intellect waging war with my emotions. I performed those macho heroics in my teens, when I was objective enough to see, and sometimes scorn, my need to play, yet not strong enough emotionally to overcome it. That's part of what makes adolescence so hard: your desire for approval overwhelms your good sense. Logic doesn't help because reason can't solve problems of intuition and emotion. In fact, thinking too much seems most often to make things worse.

Although unreasonable, the thought that I had disappointed my teammates brought me lower yet in my sudden spiral of self-doubt. What I had done out of prudence seemed selfish now. After only three days on Mount Teine, I had hit rock bottom.

twenty-three

Finally, after a long snowy week, the weather changed. For the first time at Teine, I woke to see blue sky out of the window. My knee, elevated each night on pillows and a heating pad, felt noticeably better. I sat up and flexed my leg slowly. The joint felt tight but it worked. There was even some evidence of a kneecap.

I looked outside again. After the ubiquitous white of that first week, the sudden color was startling. A single branch, leafless and frosted white, stretched across the window, its tiny twigs like Chinese writing, etched against the blue parchment sky. I wondered what the other trees looked like, or the entire ski area for that matter? Although it somehow seemed I had been there a long time, I had not yet seen Mt. Teine in its entirety.

I climbed carefully from the bunk, slipped into my sweat suit, and padded down the hallway to the huge lounge windows. My view of the mountain grew as I approached the glass until finally it loomed above me, majestic in the morning light. The forest was a winter wonderland, molding with the contours of the mountain, glazed down to the tiniest twig by the storm. The curving white runs looked like the fairways of an angulated golf course.

I saw the clean slash of the cutline below the gondola, and moving right, the great wide bowl, Bougisawa, and further yet, Takao's favorite, the closed site of the Men's Giant slalom. These runs were on the steep, straight part of the mountain that faced the day lodges. On the left of the gondola, the cliffs of Kitakabe could be seen in the scattered trees beneath the chairlift. Beyond that, in the heart of the area where the mountain curled around on itself, was huge run that had once housed the Ladies' Giant Slalom. On an adjoining flank, facing the Olympic Center, was the straight and steep site of the Men's and Ladies' Slalom course. There were intermediate slopes higher up on top and tree skiing throughout, but I saw, for the first time, that Teine was not as large as it had seemed originally.

I felt my pulse quicken as I thought ahead to our favorite spots, lying in quiet perfection. Though sore and still nervous, I couldn't wait to see what they looked like up close. I hurried downstairs to the kitchen where the mood was upbeat. For once, the television received scant attention. We ate, dressed, and rushed out, trying to get two runs before the ski school opened.

But it was not to be. The morning took a twist when Miura appeared in front of the lodge, looking regal in a cobalt blue coat and red stretch pants. Tom and I hadn't even heard that he was back from Alaska, but there he stood, talking with Hiro, Saito, and Makoto while the rest of the staff readied themselves. I wondered if the topic of my trial period had come up yet? Would they make a decision soon?

Naomi slid over next me. I asked what was happening. "This morning we have photographs," he said.

"Really? Where are the photographers?" I asked.

"Over there," he said. Ozaki, looking like a sunburned Cheshire cat, was crouched over his camera bag. Miura's father waited beside him, skis on, a small backpack over his shoulders.

Tom slid over. "What's going on?" he asked.

"A photography session."

"Are we involved?

"We'll find out, I guess."

That's the way it was shaping up on Mt. Teine. We knew so little—from Miura's activity and the daily itinerary to the sub-surface group tension. This was due, in part, to our inability to speak Japanese, but it seemed also that no one attempted to keep us informed.

When everyone was ready, Miura led us to the lift. We rose in order, Miura in blue out front, then Daichiro, the senior three, and the rest of the bright red troop stretched to the rear. Their uniforms were vividly colorful in the morning's clean light.

Looking around as we climbed, it thrilled me to finally see the terrain we had been skiing. With every foot the chairlift rose, I had a slightly new vision of Mount Teine. I saw for the first time how the different runs, glades, and gullies connected with one another, each now more beautiful yet. Sunlight glinted and refracted off the trees, cross lighting the shadows, transforming the woods into a sparkling playground. Every trunk, branch and twig, every shrub or treetop still visible, was glazed in frost and laden with snow.

Beyond and below the mountain itself, with its virginal whiteness and wonderland shapes, were the sweeping plains of Hokkaido. Sapporo looked like a tiny grid upon them, like a microchip on a white tabletop. To our left, the steely gray water of the Sea of Japan merged hazily with the sky. The coastline split the scene, arcing toward huge, snow-capped mountains on the horizon.

Minutes later at the top, Tom, Takao, and I stood behind the others while Miura perched on the crest of the steep mogul field, looking down at the cameras and up toward wisps of cloud that drifted near the sun. When the photographers were ready and the sun shone clear, Miura nodded to Daichiro, Makoto, Saito, and Hiro, then led them over the ledge.

They dropped quickly from view but looked, in those few seconds, as smooth and polished as five skiers could in such close quarters. Miura, out front, was absolutely unhurried. He rose, sank, and swiveled down a direct path toward the cameras, never once pausing or deviating. His skill and utter sureness was accented perfectly by the group behind him, his dominant blue against their moving red backdrop. Miura had chosen and costumed his supporting cast well.

Seconds later, they reappeared down the valley, streaking toward the lift to get back up again. Igarashi took charge, stepping to the edge and waving his pole to the photographers. With one eye on them and the other scanning for errant clouds, he waited. What's next, I wondered? I looked to the others, searching for clues.

A second later, Igarashi pushed off alone. His was not the smooth, strong style of Miura, but he certainly showed why he was Japan's mogul champion. He bounced, hopped, skipped, and skimmed straight down the steepest pitch possible, gathering speed constantly. The racer, Ogata, stepped up, raising his pole and checking the sky. He too got the go-ahead wave and began a direct descent. Yasu slid up and waited.

As they skied, one after another, I realized how much better I knew them already. When I met them in rapid succession, they seemed like characters in a Russian novel, too many names sounding too much alike. But as we shared hours upon skis, I discerned a great deal more about the characters I had come amongst. Interestingly, my assessments were based more on their skiing than their social behavior, which was, to me, largely indecipherable.

Daichiro was smooth and elegant, as befitting his role as Miura's on-hill general. Hiro skied powerfully but sporadically, with sullen bravado. Makoto was quick and fluid in difficult situations, while Saito's strength lay in an unwavering directness that carried him through moguls and conversations in a straight line.

Igarashi, in keeping with his lifestyle of skiing all day and drinking half the night, simply trusted his reflexes on a ricocheting path down the fall line. Ogata was a hawk, with narrow slits for eyes and a predator's economy of effort. In his travels, the photographer, Ozaki, had developed an abandon in his skiing that was unique amongst the measured Japanese.

The two female instructors, Emiko and Hide, seemed stereotypical of the new and old roles for women in Japan. Emiko was game enough to follow the men, but she sometimes found herself in uncertain territory. Hide, on other hand, was reserved and efficient, attempting only what she could do well. Only one aspect was similar. Although Emiko had special status as Daichiro's fiancée, it was apparent that both women had an auxiliary role on the mountain, one excluded from the possibility of promotion.

The diminutive Yasu, who had a year less experience than Emiko and Hide but the same relative power within the group, was the epitome of Japanese competence. No matter how steep or difficult things became, he would be there, wordless and waiting. Two of the younger instructors displayed confidence, Naomi with a fluid style that reflected his lightheartedness, and Yoko, who displayed solid consistency.

The other two newcomers stood out for opposite reasons. Miya, the youngest and least assertive, trailed behind always, eager but hesitant, like a young pup among a pack of wily dogs. Sasaki, new to the team but older in years, displayed bravura inconsistent with his ability and rank. While Miya and his faults were apparently forgivable, reaction to Sasaki's behavior made a second season for him seem unlikely.

More than anyone else though, Miura's personality and skiing style seemed to mesh most consistently. Although I didn't yet know him well, and he was obviously too busy to spend much time with us, the depth and strength of his character was apparent. From his presence and gently elegant manner that first day to the respectful tone of his skiing protégés, his mastery revealed itself in many ways. The monk, Nobu, had been right after all.

Soon it was my turn. Feeling conspicuous in my peacock blue suit, I slid forward, raised my pole, and squinted at the two tiny figures below. Neither moved. Several seconds passed and still no signal. Puzzled, I looked back to the others and saw Naomi and Tom looking upward. I checked, a little sheepish, and saw a wispy cloud veiling the sun. In my nervousness, I had forgotten to check. When the cloud passed, I raised my pole and looked toward Ozaki. His arm rose and fell. Time to go.

Exhaling forcefully, I plunged off the crest into a deep gully. It narrowed and squirted me quickly around a small mogul where I pumped and swiveled softly on the backside. A half turn brought another large mound. My knees came up hard to slow me down, and I sliced my two quick mogul-top turns before my speed gathered again.

The cameras didn't bother me, not in the moguls where I felt comfortable, familiar enough to enjoy the added pressure. Just as in football, where the stadium roar had filled my ears, or in hockey, where people pressed against the glass scant inches away, the camera's presence made everything doubly vivid—the blue sky and firm white snow, the rush of gravity, the delicious breeze of speed.

Instead of distracting me, I realized, the significance of the moment was helping me to concentrate. *I'm more aware, more involved, more able to expand the seconds and use them effectively. My mind is a benevolent coach now and not a harsh judge.*

But these thoughts came too soon. I crossed a tip on my last turn and went flying, bouncing and rolling the last few feet. Ozaki laughed and kept shooting. Miura's father just lowered his camera and looked at me, his expression neutral. Finally, they turned uphill, leaving me to reassemble myself.

Damn, I thought, *falling on film, directly in front of Miura's father!*

I dusted myself off, seething with shame. It reminded me of a childhood hockey experience, when I had practiced to perfect my wrist shot, then bungled it when I tried to show my father. It's frustrating to know something, to learn a skill, and yet fail in the presence of others. I knew why intellectually but that knowledge didn't enhance my body's ability. If anything, it hindered me. At times, my thoughtful side was so developed, so dispassionate in its lens-like capture of my actions, it was like watching myself from a distance. Too often these self-critiques were incessant and instantaneous, pervasive to a point of interference.

These thoughts simmered until Miura and the senior skiers appeared on the ridge high above us. With a wave from Ozaki they set out, giving us a preview of how the photographs would appear. Tiny at first, then growing steadily, the five colorful skiers wove downward. With the textured white foreground and the yawning blue-sky backdrop, Miura and his skiers were like modern dancers, the scene a graceful merging of sport and art.

Miura was all business when he arrived, explaining what he wanted in a few short sentences. Daichiro called out to his brother, who stood near me. Hiro listened and nodded, then turned to Tom, Takao, and me and spoke with a mean sliver of a smile. "We're going to have everyone in uniform skiing together."

Surprised and a little embarrassed by the pointed exclusion, we skied off to the side of the run. There, out of camera range, we watched Miura and his team, the Snow Dolphins, begin their descent. Thirteen of them fanned out behind Miura, sending an icy white mist billowing into the sky. Miura looked like the bow of a ship, sending up froth to either side. I imagined myself amongst them, straining to see and breathe in the maelstrom of cast up snow, glowing with the energy of a coordinated group. I had enjoyed this feeling so often, especially when an opponent forced my team to fuse together as a single entity. To unite with others in this manner is not to lose oneself but to gain the strength of the whole.

But to be excluded was painful. I had felt this in sports also, when cut from a team or injured or simply too old to play any longer, or in other situations when I had left school friends, work groups, and traveling companions. It was the sudden separateness that hurt, the loss of people I cared for, the sense that things were proceeding without me. Each time it happened, it felt a bit like death.

I looked over at my friends. I knew Tom felt the pressure; we talked about it at night. But Takao was an enigma. What did he think, or feel, about all this? He understood Japanese behavior, of course, and had rebelled already against it, but at what cost? True individuality is difficult in any country, but particularly so in Japan.

It was time for the ski school line-up. As on the first day, Miura addressed the students and assigned the instructors. Tom, Takao, and I were again excluded from duty, left to stand there conspicuously in front of Miura. As much as I loved to free-ski, I felt useless. But I had a surprise coming. Miura approached me with a tall, erect foreigner at his side and graciously made introductions.

"Rick-san," he said. "This is Bob Drummond, a friend of mine doing business here in Japan. He and his family are our guests here today."

Turning to the man and his family, now standing behind him, Miura said, "Rick is a Canadian ski instructor, with us for the winter."

Bob leaned to shake my hand, but I was frozen for a moment. Miura had said, "With us for the winter." Was this the verdict on my trial period?

Finally, I extended my hand, which he shook with a warm smile. The group behind him came forward on cue, led by an elegant blond woman. "This is my wife, Mary, my son, Jeff, and my daughters, Nancy and Brenda."

I shook the hands of his wife and son and simply nodded toward the shy girls. Jeff was roughly twenty and the girls were in their early teens.

Seeing the introductions completed, Miura spoke again to Bob and his family. "I apologize again that I have business now, but Rick will escort you around Teine."

At that moment, Tom and Takao waved to me from the chairlift, grinning widely, but it really wasn't hard to swallow my disappointment. It felt good to be given responsibility.

I rode up with Bob and his family and, upon arriving at the top and heading to the intermediate slope, was quickly reminded of two more lessons about powder. In snow up to your thighs on a gentle slope, you go nowhere fast. In fact, when resistance overcomes gravity completely, you go nowhere at all. That's how the morning started. With Tom and Takao's hooting, real or imagined, in the distance, I literally walked my way down parts of the intermediate run. Nothing, except a steeper hill, could make us slide. I also rediscovered that many people fear the unfamiliarity of powder. Once the snow tractors had packed their swaths, there was no luring the family back into the fresh snow.

Mary Drummond skied well but the others needed help. I watched before commenting, first to allow them to warm up and find their rhythm, then to perceive their respective problems. Often, when teaching skiing, there are so many aberrances happening at once they become hard to distinguish. Even if you can identify them, there is a danger in separating these problems in the mind of a student. Although you can usually teach the correct technique in each instance, students must be able to integrate the various solutions that you demonstrate. The challenge to coaching, true in all sports, is to draw attention to one or more aspects without rendering athletes overly self-conscious and unnatural.

I had to laugh at myself, trying not to make them think too much. I needed to learn, or relearn, that same lesson. The irony deepened over the course of the day, as I repeatedly caught myself teaching what I had lost touch with personally.

Neither of the girls was using her poles effectively, but I caught their attention with a question: "Do you move your arms so carefully when you dance?"

They shook their heads.

"Of course not. Dancing involves your whole body, one movement balancing another. It's the same with skiing. Let yourself go. Pretend that you're dancing your way down the mountain."

Jeff skied well in the smooth areas but grew tentative in the moguls. He wasn't watching them carefully or using them to his advantage. "The mountain will help you, if you let it," I said. "Bumps give you the moment of weightlessness you need to make a turn. Use it. Think of moguls as aids not obstacles."

Bob was a longtime ski student. "How's my pole position?" he asked. "My last instructor kept working on that."

I left his question unanswered. "Let's try a different approach. What other sports do you play?"

"Tennis mostly."

"What's the 'ready' position in tennis?"

"Feet shoulder width apart, weight on the balls of your feet, slight crouch, hands and eyes forward."

"That's right," I said. "Same as most other sports. Why? Because from that position you're best able to move in any direction. It's the optimal position for athletics."

"OK, I see that."

"So let's relax, forget specific techniques, and just think of skiing as simply maintaining the ready position."

They all looked slightly uncertain at first, but they gained confidence steadily. We skied run after run, stopping only briefly for lunch, and by the end of the day they were all skiing much better. Bob looked especially pleased.

"Mary's been skiing all her life," he said, "and I couldn't keep up no matter how hard I tried. Now, by essentially telling me *not to try*, you've helped me do just that. I don't understand, but I'm grateful."

"Glad to help," I said.

I was too. "Just relax" wasn't conventional instruction and I felt like a hypocrite saying it, but this advice seemed the most important of all. Students often get so caught up in specific instructions that they tense up and lose the bigger kinesthetic picture. The integration of sporting motion, particularly for a beginner, is too involved and simultaneous to focus on one specific motion. A broader suggestion, "Maintain your balance," works better because it broadens their intention instead of narrowing it.

I just wished I could hear myself. I advised them to move spontaneously, to use the mountain wisely, to trust their reactions—all things I was not doing. The Drummonds couldn't see the flaws in my skiing; my challenges were at a different level and their perception wasn't yet acute enough. But the instructors and Miura certainly could and, as a result, I couldn't help worrying what I looked like. I knew rationally that worrying hampered my skiing, but simply knowing this didn't help. If I was to learn from Miura, both on skis and off, I had to overcome my self-consciousness.

That night the Drummonds were dining with Miura and his wife in Sapporo, and it was arranged that I would join them. I washed, shaved, changed, and headed down to Miura's house at seven o'clock, acutely aware of the looks I got from the other instructors. No one else had been invited.

I arrived to find Miura working on blueprints. Having just become a partner in a new ski area on Hokkaido, he was busy planning thirty-two runs, six chairlifts, a huge day lodge, and an eight-story hotel, all in addition to roads, parking lots, and support facilities. Construction and ground clearing was to begin that spring, as soon as the snow melted.

"When will you finish?" I asked.

"November 21st," he said.

"Which year?" I asked.

His confident reply taught me more about Japanese business that anything I had yet heard. This was a massive, complex project, not yet even begun, and he predicted, matter-of-factly, "This year, of course."

As a businessman, Miura was part visionary, part celebrity, part showman. In addition to his planning expertise, he would bring prestige and publicity to the new resort before it even opened. Through his office in Tokyo, manned by his brothers, he would promote the Miura Special Ski Tours to this new destination. He would also operate the ski school, staffing it partly from his ranks on Mount Teine. Then I learned one last, telling fact: One of Teine's senior staff would be chosen as Head Instructor of the new resort. A sudden thought struck me: Was it this competition that was affecting Hiro?

I saw Miura's celebrity persona later, in a Bavarian-style restaurant with tiny barmaids carrying huge steins of beer and a six-man band wearing the peaked hats and leather shorts of the Alps playing lively polkas. Evidently accustomed to the limelight, Miura moved within it comfortably, making conversation easily with his guests and well-wishers. Apparently, guests of considerable rank came frequently to visit Miura: movie stars, industry leaders, politicians, even members of Japan's Royal Family. Miura Yuichiro had become more than a celebrated sportsman, I realized. He was a living legend.

Near midnight, we bid goodnight to the Drummonds and wound our way up the mountain. As we drove, Miura listened to his wife's light chatter with the same calm expression he wore all evening. Nothing seemed to faze, agitate, or excite him. He watched carefully when people spoke yet never seemed judgmental. Strange to say, since he was the venerated Master, but I found Miura the easiest of all the Japanese to relax with. I enjoyed being near him, bathing in his remarkable energy. The more I learned about life on the mountain, particularly Miura's dauntingly busy schedule, the greater a privilege that seemed to be.

twenty-four

Despite the good weather, which lasted a week and then two, things didn't get any easier on Mt. Teine. Only the skiing conditions changed. Our tracks had long since crossed and crisscrossed until there was none of the soft powder anywhere. Instead all the runs developed deep moguls, called *kabu* by the Japanese, which grew hard then icy. The crests were scraped hard; the troughs grew deep and long.

At least I knew the techniques and tempo of this kind of skiing. Although my knee was still wrapped in a bandage, I could finally challenge the slopes and the Japanese. I could ski head to head with everyone except the mogul champion, Igarashi, with his head-on, hell-bent style. Despite this distinct progress however, there were still way too many times when I found myself holding back amidst the Japanese, shackled by self-consciousness. Instead of expecting success, I feared failure. The harder I tried, the worse I skied.

Meanwhile, the non-status of Tom, Takao, and me was increasingly clear. Takao was assigned lessons on busy days, and I hosted all the English-speaking visitors and celebrities, but usually the three of us were left alone. While this allowed us to ski as we pleased, it also meant that we weren't contributing. Perhaps worse, we enjoyed a unique freedom among the instructors that made me uneasy.

Our advantage was unwittingly compounded by Miura, who rotated his lunch invitations among the group, but asked Tom and me almost invariably. On the positive side, Miura was a pleasure to be with. Less enjoyable was the cool reaction of the instructors, especially Hiro, who resented the attention we received. For us then, Miura's invitations were increasingly awkward. We couldn't refuse to ski or eat with Miura, nor did we want to, but it was hard to ride with him on a chairlift above the instructors and their classes, or to call over from Miura's home to say that we wouldn't be dining with the instructors. Nothing was ever said, but the vibration was unmistakable.

On one such afternoon, I came into the ski school and called out the Japanese phrase *"Otskurei sama deshita,"* which politely thanked all my fellow workers for their work.

There was no reaction from the seated group until they noticed who had spoken. Rick-san! It wasn't possible. They all thought I sounded Japanese. They made me repeat the phrase, then shook their heads in amazement that I could parrot this stock phrase so accurately. There was a moment of real warmth until Hiro barked something and they all fell silent, like a curtain had been drawn across the room.

When I looked at Tom, he shrugged slightly and pointed to the desk. "There's a letter for you."

This perked me up, especially when I saw Brian's handwriting. It began well too, lots of news about comings and goings at Yoshida House and ESS, but it finished on a sad note. Yumi's father had grown much worse. He had stopped working entirely, and Yumi spent most of her days at his bedside.

This wasn't the news I wanted, especially at that moment. I sat among the instructors, listening to their casual banter and locking eyes once with Hiro, but my mind was back in Tokyo. I imagined Yumi's father lying tiny in his futon, his workshop silent, Yumi tending to his needs quietly. I thought of Brian and the bustle of Yoshida house, of my little room and the long nights I spent there, thinking and writing at the low table by the window.

Where are those thoughts today? Have I learned anything? Do I even know anymore what I'm looking for?

It was easy to chastise myself. I was obviously more concerned now with physical challenges and social striving than I was with my search for spirituality and God. This realization made me restless. I put on my jacket and headed for the door. As I left, Tom followed me out and walked with me back to the Olympic Center.

"It sounds weird," Tom said, "but I've been traveling for twelve years now and I'm finding this—living on a mountain with Japan's top young skiers—one of the hardest experiences I've ever had. You're expected to do things a certain way, but no one ever tells you if you're making a mistake."

I told him about Randy's hockey team in Tokyo, and about the foreigners who play baseball for Japanese teams. For them it's even worse, I said, since their every move is reported in the press. The imported players all eventually react one way or another, namely, they either try to fit in or they don't.

"Well, we're definitely trying," Tom said. "But whether we're succeeding is another question."

His frustration was evident. "It's hard for you, Rick, I know, because they see you as a fellow instructor and expect you to ski up to their standards. But it's difficult for me too, in a different way. They don't expect anything from me. They hardly even watch me."

It was true. While the Japanese scrutiny was excruciating, their indifference was worse somehow. Strangely, this seemed to be the glue of their culture. Their collective ability to include or ostracize people is so highly developed, and the accompanying anxiety so great, that individuals strive to ensure inclusion by tailoring their every behavioral nuance to the norms of the group.

"I just wish I could ski like you guys," he said.

"But you're skiing well, Tom. Much better."

"Yeah, thanks, but it's not enough." After a long pause, he spoke again. "I can't figure it out. I know all the techniques and I'm really trying to link them all together, but . . ."

"Maybe you described your own problem. You're '*really trying*.'"

"What's your point?"

I felt like a hypocrite, but continued. "At a certain point you have to stop trying. Once you've trained your abilities, you need to let go and trust them. You just let it happen."

Tom caught the contradiction immediately, but not quite the same way. "Listen to what you just said. We've been talking about *trying harder* with the Japanese, then suddenly you say that I'll ski better if I relax and let my body take over."

He was right. We were forcing the situation, both on skis and socially. Like a pair of teenagers, we wanted acceptance so badly we had become self-conscious and overly eager. But realizing this wasn't enough. It is far easier to say, "Trust yourself," than it is to actually do it.

Frankly, I was tired of thinking about it. When we reached the lodge, I went upstairs and pulled on my sweat suit and went running. Since my knee healed, I now stretched each morning and jogged in the late afternoons. It helped to forget everything and just get into the flow of it. It was also fascinating to feel myself getting stronger, largely because the decline in my physical condition had been too gradual to notice. It wasn't until I could again bound up a set of stairs, or rise with a sense of power from a sitting position that I thought: "I remember this feeling." Only then did I realize the vigor and zest I had been missing. This sensation was exciting and self-sustaining. The stronger I felt, the more I wanted to exercise.

But at that moment, distracted as I was by Brian's news, my talk with Tom, and the maelstrom of thoughts swirling about my head, it took everything I had to force myself out and down the long road a couple of miles. When I turned around however, and headed back up, my mind renewed its protest and arguments that I should walk. I kept running, but as I chugged my way upward, I played host to a mental debate. While one voice urged me to quit, another voice, even stronger, insisted that I keep going and finish what I started out to do. That was precisely how I felt regarding the Japanese. Life on Mt. Teine was stressful, confusing, even dangerous, but I wouldn't give up.

I realized early in life on that strength is both mental and physical. In fact, physical strength seemed to be the result of mental discipline. Exhausting exercise generates messages to your brain that the muscles are straining. While the mind knows that training will strengthen you and take you past previous thresholds, it also hears the problems, fears, and excuses that grow louder with fatigue. Your mind can either listen and stop, or simply overrule the muscular protest.

Your reactions shape your destiny. Quit in the face of difficulty, choose the path of least resistance, and you will atrophy mentally and physically. But if you persevere, then adversity creates the capacity to overcome adversity. You grow stronger, more confident, more capable of meeting the next challenge.

It was all too ironic. At Teine, instead of seeking to have, and understand, peak experiences, I had been reduced to a more basic concern about social status, about acceptance. Despite my improved skiing, my training program, and my increasing facility with their language, I was still frustratingly self-conscious. Only stubbornness kept me going, and this long held lesson that you never win if you quit the game.

So despite everything I stepped up my pace and finished my run with a sprint. My chest was heaving when I came into the Olympic Center. Most of the instructors were in the kitchen watching TV, so I kept walking and went upstairs, grabbing my towel and notebook on the way to the upper lounge.

Catching my breath, I sat by the window and stared out at the mountain. It glowed blue in the moonlight, with the forest like a dark robe on its shoulders. As I studied its sloping contours, images of my favorite gullies and glades flashed easily into my mind's eye. On the nights when snow fell or the wind blew, I loved to imagine how the snow was settling into our ski tracks, collecting on the branches and in the bark of the trees, drifting with the wind's whimsy into infinitely new variations. On clear evenings such as this, it was just as pleasant, just as reassuring, to visualize the calmness of each locale, the shadows stretching in the early moonlight, the wind whispering through the trees.

Mt. Teine was taking on life for me. As my eyes opened, I saw its character and mood varying daily with the light and weather, and evolving slowly over the seasons. How will it look in a few months, I wondered, with tiny streams of spring water and the first vibrant green buds, or in summer with a full cloak of leaves and those same gullies and glades filled with small animals and birds? In autumn, the Siberian winds would throw a colorful patchwork quilt over the mountain, until finally the snow would return and gather and the cycle of the ages would begin yet again.

I thought about the Shinto beliefs that link the Japanese to nature, and hoped that this ancient wisdom would survive, and perhaps temper, the nation's economic progress. Too many cultures try to subjugate nature, to harness her to the technological plow of progress. Not just Japan is at risk either; other societies throughout the world that have co-existed for centuries with nature are now losing that precious, perhaps irretrievable, balance.

Years earlier, I'd worked briefly with an environmental group, walking door to door talking to people about clean air and water and the preservation of ecosystems. There were three groups of respondents: the like-minded, who gave what support they could, the ignorant, who simply shook their heads, and the antagonistic, who acted like I was trying to harm them. The last sad group had clearly spent too few days in the woods, thought too little about biodiversity, and lost too many of their primal instincts to atrophy. Such people, from welfare recipients to board presidents, have virtually no concern for the vast precious thing that needs protecting.

I opened my notebook and glanced back to the entries I'd written at Yoshida House when my mind was filled more with global problems than the desire for respect and acceptance. Perhaps because the sound of a television again filtered up from downstairs, my eye caught this passage:

As a result of television, social and mental ecologies the world over are changing in mere decades. Television has supplanted the fireplace as the hearth of modern culture, drowned out the elders as the teller of stories and the source of information. Television and movies fill minds everywhere with ideas and images—not ones the populace might necessarily choose, but ones selected by businessmen to earn money and boost market share. The stakes are fantastic, so high that there is now a global race to produce, control, and profit by, information.

There are a lot of good elements too, but the flow of information, and the rate of change it is evoking, is not only without precedent, it is too often without forethought or moral concern. At its worst, media implant fear and desire both collectively and individually. Television, especially, attracts attention with news and programs about danger, misery, and violence, then capitalizes, quite literally, by displaying advertisements that fill us with desire. Why? Because bad news sells better than good, thanks to our strangely masochistic nature, and because we will never buy anything new if we are still satisfied with what we have.

Worse yet, modern nations like America export and advertise Mickey Mouse and MTV just as surely as McDonald's hamburgers and Marlboro cigarettes. While it's good for business to create demand and alter behavior in foreign nations, it is also disruptive to ancient cultural ecologies. While it is certainly true that most countries want "progress," people are bulldozing centuries of social architecture without considering that many new ideas are just bad ones not yet proven so.

America has been the world's great laboratory for change. There has never been such a free and dynamic culture, and its collective achievements are truly remarkable, but there have been painful and unprecedented social costs. Crime, domestic violence, substance abuse, alienation, and a host of other mental and social disorders—these too are irrefutable results of this grand human experiment.

Historically, Japan's experience has been quite different. While they have several times changed dramatically, usually in response to foreign influence, these transformations were always studied and controlled by the ruling powers. Concepts and technology were selected and adapted in a controlled process. But this filtering and grafting appears to be no longer possible in modern Japan, not with global travel, commerce, and information exchange. How long can the Japanese retain their cultural heritage?

I got up from my chair and paced the room. *Where am I going with all this? What is the connection between meditative awareness and global media bombardment?* My mind was moving in several directions at once, making comparisons and connections. I returned to my chair, opened my notebook, and began to write.

Meditation helps us transcend the world, while media seek to enter our consciousness. Our minds are invaded daily by far more ideas, images, and enticements than we could possibly want or need. This would not be so bad if it didn't distract us from what is subtle but truly more important, such as this intimacy with nature that I have regained at Teine, or the spirituality and knowledge of self that I am developing while traveling.

That is the critical connection. Serenity and spiritual strength are too often diminished by the busy, changing, acquiring, worrisome world and, as a result, we need to regain our mental balance. This is precisely the reason why sports have become so important in modern culture. When we are on skis, or on the court, field, rink, or trail, there is no worry about global warming, recession, inflation, or personal security. In fact, there is no past or future at all, only the here and now of the game, demanding our attention. Sports provide a respite from the world, a total focusing on one thing that leads, paradoxically, to a greater understanding of, and compassion for, all things.

I walked to the window and stood staring out. I was close to something, but it wasn't quite coming together. Thoughts and intuitions were aligning themselves, like black and white dominoes, in complex and interrelated patterns over the board of my being. I kept adding new ideas and impressions, waiting for the key piece to fall and trigger what I sensed would be a collective realization.

I thought back on my own advice to Tom, essentially to "stop trying so hard." In fact, this had always been the hardest lesson for me to learn. I fought my way up to the highest levels in sport, but I didn't excel until I learned to let go, to release my striving and let my body take over.

But awareness was a mental thing, not something to be solved by the body. Or was it? If I listened just then to my body, it was telling me lighten up emotionally, to relax intellectually. Already I was running and stretching instead of thinking and writing all the time. The more balanced I felt physically, the greater my emotional evenness too.

Suddenly, I had an idea. I turned from the window and strode to a clearing in the center of the room. With my feet shoulder width apart and my hands at my sides, I began the slow motion movements of *T'ai Chi,* the ancient martial art that I had studied from a Chinese master when I returned home from Asia. I went to his studio nearly every day and found the flowing motions and his calm presence to be greatly soothing during those difficult days.

In terms of skill, I was little more than a neophyte. It had taken me months simply to learn the subtleties of the maneuvers, longer yet to link them in the extraordinarily slow tempo of the art. Intellectually, I understood it better. At first, the movements were a meditation only, and of little value in self-defense. Only gradually would they be engrained deeply enough in a student that they might surface through the enormous distraction of a fight.

Teaching in slow motion was an interesting approach. Boxing, wrestling, judo, karate, and the various other fighting skills also separate their techniques, but usually they practice them in real time.

That is, full speed. Once again, however, since an actual fight happens so quickly, and there is so much fear and distraction, a student often can't access his or her trained abilities.

Fighting ability begins to emerge when the student doesn't allow him or herself to be mentally rushed, but instead sees things as they occur, or better yet, in some measure of slow motion distortion. That was the fascinating aspect of T'ai Chi. They taught us to see ourselves moving through the techniques in slow motion, effectively laying down the circuitry not only for the physical activity, but for the focused perceptivity as well.

I returned my mind to my body, just then performing a motion called: *"Hands Like Carrying Clouds."* It was repeated four times, and each time I pivoted my torso, I stared at the fleshy grain of my fingertips and imagined myself cradling a fluffy cumulous cloud. How gentle it felt, like hugging a spirit. As I flowed into the next form, I sensed immediately the difference in my attitude. It was so easy. In seconds, I had literally "changed my mind." But I had to laugh too, since I suddenly visualized another domino, settling into place.

twenty-five

On the eve of the long-awaited race between the instructors and the lift operators, I gained more firsthand insight into the *"Japanese way"* of learning. A dozen of us, skis over our shoulders, trooped down through a heavy snowfall to the main chalet, then down the stairs to ski rental tool shop. Miura's father, the author of two books on ski maintenance, was to teach us his ski tuning techniques.

At seven o'clock exactly, the door to the shop opened. Miura's father, a slight man with dark glasses and a deeply tanned face, bowed slightly to acknowledge our presence. We bowed silently in return, then parted to allow him access to the workbench. He used one of Naomi's skis as an example, securing them in the clamp and examining them carefully. Besides the overall condition, he checked the sharpness of each edge and, with a straight piece of steel, the relative flatness of the base.

Miura's father said nothing as he discovered the various flaws. He proceeded instead to the remedies, taking a file and a two-handed steel scraper out of the bag at his feet. Where concave, he used the file to grind the metal edges down; where convex, the ski's base material yielded to the steel scraper. Whichever tool he used, he pulled it slowly and steadily, in overlapping one-foot sections and a rearward direction only, along the ski. Periodically, he paused, either to sharpen the scraper or to clean filings from the grooves of the file. He was extraordinarily fastidious about this, and I realized again that craftsmen, like skiers, are only as good as their tools.

Once flattened, the ski needed filling, scraping, sharpening, and waxing. I had seen these techniques before but never with the sureness and grace of this man. His hands moved unerringly, without pause or wasted motion. It reminded me of Mrs. Morita performing the tea ceremony. Every move was measured, firm, exactly appropriate.

When the ski was finished, he straightened and looked around for questions. There were none. Our turn. There were other clamps on smaller benches round the room, enough for three pairs of skis. Sasaki, Emiko, and I were nearest the respective benches and so went first. The others split between us to watch.

Although I was enjoying the pair that Miura had given me, I had decided that my own skis would be better for the downhill-style race the next day. But as soon as I laid them out, I was embarrassed by their condition. Naomi's skis were in far better shape, even before repair, and Miura's father had made the ideal condition very clear. My skis—with cuts, gouges, dull edges, and irregular surfaces—seemed to me, and to the others watching I was sure, a damning indictment on my state of readiness.

Although a poor excuse, I had an almost total lack of experience with tools or technical work. The mounting, adjusting, tuning, and maintaining of skis, in fact the entire shop and its procedures, were as foreign to me as automobiles and garages or chemistry and laboratories. Having so little technical experience therefore, I tended to shy away from these places. Like most people, I stuck with what I knew and got better at that, even though I realized that this skewing of behavior and knowledge makes us even less inclined to try something new. Risk avoidance can be a powerful motivation—protecting oneself from injury, anxiety, pain, or embarrassment simply by pre-empting the potential cause.

Flattening the skis came first. As I drew the different tools down the surface of my skis, trying to emulate the rhythmic motion of Miura's father, I sensed the variables in the surface immediately. Where convex, I felt the buttery resistance of the wax base, yielding in white curls to the scraper. Where concave, I felt the firm, linear contact of metal on metal instead. Anticipating this, I learned to steady my motion and watch for clues. My mood changed from mortification to curiosity. The work lost its daunting aspect and the presence of others around me seemed less intimidating. By the second ski, I became almost proud of my improving technique.

Thus began another lesson in humility. Just as I started adding flourish to my filing motion, I noticed the old man's head lift and turn. He didn't look at me, but off into space instead. His cocked his head, listening. I repeated the procedure, a little nervous now. The old man straightened from Emiko's ski and walked slowly toward me. He replaced me at the bench without speaking and repeated the technique twice. The first time as I had done it, the second as he had shown us originally. I saw, and heard, the difference immediately, especially now that I had tried the technique myself. Still silent, he indicated that I should try again. When I did, he seemed satisfied; it looked right, sounded right. He returned without a word to Emiko's ski and resumed his work there.

I went back to my skis, occasionally stealing a glance toward at the Master. I studied his face, the dark furrows and unwavering gaze. He hardly spoke a word, relying completely on demonstrations, yet he noticed everything, even the sound of my file on the ski's edge. His teaching was completely nonverbal. When I made a mistake, he simply repeated the correct method, slowly and quietly. Even beyond his flawless technique, it was his manner that affected me, the calm sureness and unhurried efficiency. The attitude of the instructors was equally remarkable. Their attention to Miura Sr. was absolute, unwavering; their respect for him and his knowledge was total. He knew; they wanted to know. He demonstrated; they emulated. He spoke few words, but they heard his unspoken communication.

Based on what I had learned in Tokyo, I knew that this wasn't a singular instance. This was the Master-Student relationship of Japan, centuries old but effective still. In fact, I now saw the historical pattern that pervaded Miura's organization. Having himself succeeded his aging father, he now groomed his sons as skiing heirs, employed his brothers as publicity envoys to Sapporo and Tokyo, and chose fine skiers from all over Japan for his entourage. With royalty, dignitaries, and businessmen coming frequently to see him, it finally seemed clear that Miura held court on Mt. Teine as his warlord ancestors once had in their high castles.

I kept working, trying to focus with the elderly Miura's intensity upon my skis. I visualized the surface in the tiniest scale as I worked, seeing the burrs yield slowly to the file, watching the excess base material curl up like snow off a street plow. Strangely, the energy I devoted to my skis gave me an intense new empathy for them. I seemed to understand them more intimately, to care more specifically about their details. For the first time, I sensed what craftsmen must feel when they labor long and carefully over a piece of work. I gained a glimpse also of the meditative work patterns of Miura's father and the heritage he personified: to the Japanese, all focused endeavor, from the loftiest to the most mundane, is an art form.

Most of all, Miura's father was aware of the inner edge of each ski, those critical few inches where safety and control reside. At first, this seemed fastidious, but again I saw the historic pattern. With his grinders, scrapers and files, he worked on those thin strips of steel with the care of an Imperial sword smith. Miura's heritage, his hierarchy on the mountain, his father's ritualistic preparation of the ski—it all fit together: their penchant for the ski's perfection was a philosophy, not an idiosyncrasy. It was a continuation of the traditions of the Samurai, to whom the sword was more than a mere weapon. It was the embodiment of their spirit. The forging and the wielding of the sword required a pure heart as well as the utmost skill. Like the clay of a potter, a sword was imbued with the energy of those who worked with it: first the craftsman, then the warrior.

More than any other feature—the length, curve, balance, or weight—the edge was deemed most important. To hone that edge, that epitome manifest, the sword was heated, pounded, and cooled over and over, through a process seeming redundant to most westerners, but respectful and essential to the Japanese. In their understanding, as long as the work was done purely, those hundreds of hours spent on a single sword were adding to the sum total of its latent energy. This effort was not calculated for efficiency but invested with sincerity.

In this bright new light, I saw things clearly. Yuichiro Miura, The Man Who Skied Everest, my benefactor and master in an era when clans have given way to corporations, was fighting to retain some semblance of this tradition. Instead of swords, he wields skis; instead of men, he battles mountains. These are duels he can never win, yet Miura repeatedly risks his life in them. He does so as a human being for the demands and insights of ultimate challenge. He does so as a Japanese to demonstrate that things integral to the national soul—forthrightness, courage, and mystic vision—have not been lost or sold. In this way, in this day, Yuichiro Miura has truly become a "Samurai of the Snow."

twenty-six

Snow fell through the night and all the next day. By late afternoon, as the instructors gathered for the race and the day skiers streamed down to the parking lot, a fresh foot of snow had fallen. Our team sat in the ski school, a few chatting but most sitting quietly, wearing numbered racing bibs from a pile on the table. I rummaged through them and found forty-one, my old number from football. With the wry smile of a superstitious sportsman, I plucked it from the pile and moved to a seat near Naomi.

"Where are the lift operators?" I asked.

"They are using the small lodge as their team room," he replied. "They will ride the gondola first."

I nodded and sat back, watching Naomi's earnest behavior. I liked him. By now, he was the closest I had to a friend amongst the Japanese. Being a newcomer as well, and close to my age, we had a few things in common. He seemed to be an ally, even though his easy laugh came only when away he was away from the older skiers.

Looking around at the men and women on my team, I saw quiet determination. I felt it too. The mutual challenge brought us closer. The first place racer, the coveted number one, would make Miura's team the collective winner. Conversely, to allow a lift operator to beat us, the professionals, would be a huge loss of face. Our opponents had been given a thirty-second handicap, a huge lead in a five-minute race.

In their identical red jackets and black pants, with numbers front and back, Miura's Snow Dolphins reminded me of teammates and challenges past. I had so often enjoyed this drama, regarding teammates around me as an extension of myself. Sports can do this, replace personal barriers with empathy, with a harnessing of collective will that is greater than the sum of its parts. The better the team, the stronger its integration, since a firm sense of belonging draws out the supportive instincts of its members. Team spirit, in its finest form, is a love—a love that brings people close and binds them in the sweetest, most comfortable bonds.

Groups of all types feel this kinship. Although they might vary in size and purpose, the same sense of mutual responsibility and belonging is possible. The Japanese have certainly learned this. The associative urge is the bond that creates their national consciousness: small groups forming large groups, large groups forming Japan. Being at Teine, living within one of those groups, I finally saw how this small contest with the lift operators represented, in miniature, the motivation of all Japan.

The games and players differ—from baseball to billion dollar deals—but in the eyes of the Japanese, the prize at stake is respect. They suffer without it. They will work incessantly, sometimes die, rather than let themselves or their group be humiliated. The entire Japanese conception of life, death, and duty is foreign to westerners. The world learned the sensational aspects of *kamikaze* and *hara kiri* during the Second World War, but they knew little of the history behind it, nothing at all about Japanese loyalty. Though westerners are astounded by the rapid growth of Japan, few realize the social force that propels it: personal sacrifice to gain or maintain respect by association.

Daichiro strode to the center of the group, giving instructions as he walked. We listened attentively until he finished, then rose and readied ourselves to leave. Naomi turned to me. "We go up by gondola—the lift operators first, then us."

"We'll alternate on the starting line though?" I asked.

"Yes," he replied. "We start in order of our numbers. They have even numbers. We have odd numbers."

I looked down at Naomi's bib. He wore number nineteen. At number forty-one, I would be one of the last to race. *Great,* I thought. *I'll be racing in darkness as well as a blizzard.*

Naomi read my mind. "Don't worry," he said. "They have seven timers working so we leave one every minute from the top. We're all finished in one hour."

"Thanks, Naomi. Good Luck."

"*Gambatte*, Rick-san." Seeing my puzzled look, he translated. "I think you say: 'Go for it.'"

I laughed quietly. "*Gambatte*, Naomi."

We merged with the throng at the door and filed out into the storm. Squinting against the blowing snow, I could see the lift operators in a long line, marching up the gentle slope toward the gondola station. They were evenly spaced, like a platoon, with skis balanced on their shoulders like rifles. As I retrieved my skis, I watched my own group forming. Sure enough, Makoto, Saito, and Hiro and the rest fell into formation behind Daichiro, and we climbed to the gondola the same way.

The first car, loaded with operators, pulled away as we arrived. Still following Daichiro, we snaked through the metal labyrinth that guided lines of skiers each day. Above us on the wall were plaques honoring the medal winners of the 1972 Olympic Games. I read the names as we shuffled around, trying to imagine how they felt, skiing for their country against the best in the world, knowing that the long years they had trained and hoped and prayed had all come down to the task before them. What went through their minds?

I let myself drift, fantasizing myself in the Olympic Downhill. My breath slowed even more, filling and emptying the lowest regions of my lungs. My skis were reassuring as I lifted them; my movements felt purposeful yet relaxed, exactly appropriate.

The gondola lurched forward until we were swept away and engulfed by the nothingness of the storm. All we could see was the single cable above us, disappearing into the cloud. Except for the gentle humming of the cable and the occasional shuffle of a ski boot on the metal floor, there was silence.

I stared out into the whiteness, energy surging through me. I visualized myself on the course: holding a tuck through the first set of curves, pre-jumping the ridge, and holding firm in the sharp turn and the long straight-away, carving the huge S turn into the gently mogulled stretch, and then curving right at full speed to the finish line. The course wasn't dangerous or technically difficult, but it was long. Endurance would be critical, especially towards the end on the bumpy straightaway. I tried to psyche myself for the inevitable fatigue.

Like the yawning mouth of a great beast, the gondola entrance drew near. We slowed and swayed on the cable, bumping against the rail that guided us inward. At first, the station seemed dark, but our eyes adjusted quickly from the glare of the storm to the shadowy fluorescence. Wizened lift operators, too old to compete, opened the door with welcoming bows then escorted us to the exit.

Outside, visibility had worsened to less than fifty feet and a thickening mantle of snow lay everywhere. The crest was smooth and softly contoured, untracked except for the marks of the operators before us. Like sleepwalkers in the hazy silence of a dream, we readied ourselves as the snow blew past, then slid quietly together to the starter's building. The elevated concrete structure, left over from the Olympics, looked ominous as the first group of skiers climbed up toward it. Used only a few times each winter, it stood cold and silent, like a gun emplacement from a forgotten war, still guarding the mountain.

Even as the first racers bolted from the starting gate, I kept imagining the course, anticipating problems and overcoming them, preparing myself to ignore the tired protests of my body. It struck me suddenly how little visualization I had actually done that winter. I had been worrying about "fitting in" with the group instead of seeing myself ski well. After thinking positively for much of my life, I had missed its guiding reassurance totally those past few months.

It was a stunning realization, and undoubtedly true, but little time remained to ponder it. Daichiro had summoned the second group and I felt a fresh surge of nervousness as we climbed up the steps. Daichiro took note of our numbers as we passed, directing the lowest five towards the starting gate.

In the sheltered darkness, my breath billowed out big and frosty white. The fresh air came in cold, down deep where the juices of excitement and fear were brewing, then rose out again, warm and lazy. Twelve racers to go.

I moved to the rack to retrieve my skis. When they were down to six, I put them on. I slid into line when number thirty-eight took off. Now almost every racer was gone. Only one lift operator and Hiro, who had chosen to go last, remained behind me.

Number forty slid into position, poising himself like a predator in the gate. Bobbing to the cadence of the starter, he sprang into action and dropped quickly down the steep ramp into the blizzard. I took his place.

The starter first did a double take at the sight of a foreigner, then checked my bib number and called for a confirmation on his radio. A few seconds later, hearing the reply, he muttered in Japanese and nodded.

As he relayed the ready signal, I took several long breaths, deep into my abdomen. I tried to empty my mind. *Just trust your reflexes,* I thought. *Stay calm. Relax. Empty now. Empty. Breathe. Again. Breathe. Empty. Just ski . . . Just ski . . .*

The starter began a cadence, "*Ju . . . Kyu . . . Hachi . . .*" but I was confused. The numbers sounded strange.

Damn it. What's happening?

The starter's voice grew louder and he began gesturing rapidly.

Suddenly, I realized he was counting backwards! And now he was yelling, "Go . . . Go . . . Go . . ."

Feeling foolish, I burst into action. Gravity took hold, speeding me quickly down the ramp and onto the mountain. Pushing off one ski, then the other, in an exaggerated skating action, I gathered speed into the first turn. I carved through nicely and carried my momentum, but I couldn't see the next gate. Squinting desperately into the white maelstrom, I saw the flag too late. I turned sharply, fighting panic, and managed to get back on track, but I had lost a crucial second.

The next few turns went smoothly and I settled into a relaxed concentration. No fatigue yet. I prepared for the sharp veer and the quick drop off the Waterfall, searching steadily for the red course marker. It appeared suddenly, like a sign on a foggy freeway, and I cut sharply past it and over the ledge. I dropped fast, bouncing off unseen bumps but keeping my balance.

Next would be a critical arcing turn to the left. Besides staying out of the trees, I needed momentum and a good line toward the flat stretches ahead. At the last instant, I saw the flag and sliced through the turn with a good angle. The next stretch—an easy bypass trail—was so gradual that the new snow made it hard to hold speed. I was forced to start skating. Protest rose from my legs and my breathing grew louder. I had been racing for three minutes, and for the first time I heard negative thoughts, urging me to relax: *No one will see; no one will know that you coasted.*

But I kept at it, pushing myself until I came over a rise and again received gravity's assistance. I tucked hard, feeling the burn. My thighs cried out, heat seared my buttocks, the back of my neck ached and wanted to let my head hang down *"just for a second."* Anticipating these traitorous appeals, my mind shut them out. I focused totally on keeping my skis flat and on line. When forced to skate again, I strove to push off smoothly and transfer my weight gradually.

Focus.
Get into the motion.
Smoothly, smoothly.
Don't think, just ski.
Just ski . . .
Ski . . .

But strange demons haunt the delirium of intense fatigue. Even while I felt pain and discipline fighting for control, I also noticed urgent thoughts in bizarre combinations flashing in and out, playing tricks, singing siren songs. I saw the past and the future in chaotic order; I dreamt outward and flew inward with each loud breath. All things seemed possible yet nothing was real.

Through it all, I watched the snowy trees pass hazily by and wondered if I would ever see the next marker. Suddenly, there it was, approaching fast. Now the course would get bumpy and steep, but at least the movements would be different than the crouch that was scalding my body.

With a hard edge set, I cut sharply downward and picked up speed into the final straightaway. Accelerating, flying over the bumpy terrain, I caught only the crests of alternate moguls. The pain, briefly absent, returned mightily, bombarding my muscles and joints with protest. My legs, hips, back, neck—my entire body cried in chorus for rest, but my will held fast. Through the blue shroud of agony, above the rising urge to quit, I squinted with my mind's eye toward the target.

When at last it appeared, the thin banner at the finish line looked beautiful. Just seeing it gave me strength. I tightened my stance, holding firm against the jarring force. *A few more seconds,* I thought. *Hold on, hold on.*

I tried to squeeze every last millisecond out of the mountain, wishing now that I had been stronger earlier and not succumbed, even the slightest bit, to the strain. It seemed I had been alone a long time, struggling in the dreamy whiteness. I was coming home.

I was glad crossing the finish line: glad it was over, glad I had done my best, glad I could finally relax. My throbbing thighs did their last duty, holding my jelly-like legs firm until I shuddered to gasping halt. I collapsed on the snow, chest heaving, mind reeling. A pair of legs approached. I looked up through the clouds of my breath to see Naomi.

"Great, Rick-san," Naomi said. "*Sugoi.*"

Curiosity overcame fatigue. I managed to gasp, "How'd I do?"

"Five minutes, three seconds," he said. "You're in third place."

Third place! I couldn't believe it. "Who's winning?"

"Saito finished in five minutes, one second. Yoko came right behind, five minutes, two seconds."

Two seconds. One . . . Two . . . A pair of blinks was the difference after a mountain of effort and agony. Despite silly errors, I had nearly won. My mind flashed back to the excited gestures of the starter and my confusion when I was skiing off course.

Now I wanted another chance. I wanted to pull those moments back and make the most of them. But I couldn't. I simply had to accept Naomi's congratulations on a respectable showing. I stepped out of my skis just as the next racer crossed the finish line. He had lost control completely and was sliding to a halt. As people rushed over to him, he rolled over and let out a dramatic moan.

Breath returning, I turned back to Naomi. "How did you do?"

He blushed. "Not so good. I went off the course near the beginning."

"Really? I nearly did too." It surprised me somehow that others suffered the same difficulties.

The other racer had been helped to his feet and steered toward the festivities in the lower lodge. The warm yellow lights looked inviting against the deepening gray of the mountain. Most of the previous finishers were standing by the window, cupping their hands against the glass to look out. Behind them, laid out on long tables, were piles of food, liquor, and prizes.

"Here comes Hiro," Naomi said, tapping me on the shoulder. I turned back uphill and squinted to see through the formless swirl. A small, dark figure approached rapidly and we stepped up near the finish line to watch him streak past. He, too, was exhausted, but he kept control until he stopped. He sagged onto his poles, his face contorting in a pained attempt for more oxygen. When an official ran over and related his time, Hiro jabbed his pole at the ground in a feeble show of anger.

"What's his time, Naomi?" I asked. The slim instructor was reading the last entry on the timer's sheet.

"Interesting, Rick-san," he said. "Hiro also finished in five minutes, three seconds also. You two are tied."

Tied with Hiro! Of all people! By this time, he was looking at the timer's sheet himself. As I picked up my skis and headed to the lodge, Hiro turned to face me, eyes smoldering in the growing darkness. Feeling no ill toward him, I could only absorb his energy, but I think that angered him more. I wanted to tell him that his fears or resentments were unnecessary, but I didn't know how.

The lodge felt warm and comfortable. The food and drinks were untouched; the prizes lay under wraps on a table behind the podium. Saito, as the winner, would receive a pair of skis, but the rest of the prizes were a mystery. I hadn't expected to win or even place well. *Had the Obi Corporation made provisions for a tie? Were award-winners expected to say something when accepting?* I grew a little nervous.

A tall Caucasian woman sat with Takao and a young girl against one wall. I turned to Naomi and asked about her. "That's Nancy, Takao's wife," he said, "and their daughter, Yuuki."

I had forgotten about Takao. How had he finished? As the instructors took seats for the awards ceremony, I went over.

"Hello," I said.

Nancy looked up from the young girl. "Oh," she said loudly, pushing her glasses up on her nose to look at me. "You're the other *gaijin* up here."

"That's right. My name's Rick."

"Takao told me about you. I'm Nancy." She thrust out her hand.

I shook it, a little taken back. After awhile in Japan, such an abrupt manner is startling. I was no longer sure, but she seemed effusive even by Western standards.

"How did you do, Takao?" I asked.

He shrugged. "Not so good. Eighth place or something. But you did great, Rick."

"Sshhh . . . they're starting," Nancy said, pointing behind me.

The Obi district manager prepared to open the festivities. He raised his glass to the crowd gathered round, said a few words, then gave the customary toast: "*Kampai!*"

"*Kampai*," came the voices in perfect unison, and they all drank up. Until that point, not one person had touched their drink. *Not much chance of that*, I thought, *among Western ski instructors.*

Miura was in Europe, so Daichiro joined the Obi manager at the podium. They each spoke a moment, then reached back together and picked up the brand-new skis. Everyone cheered or called out, particularly in the area near Saito. He blushed as people teased him, but looked pleased to have captured the victory for Miura and his team. As Daichiro called him up to collect his prize, there was a large round of applause and friendly heckling.

My palms were growing moist. For some reason, the prospect of collecting a prize was embarrassing. I hardly had time to prepare any Japanese remarks, especially with my limited vocabulary. As I imagined walking to the podium, the cafeteria started to seem large and very full.

Saito stopped to crack a few jokes, but Daichiro soon came back to the microphone. The second place award, a set of bindings, went to Yoko, but he was shy and accepted without speaking. Daichiro returned. I readied myself to rise and go forward as he called my name.

But he didn't. Daichiro instead called up Hiro alone and awarded him a new pair of gloves. I was surprised, and only just caught myself from standing. I sat back, thinking that they would award me next.

Wrong again. A lift operator's name was called, and he went up, beaming and bowing, to receive another pair of ski gloves. I settled back further in my chair, stunned. Fifth, sixth, seventh, and on up—the same thing.

I looked around. Only Nancy had noticed me preparing to stand. She gave me a knowing look, and I felt pressure in my chest and blood in my cheeks. To be excluded so blatantly was painful. I tried to let my intellect counsel my emotion. It was an Obi event officially, and I shouldn't let their judgment call upset me. But it did.

As the ceremony concluded and attention shifted to the food on a long side table, Nancy turned to me. "So they passed you over?"

"Apparently," I said, feigning nonchalance.

She wasn't fooled. "I wouldn't worry about it. It's just the Obi people saying that you're not in the *kaisha*."

I must have looked confused.

"It's the company, the group, the house. You're either part of a *kaisha* or you're not. Here, in the eyes of the Obi paper company, you're not."

I grasped the concept but didn't feel much better. Seeing this, Nancy turned and spoke rapidly to Takao in Japanese.

"You should come to my house some time, Rick," he said, in his simple, endearingly direct manner. "We don't have much furniture, but Nancy is a good cook."

Nancy rolled her eyes and softly scolded him in Japanese. He smiled broadly and amended his offer. "Why don't you come with us now? Nancy says we have lots of food."

I looked into his dark eyes, realizing how little I knew about this strange, childlike renegade. Nancy, at his side, was equally interesting with her frank opinions and manner. I yearned to go with them, but I was pulled the other way as well, back into the vortex of the group.

Over their shoulders, I saw Hiro trying on his new gloves. Around the room the instructors were mingling with the lift operators. One part of me wanted to wade out there and try once again to understand them. But the other part knew that I had been "trying" all winter. The harder I tried, in fact, the more anxious I became. It was clear in a flash: I needed to get away.

twenty-seven

The snow groaned beneath the tires as the car began to roll. Looking back through the frosted window, watching the Olympic Center fade from view, I felt an unmistakable surge of relief. Turning forward, toward Takao at the wheel and Nancy beside him holding Yuuki, I had that feeling one gets before a strong electrical storm—of strange winds and high energy.

The heater poured out a warm, noisy reply to the chilled silence of the night. Yuuki drew with her finger on the frosty window while Nancy whispered in her ear. Within minutes, we were down from the mountain road and merging into the slow moving city traffic. Car tires were spinning to get started then sliding to a stop, over and over on the icy roads. There were headlights, taillights, and flashing signs, and clouds of moisture escaping from cars and manhole covers and sewer gratings, all mixing under the dark canopy of the night. It all seemed bizarre after weeks in the natural serenity of my mountain home.

Nancy turned in her seat. "It's getting to you, isn't it?"

Taken aback, I stammered, "Well, I wouldn't say—"

"Hey, don't worry about it. All foreigners in Japanese companies complain about this, and very few actually live within a group of coworkers. Face it. You're with high-powered people in a confined space. It's got to be tough."

"What were you saying earlier about the *kaisha?*" I asked.

"Well, the easy translation is "company," but it's a much broader concept. It's similar in the word *uchi,* which means house, but in this context it's a social grouping. You're either part of a group or you're not."

"Like being a *gaijin?*"

"Exactly," she said. "You're either Japanese or you're not. Same thing."

"So they wield this pressure on other Japanese also?"

"Of course. Both outwardly and inwardly. Since no one wants to be shunned or rejected, they all abide by the rules and act for the good of the group."

"Why do the younger instructors act so weird around the senior guys?" I was also thinking about Randy's hockey players back in Tokyo.

"Well, that's pretty complex. Japanese culture is organized according to the five relationships of Confucius, the most important one in this context being that of *Sempai* to *Kohai*, or older to younger."

"Modern Japan runs on the dictates of Confucius?"

"It's not that different from Christian ideals infusing Western culture, or the effects of Islam in the Arabic world."

She was right, of course. "What was that again about *Sempai* to *Kohai?*"

"The *Kohai*, or junior man, must always pay deference to the older or more experienced person, called the *Sempai*, even if he is wrong or weak. The youngest *Kohai* does all the dirty work basically, acting practically like a personal slave, but the next year there is someone below him. Gradually he climbs the seniority ladder, receiving the same obligatory respect from below as he gives those still above him."

This was like sunshine through the clouds. It explained why the young instructors had to work virtually every day, especially with the raw beginners, then come to the lodge in the evenings and clean the bathtub and wash the dishes. It also made their timid behavior around the older instructors more understandable.

Nancy continued her explanation. "Since everyone has been a *Kohei* at one time, there is nothing demeaning about starting at the bottom. It's accepted as the way things are done. The process is usually linear, age equaling experience, since job shifting is minimal and promotions come more with time than merit. It's rare and awkward in Japan to have someone younger as your superior or, conversely, someone older as your *Kohai*."

"What about Sasaki?" I asked. "He's thirty and this is his first season."

Takao cocked his head to the side and spoke slowly. "Sasaki-san, yes, it's a problem."

That was it from Takao. No more explanation, as if his statement was sufficient for me to understand. Inference from understatement is a critical skill in Japan. I also noted his addition of the respectful suffix *-san* to Sasaki's name, like calling him *Mr. Sasaki*. As I thought back on it, the others instructors did the same.

Takao turned onto a snowy side street, a barely discernible track between parallel brown buildings. People plodded through the drifts beside the road, many carrying parcels and shopping bags. Several of the low wooden homes had a bundled figure clearing the sidewalk or men on ladders shoveling the heavy snowdrifts off the roofs.

Nancy spoke more explicitly. "Sasaki is an example of the system in adjustment, something more common now with rapid growth in Japan and the beginning of promotion by merit. This all makes it harder for the traditional system to work properly."

"Which is how?"

"Ideally, the *Kohei* are patient, obedient, and selfless and the *Sempai* are worthy of the respect accorded them. It's a simple system, almost like bartering. In return for their obedience, *Sempai* teach *Kohei* the wisdom of their years. But now, with prosperity, the process is no longer a certainty. There's too much materialism and foreign influence giving the *Kohei* new ideas and freedoms. Besides that, many of the *Sempai* are not so benevolent. Way too often they're petty, jealous, and manipulative, real assholes basically."

I sat silent, remembering how the older hockey players on Randy's team suppressed the rookies. I thought of Hiro too, and how uncomfortable he made the younger instructors. Being so conscious of my own struggle, I had never before this recognized the similarities.

Nancy spoke with the practiced air of a professor giving a familiar lecture. "This is hard on their subordinates. Japanese can handle hard work, long hours, and endless commuting, but when human relations get strained, they really suffer. Even if something is wrong, the system doesn't allow dissension. Frustrations and anxieties must be hidden for the sake of outward appearance and harmony."

"That can be pretty tough," I agreed.

"Absolutely. And contrary to Western opinion, the Japanese are not identical or emotionless. Quite the opposite. They just suppress their differences in the common interest."

"Is the system eroding?" I asked.

"Well, young Japanese have less discipline and more foreign exposure than their parents, that's for sure. Right, Takao?" She was chuckling now.

At first Takao looked over, eyebrows furrowed, as if he didn't see the pointed humor. Then he smiled impishly and said, "Maybe."

"But . . ." Nancy said, holding up her finger.

"But what?"

"They're all still Japanese."

She said this with the same finality that Takao used when describing Sasaki as "older." As if that were enough to say.

"What do you mean?" I asked finally.

"Well, Takao's a hopeless case, but ordinary Japanese still have to conform within this culture. They still go to school, university, and work, and in each stage, the yoke of precedent weighs more heavily on them."

I described the boulevard dancers I had seen in Tokyo with Junko, changing out of their bohemian outfits when it came time to go home. Like pretend radicals.

"Right. They're stuck, despite their frustrations," Nancy said. "They can't change the system and they can't quit either."

"Why not?" I asked.

"Quit?" Nancy scoffed. "You can't quit anything in Japan. Well, actually, you can quit, and more young people do now, but there is a price, a stigma attached. If you leave school, forget about getting a decent job. If you leave a company, prospective employers will always ask why. If you leave Japan, it's as if you're tainted then, no longer pure Japanese.

"It affects decisions and behavior profoundly. For example, during the first few weeks of university, Japanese students choose their clubs and teams carefully. They know that the people they meet there will be their companions throughout their school years and, in many instances, their whole lives. You simply can't quit these groups, these relationships."

I told Nancy about the father who chose to live alone when he was transferred rather than uproot his son from his school and friends.

"That seems strange to Americans," she said, "who aren't nearly so reluctant to relocate themselves and their families. We feel confident that our kids will make new friends. That isn't so in Japan. Changes here are thought to put children at a severe social disadvantage."

"But they seem to fit together anywhere, like interchangeable pieces."

"It looks that way, but what you're seeing is social choreography. They've been taught to value outward appearances and collective harmony more than their own individuality."

"Does harmony exist?"

"Yes and no. The group interactions are so patterned that these forces tend to remain static, like electricity in clouds."

"Doesn't alcohol play a role?"

"Sure," she said. "Booze as therapy. Especially for businessmen. You have to feel sorry for those guys. They commute an hour or two both ways, work five or six long days a week, then they're practically forced to drink at night too, so they can communicate with their coworkers and clients."

"What about Takao?" I asked. "He doesn't drink with the gang."

"You're right, but look where he stands with the group. He packs a bag lunch, wears an old uniform. He's an outsider."

We plowed through a small snowdrift and into a flimsy plastic carport. While Takao and I unloaded the car, Nancy took Yuuki into a squat, stucco building. She had the kettle warming when we came in. We slipped off our shoes and crossed the *tatami* mats to the *kotatsu*. As we settled on the thin square pillows and tucked the quilted fringe around our waist, Takao found the switch for the heater underneath. It glowed to life instantly, warming our chilled legs and feet.

Nancy's arm swept the room. "Not much but it's home."

"Lots bigger than apartments in Tokyo," I said. Besides the large room where we sat, there was a second of equal size past a partition, and then a bedroom beyond that. The plain white walls and lack of furnishings added to the sense of spaciousness.

Nancy served us steaming hot tea as the warmth and aroma of dinner filled the apartment. Takao lay back on the carpet, playing with Yuuki.

"Did the apartment come with appliances?" I asked, pointing to the stove, refrigerator, and gas heater.

"No, we found them," Nancy said.

"Found them?"

"Sure," she said. "Just sitting on the curb. Same with the *kotatsu*."

"But it's all good. Why would anyone throw it away?"

"They wanted new stuff."

"Wouldn't they sell it or trade it in?"

"Not likely," she said. "Japanese don't like used things. It's a carryover from their Shinto beliefs—they feel that objects take on the energy of the people that use them."

"That makes a friend's business in Tokyo more understandable. He buys beautiful old kimonos at estate sales and exports them to the States. I always wondered how he got them so cheap."

"Well, that's half of it," Nancy said. "Besides that the Japanese have the *ichi-ban* mentality."

Cradling the warm cup, I said, "I've heard about this. The importance of being Number One, isn't it?"

"Right. Everyone wants the new or best thing, or to associate themselves with it. Isn't that right, Takao?"

He was half-listening while he played with Yuuki but he looked up and casually confirmed her words, "Yes, very important."

"Like Miura?" I asked.

Now Takao brightened. "Yes, Miura's great. Number One skier in Japan."

Nancy rolled her eyes. "That's why we're here. Takao admires Miura.

"Was it prearranged?"

"Prearranged? Takao can't plan his next meal. No, he was a walk-on at Miura's preseason camp. We came on a wing and a prayer."

I looked over at Takao. "How did it happen?"

He thought for a long moment, as if he were considering this for the first time, then said slowly, "Pretty lucky, I guess."

Takao was intriguing. He had hardly spoken in the car. In fact, I couldn't remember him ever saying more than a few words in a row. He wasn't absent-minded or unintelligent. That was clear. He was just so . . . simple.

"Tell me what happened," I asked.

"Well, . . . I came with Nancy to Tokyo and, uh, . . . first I checked all the ski magazines." He spoke incredibly slowly.

There was a long pause, as if he had to store up energy for the next sentence. He cocked his head and sighed. "I found plenty of advertisements for ski instructors but everyone wants some paper or something."

Nancy jumped in. "Certification. Japanese ski instructors have more ranks and certificates than the military. Everyone buys into it, even the students. If you say you're an instructor, they'll immediately ask 'What level?'"

"Not Miura," Takao said, almost scolding Nancy. Then to me, he added, "That's why I like Miura. His advertisement said only this: '*If you think you're a great skier, come see us.*'"

"Really?"

For the first time in the conversation, Takao showed real earnest. "I read this and feel so much freedom about this school. I feel really happy. Miura's great."

"So you came up to Teine," I said. "Then what?"

"Kind of a training camp. I skied together with the instructors for one week."

"And then they picked you?"

"Not . . . exactly," Takao said slowly, starting to laugh. "Miura picked me. He saw me skiing, first time, on Ladies' Giant Slalom, and I was going veeerrrry fast. When I stopped, Miura looked at me, kind of strange, and said '*Osorubeki skier.*'"

"What does that mean?"

Takao laughed again and scratched his head. "Hard to say. Sort of like, '*Skiing like scary,*' I guess."

Nancy snorted. "It means more like: '*I am awestruck by this frightening thing.*' Like meeting Godzilla."

We all laughed at the thought of Miura saying this to Takao, then still dressed in his tattered ski garb. He certainly made an impression.

Nancy served up soup, rice, fish, and vegetables, all the while bantering with Takao in Japanese. Nancy was sarcastic with him, but also loving and supportive. I studied her against the backdrop of shelves and steam. She was not one to dance lightly across the surface of subjects; she preferred to dig in and turn the soil.

Between bites, I asked, "What makes Takao immune to the group's influence?"

"Takao?" she laughed, with mock incredulity. "He doesn't care if he belongs or not, so the Japanese way has no hold on him. It drives those instructors crazy though, as if they were playing some game and he was ignoring the rules. Right, Takao?"

He looked up from his plate and shrugged, a mischievous half smile on his face.

Nancy was far more opinionated. "The instructors don't understand Takao. They resent his freedom."

"How about you?" I asked. "How do you feel as a *gaijin* wife?"

"Well, things are a little *strained* around his parents. As oldest son, he was supposed to take over the family reins—the *aikido dojo*, the family responsibilities, everything. Instead, he married a foreigner, got interested in skiing and surfing, and they've hardly seen him since. You can imagine how popular I am in that house."

"Are they hostile?" I asked.

"His father treats me all right, probably because he knew me when I studied *aikido* in his *dojo*. But his mother and two sisters—they just tolerate me."

"It must be awkward around their house," I said.

She arched her eyebrows, giving me the "You must be kidding" look, then added, "We lived for six weeks in their house before coming to Teine and I went crazy. The women would all be in the kitchen together—a tiny Japanese kitchen, mind you—yet they made me feel like I wasn't there. It was like I had done something wrong but could never figure it out."

"But you speak Japanese."

"Didn't matter. They wouldn't talk to me anyway. There's a historic rivalry in Japan between women and their mothers-in-law, mostly because a Japanese bride traditionally comes to live in the house of her new husband. Because she is an outsider, she is often subjected to strict and silent treatment."

Nancy's words were insightful, but I couldn't help but notice how Takao sat so quietly, aware of us, yet content to play with his daughter and fiddle with his ski boots. Like Miura, he had a wonderfully calm manner.

Nancy lifted the teapot and refilled our cups. I watched the steam waft off the tea and felt a growing sense of ease. There were no pretensions or codified courtesies here, no tension in the air. They just lived.

Nancy went on. "Whether it's a family or team or a company, it's still an *uchi* that you either belong to, or you don't. The loyalty of the Japanese, their willingness to sacrifice, the group organization—these are all carryovers of ancient disciplines."

I whistled. "Still at work in the late-twentieth century."

"For better or worse," she said. "Probably worse. Things get done at a tremendous psychic cost."

"Can they change?"

"We'll see. Right now they're dealing with a Catch-22 situation. Japanese want more freedom, more creativity, and spontaneity of thought, yet they want social harmony also. They haven't realized yet that the two don't mix well. Individuality breeds differing opinions and lifestyles, two things that are indigestible in Japanese culture. The saying here is: 'The nail that sticks up gets hammered down.'"

"That hits home for me. I've been hammered down all winter."

"Of course," she said. "You're a non-Japanese. You're not in the group and you never will be. It's that simple."

"How about Takao?"

"Like I said, he doesn't care. He focused on his own priorities a long time ago."

"How do people react to this attitude?"

She waited before answering, studying her husband as if seeing him for the first time. Finally, she turned back to me. "It doesn't go over well with traditional types like his father and Daichiro, but he gets support in strange circles. Miura, for instance, sees in Takao the rebel he was when he was young. Miura knows that it takes guts to be different in Japan. And Takao was a hero in university, too. Not only was he an *aikido* master, but he also had the boldness to really be himself. It's a funny thing in Japan. People scorn the recalcitrant but admire the renegade."

Nancy looked again at her husband, who was checking the snow report, and mused, "Maybe if I hadn't turned him on to skiing, he'd have a famous *dojo* and be Japan's eccentric *aikido* master."

At this, Takao laughed and said, "I would have found skiing anyway. Don't you think so, Rick?"

"You're probably right," I said, believing it. I had seen his passion all winter. He always wanted to ski the most difficult moguls, jump off the highest cornice, or traverse out of bounds to some narrow chute or forest cutline. Takao had the thirst for challenge of a young boy.

"I just like to have fun," he said. "And get a little better ever day. That's all."

No simpler philosophy could be derived. "Have fun, get better, don't worry." Childishly simple and that was the beauty of it. In contrast, my exhaustive self-examination was fragmenting and mul- tiplying my fears. I cringed to recall what I had advised Tom: "Don't think. Trust yourself." I felt like a false prophet, deaf to his own message.

I recalled my thoughts before the race, when I noticed my poor mental posture. Instead of expecting to ski well that winter, I was trying not to embarrass myself. In powder, instead of skiing through the open spaces, I was worrying about avoiding the trees. With the Japanese, I feared rejection more than I expected acceptance. My attitude was diametrically incorrect.

Takao was doing something far better than conscious visualiza- tion. He just expected to learn and have fun, as would a child. There was no need to overcome fear because there was no fear. Instead of trying to win, he expected to win; instead of working at his skiing, he skied for the joy of it. These differences were crucial.

I returned my thoughts to Nancy, and found myself admiring her for supporting Takao in his athletic bohemia. Not many women would agree to such a lifestyle. "I never worried about being rich," she said, as if in explanation. "Besides, Takao's a good father and husband

and a fine human being. I think of him as a purifying force in the Universe."

"That's an odd description."

"Maybe, but it's the truth," she said. "Sort of like the saying: 'If you're not part of the solution, you're part of the problem.' Well, the *problem* is that the world is a messed-up place right now, full of messed-up people, and the *solution* is more human beings like Takao. People more concerned with their spirit than their pocketbooks."

"Do you normally talk about Takao when he's sitting beside you?"

"Oh sure," she laughed. "He doesn't care."

"That's right, Rick," said Takao, equally cheerful. "I don't care."

His impish manner was convincing. Nancy piped up: "Hell, when Takao gets talking—which isn't often, mind you—he'll tell you he's the Buddha."

Takao at first looked stern, as if angry to be mocked, but then he looked back with those laughing eyes and said mischievously, "Of course. I am the Buddha."

I smiled. Seen with the clear vision of serene empathy, Takao was the Buddha. I was the Buddha too. We are all the Buddha or, rather, a-part of the Buddha-nature that pervades all things. If we were Chinese we would be a-part of the Universe, or of The One if we were Hindus. Somehow, in our quietest moments, we are all God, or part of God, or God in action. Labels and theories and dogma provide more confusion than clarity. Explanations create a maze, a hall of mirrors around the truth.

We talked until Yuuki fell asleep, then Takao pulled out a blanket for me while Nancy put their daughter to bed. I bid them goodnight, straightened my legs under the heated table, and lay back in the darkness. I was glad I had come away. Nancy made things clearer for me, especially about the exclusionary, vertical nature of Japanese groups. And Takao, how I enjoyed his simple laughs and gentle manner. He hardly said a word all night, but played instead with his daughter or his ski equipment. Even after skiing every day that winter, he still looked forward to the next.

The funny thing was that, being near him, I did too.

twenty-eight

I awoke with a freshness I hadn't felt in weeks. The storm had cleared overnight and blue sky could be seen through the kitchen window. Nancy stood by the stove, cooking breakfast quietly while Takao made his sandwiches. When I bounced up and said "Good morning," I really meant it.

Takao flew through his breakfast. Another foot of snow had fallen overnight and he was positively ecstatic at the prospect of a sunny day in powder. His excitement was contagious. For the first time in a long while, I felt keen to ski.

I barely had time to thank Nancy before we loaded the car, plowed back down the snowy lane, and spun our way through the snowy city streets toward Mt. Teine. Drafting behind the snowplow, we made good time up the mountain. Once at the lodge, I ran in and changed clothes quickly, emerging just in time to catch Takao, Ozaki, Hiro, Makoto, and Saito setting off. We slipped in behind them on the lift and soon stood on top of the mountain, looking down over Kitakabe.

We heard a voice, calling from below. Ozaki had already skied a hundred yards down the side of the run and was set up with his cameras. He waved us down. Makoto took the honor and disappeared in a swooping plunge from the ledge. Swiveling smoothly, he skied straight toward the lens. When he was past and the snow had settled, Ozaki looked up and waved again. Saito went next, choosing a path just right of Makoto's where we could watch his rhythmic turns. Over a few feet more went Hiro, aiming toward the circle of glass in Ozaki's hands. Then Takao. My turn.

Ozaki signaled me to wait while he changed film. My stomach was churning. I wanted to start, to turn off my mind's ramblings and my eye's searching for the best place to turn. I could see past the steep drop below me and then a few feet beyond, but there the sharp glare of the sun off the snow grew too bright. The camera made me nervous. It shot seven photographs per second, easily fast enough to capture mistakes clearly.

Seeing Ozaki wave, I took a couple of deep breaths, pulled my scarf up over my mouth, and pushed off. I felt nothing at first but gravity. I was falling, dropping through space to the first snowdrift. Then the pressure began, first on the bottom of my skis, then on my calves, thighs, and waist. I was disappearing into whiteness. The snow was everywhere, blinding, beautiful, cold. It stuck to the exposed skin on my face and burned there as I burrowed under the surface.

I was caught between bliss and terror. I loved the feel of the snow and the speed, but knew I had to turn quickly, and then again and again down the mountain. My mind was racing, fearing embarrassment.

Snap out of it.

Remember Takao:

"Have fun. Get a little better each day."

A narcotic calm surged through me. I relaxed my legs and let the snow's pressure push my skis above the snow, rising like two dolphins from the depths. I collected myself in midair and took stock. That first gulping turn had taken me fifteen yards and the second would carry me nearly that far again.

Tighten up now.

Compress your rhythm.

With clarity now, I knifed back into the whiteness and felt the whiffling of snow over my chest and face. Like the snowplow on the road, I was cutting a swath and channeling the shifted snow out behind. Deep in the second turn, I relaxed the pressure of my legs against the snow and let the unchecked resistance force me again toward the surface. Bobbing like a cork, swiveling like a weathervane, I let natural forces do the work. Instead of turning my skis,

I allowed gravity to align them with my upper body. In the subtle, weightless moment at the top of the turn, they pivoted naturally. It felt marvelous.

The second turn flowed into a third and fourth. Time started to expand. Seconds became tenths, and then hundredths of seconds. The scene ballooned into a kaleidoscope of white. The snow had delectable texture, as if I were sliding over fur or feathers. There were no skis, no boots, no poles—only me, just me, maintaining balance in an angular free-fall. I wove my path close to Hiro's, my turns identical to his, as if the mountain dictated our motion. The others grew near and I could hear the motor drive on Ozaki's camera. The clicking and whizzing filled in my ears and their attentive faces seemed to touch me.

Then I was past, stopped, gasping and laughing. The whoop of a Canadian prairie boy escaped me. Like an abbreviated yodel, it stretched up through the trees toward the sky. My exuberance surprised the Japanese, and when they laughed, I bellowed again, louder and longer. Takao started a howl of his own, and Saito and Makoto joined in with yelps. Only Hiro remained silent.

When finally I leaned over my poles to catch my breath, my mind diffused into the white expanse of snow. I could still see, and feel, how the moments opened up large and lucid, giving me time, so much time, to complete each motion. My attitude had changed completely from those early days in powder. I had faced my fear, accepted it, and let it go. I trusted myself.

Checking his watch, Ozaki waved us down toward the ski school lineup. We wove in unison through the thin, sparse trees and cut quickly across to the lodge. We found Tom standing with the other instructors, gurgling with glee. Why not? The snow was deep and light, the weather perfect, the mountain nearly empty.

As soon as the classes were divided, we three were on our way again. Our first destination was a chute near the Men's Giant Slalom. With Takao and Tom in the lead, we climbed and traversed quickly, hoping to get first tracks. We were in luck. The snow's surface was virginal, lying perfect over a shallow gully that twisted and turned toward a steep ravine full of trees. Where the ridge rose on the left to narrow the chute, I saw a lovely overhanging of drifted snow. I chortled, nervous but excited, and angled left into a clearing on top of the ridge. It ran parallel to the run but a little higher, ending just above that tantalizing cornice. My heart beat faster.

Without stopping, I set up a weaving descent. I held my legs firm and bounced lightly through short radius turns, looking toward the bottom for a gap in the trees. The cluster seemed dangerously tight and my heart beat faster as they drew near. Suddenly, seeing the space I needed, I compressed deeply and angled sharply, ducking a snowy branch on the way through. Ice crystals billowed like dust around my head, but my focus was on the approaching ledge. Ten yards . . . Five . . . Three . . .

And then I was off and out into space, soaring, falling through a very long moment. I saw the sky, the plains, the Sea of Japan—even Takao and Tom looking up at me from below. I could do nothing but be there: a terrified, fascinated participant. The ground raced upward, swallowing me in soft whiteness. I couldn't see or orient myself until I came bobbing back to the surface, my scarf off my face, my nose and mouth full of snow. Coughing and laughing, I managed to clear my throat and keep skiing. I wanted more, to challenge the hill now instead of sitting back to be beaten.

Just past Takao and Tom was a smaller cornice. With their shouts of encouragement in my ear, I flew toward it. Seeing nothing in the last seconds except the white of the ramp, I had the old feeling of throwing myself up to destiny. And then again . . . airborne.

These moments lasted longer. I relaxed and actually registered what was happening. My body position was better for the curving, blinding re-entry into that white ocean below. Down I went, into the depths. I saw whiteness, darkness, flashes of color refracting off some snowy prism, then the perfect round orb of the sun, burning through the suspended snow particles.

In a slow split second, I bottomed out and rocketed up into the bright, clean air. My momentum had hardly slowed with my landing; if anything, I was dropping faster. The trees of the ravine loomed closer and my goggles were filled with snow. Yanking them down and blinking away the tears, I cut hard past the first tree then quickly the other way. The thick trunks were tightly spaced, demanding caution, but instead of stopping, I did a half-turn to miss a stump then wove a straight, tight line through the glazed wood.

Finally I reached the return trail and stopped. My body glowed, my chest heaved, my senses were exquisitely acute. This surge of vitality and confidence felt like an old friend's embrace, something you don't treasure until you feel it again after a long absence.

Takao came over the ridge and wove a path near mine through the trees. The bobbing of his motion seemed effortless, like a dance, yet I could see the intensity radiating out from his goggled eyes. He too, was in tune, utterly focused. He reminded me of the seagull I'd seen months earlier from the deck of the Japanese ferry. Scant inches away, soaring into a ferocious wind, the bird's every feather, muscle, and sinew were aligned perfectly. The eyes had a depth, a blackness, a focus that enthralled me; they glinted, as if they were watching the wind. Takao had this same look and I had seen it before on the faces of competitors and teammates in full flight. Utter intention shows most certainly in the eyes, the eyes of life itself, and to bear witness to such purity of purpose is one of sport's most precious rewards

Takao skied no differently; I simply saw him in a new way and realized that this scruffy sports bohemian was teaching me important lessons: he never spoke a negative word; he didn't carry his concerns with him; and his unencumbered zest was a reminder of how someone could live, both on and off skis. Merely watching Takao had put my own anxieties in a clearer light. Better yet, his example—laughing, challenging, childlike—would help prevent me from lapsing again into self-scrutiny and doubt.

When Tom got down, we traversed quickly to the lift. We couldn't wait to get back up, to feel that exquisite sensation again. Run after run we skied, hardly pausing for lunch, never crossing another skier's tracks. We found all our hidden favorites untouched, perfect. Takao and I skied head to head now, bobbing, swiveling, sweeping through high-speed turns. I was pushing myself finally, sharpening my inner edge.

Late in the day, when we had skied everywhere, Takao wanted to go back and try the two cornices I had jumped off earlier. We followed my path of the morning to the small glade above the main run. Mine was still the only track visible, its rounded curves leading into the trees toward the ledge. After Tom took up position on the main run to watch, Takao took off. Three quick turns and a prolonged fourth brought him down and past the trees. Through their frosty branches, I saw his blue and white form hanging motionless in space. I heard nothing for a few moments, then a laughing shout, calling me down.

I took two breaths and leaned forward. The snow was still excellent, more like a flavor than a substance. I tasted it, digested its essence, then let it pass through me to rest again. One turn led easily and smoothly to the next. I neared the point where Takao cut right to the cornice. This had seemed to be the only way, since the other direction had been congested all winter with treetops and brush, but as I skied, full and yet empty, spontaneously, to that point, I suddenly realized that the accumulation of freshly fallen snow had created open space on the left. I had a split second to choose. Without a thought beyond curiosity, I carved back toward that new territory.

Slicing through the first bunch of trees, I found a private heaven: eighty yards long, forty yards wide, with a steep yet regular pitch. The trees were thinly spaced, like the poles of a Slalom course. The snow was soft and crisp. It was perfect. Just a turn to the left, just a chance taken, and I was alone on new ground.

I went into the rhythm and lost track of time, huge moments elapsing in each turn. After initially cleaving wide and deep, I rose to the surface and bounced lightly through a tight grouping of elms. I could hear my breath, slow and steady with the turns. Mentally, I was into and out of my motion at the same time, wondering if it was really me skiing or if I was a radio receiver for some guiding signal. I swooped down a steep mountain within inches of injury, yet there was nothing within me but utter intentionality. I was just doing it, feeling empty, feeling marvelous.

I linked up with the others and told them what I had found. They laughed and hooted and planned for a quick return, but I just smiled and skied to the bottom.

At the lodge, just as we were entering the line-up, Daichiro came by carrying the mail. I called out, "Anything for me?"

To my surprise he nodded, ruffled through the envelopes, and handed me one. It was from Brian. I stuffed it in my jacket, hurried to catch up the others, then opened it when I was alone on the single chairlift.

It was a short note. The news on Yumi's father was bad. He had died in his sleep a week earlier, with Yumi at his side. She was pretty shaken up apparently, and on top of it, she had to make all the funeral arrangements and do all the polite social things for his friends and students. I folded the letter slowly and put it away. I wanted to write Yumi immediately, but I didn't even have her address. I would have to send it to Brian and have him forward it.

When we reached the top, I didn't feel much like skiing. Tom and Takao wanted to try the new run I'd discovered, so I sent them on without me. After they left, I stood alone on the quiet blue mountain. It had been a great day until then. My joy was now bittersweet.

I remembered the fireplace in the upper chalet, and looked over and saw smoke coming out of the chimney. I slid over, placed my skis with the few still in the rack, and clumped into the lodge. It was a round building, made of logs, with exposed beams angling upward to a towering rock fireplace in the center.

I bought a cup of tea and sat on a couch beside a very old man in ski clothing. I took my boots off and set my feet on the hearth by the fire, reveling in the warmth.

The old fellow noticed this and pantomimed that he felt the same way. He smiled and smiled until, finally, he could restrain himself no longer. "My name is Fuskeigawa," he said in perfect English. "I am ninety-three years old and I have skied here for sixty years."

I smiled and nodded, unsure how to reply.

"This is my granddaughter, Kuniko," he said, introducing the middle-aged woman beside him. She smiled pleasantly, as a mother might when someone plays kindly with her child.

He pointed to my badge. "You are an instructor of Miura Yuichiro. You are fortunate."

When I nodded again, he leaned over, as if to tell me a secret: "He's the Number One skier in Japan."

His eyes had the twinkle of a child's at Christmas and his hands gestured constantly as he spoke. "Miura-san gave me a pair of skis last year, when we were on television." He seemed satisfied with this announcement and fell silent.

Studying him, I wondered how I would look when I was ninety-three? Would I be skiing? Would I be such a merry soul as this man, Fuskeigawa? One thing was certain: Your health and attitude in old age depends directly on your health and attitude in youth. I tried to imagine this man seventy years younger—at my age. How had he lived then to remain so active and cheerful now?

I stared into the fire, thinking of Takao and his unfettered positivism. If he didn't impale himself on a tree or ski off a cliff, I could see him skiing for a very long time. In fact, Takao, in his childlike simplicity, reminded me of my new friend, Fuskeigawa, who was ninety-three going on five.

Of myself, I was less certain. If I lived always as I had in Tokyo, or at other contented times, I might fare well, but if worrying became the norm then my chances of being a ninety-three year old skier, or a ninety-three year old anything, would almost certainly slip away.

Takao reminded me of an old lesson I had once struggled to learn. In my teens, I wanted badly to win acceptance, and then too I wasn't sure how. I attempted to be like others: to dress like them, talk like them, and behave like them. I even tried to see myself as they saw me and change what didn't seem right. It was confusing and sometimes heartbreaking.

Finally, thankfully, I realized that to judge yourself by the standards of others is like measuring your height by your shadow. The result would always be changing through no fault of your own. This realization was crucial. I understood finally that I could never be "all things to all people," and instead tried something simpler. Returning to my mother's most basic urging, I strove only "To do my best." Accepting this in my teens made all my activities easier: focusing on the positives, accepting others instead of judging or envying them, learning to relax and try softer. All my success, sporting and otherwise, came after this simple decision to trust myself, but somehow, on Mt. Teine, I had lost touch with that simple truth.

It came time to leave the lodge. Everyone else had long since gone and the mountain lay deep in steely shadows. I waited while Fuskeigawa and his daughter donned their equipment, then skied the gentle beginner's slope with them. With a thin smile, the old child snowplowed methodically from side to side, careful never to gain speed. His granddaughter watched from close behind. After a hundred yards, he stopped and urged me to ski on ahead. The granddaughter nodded her agreement, so I bowed goodbye, pointed my skis downhill, and gathered speed quietly on the cold snow.

It was a wonderfully eerie run, down an empty mountain in fading light. My body was warm, relaxed, and in control. My mind was quiet, enjoying the ride. I noticed the sound of my skis on the snow—gliding, biting, rasping—and the feel of my weight shifting from one ski to the other and back again. Each turn was a caress, a brush stroke across canvas.

As I slid up to the Center House, I remembered my other challenge. Takao couldn't help me in the evenings amongst the instructors. Or could he? He played the Japanese social game as if he didn't care about the score. Perhaps, since I finally knew the rules, I could follow Takao's example in this too. Play like you have nothing to lose, and very often you'll win.

That evening we watched the Sumo tournament on television. The grand champions, Chiyonofuji and Kitanoumi, were undefeated going into the final. The two huge men strutted around the raised circular dais, breathing forcefully and compressing their facial features into stoic masks of concentration. Finally they faced each other, a yard or so apart, with wide stances and straight backs. The referee sank into his dramatic pose and lifted his fan into its traditional position. After a frozen moment, they were on each other, colliding with the force of rutting moose. Each had broken the other's momentum without overbalancing, so they began maneuvering for position or for a handhold on their opponent's sash. Both pushed with their feet well apart, neutralizing any forward or twisting pressure. The first wrestler to touch the ground, or touch down outside the circle, was the loser.

Kitanoumi made a sudden grab for the sash of Chiyonofuji, but the smaller fighter got his instead and used it to heave and push Kitanoumi across the ring. Smelling victory, he backed his man against the rope perimeter, but the giant had his feet wedged against the wide cord and was proving impossible to move. After a flurry, they were back in mid-ring and Kitanoumi had hold of Chiyonofuji's sash. The larger wrestler tried desperately to pull Chiyonofuji off his feet, twisting until both men had a foot waving frantically in the air. Together somehow, they launched themselves into the air, the entire tournament depending on who landed first.

Then it was over. The cameras focused on the hulk Kitanoumi and it seemed he was the winner until I realized that he was heading off the dais into the crowd. Chiyonofuji remained in the ring, squatting in the ritual manner to receive his prize money from the referee. The slow motion replay appeared, revealing the magic of the sporting moment. From a disadvantaged position, Chiyonofuji had writhed and twisted in mid-air to bring Kitanoumi's shoulder down a split second before his own.

There was a chorus of cheers and exhortations in the kitchen. Sasaki, the older instructor, swayed and contorted during the bout, trying to influence the action. Afterwards, still pumped up, he challenged Tom to an arm wrestle. Tom waved him off on me.

Suddenly, I saw my chance. I pulled over a chair and sat face to face with Sasaki and his eager challenge.

A roar went up. The table was cleared while Igarashi raced to the cupboard and pulled out his bottle and a few glasses. I watched him pour, remembering the role of drinking in Japan, and picked up the first full glass. The group roared again, especially Igarashi, who had been trying to get me drunk all year.

After joining the others in an excited toast, I settled into position. Sasaki looked nervous now, and I could tell from his grip that it wasn't going to be a struggle. I prolonged it to help him save face, then brought his knuckles down. The room fell silent, all eyes on me. I took another large sip, then finished my gambit.

"Hiro," I said, staring over at him. "Let's have a rematch."

Everyone turned to study his response. He glared at me, then rose to his feet. The room erupted with excitement. Igarashi bustled about quickly, giving odds and refilling glasses while the others jostled for a good vantage point. Tom looked around the room, and then back at me with a wink. I gave him a slight nod, took another drink, and put my arm up in readiness.

Hiro was cool. I'll give him that. He sat and locked my hand without expression. He was strong too, and aggressive, but this wasn't the same arm he had wrestled months earlier. I was in shape now and coming off a great day.

We started slowly, wavering in a deadlock for several seconds, neither of us trying all out. The tension and noise mounted. Suddenly, he made his move, trying in forceful bursts to press me down. But he couldn't. I resisted his effort and the urge to counterattack, waiting for him to tire. When he surged a second time, more feebly, I knew it was my turn. I looked him in the eye and turned it on.

He showed a flicker of surprise, of humanness, then closed his face for the last ditch defense. His strength had left him but he wouldn't give up. I admired him for that. I even pitied him, because I finally understood his behavior. Hiro was rebellious like Takao, but since his status depended on the system, he could never break away from it. As a result, he was like so many westerners—trying to be different, to be cool, to be an individual—but ending up lonely and unhappy.

When his knuckles touched the table, I grabbed my glass, held it out before me like an olive branch, and said softly, "*Kampai*, Hiro."

I met his gaze, hoping he would see my sincerity. Slowly, he grasped his glass, brought it up near mine and clicked it lightly, saying: "Cheers, Rick."

Another roar went up. Everyone was drinking now, talking fast, and laughing. It was unbelievable. Another bottle appeared and Igarashi started singing. Other joined in merrily, creating a din that easily masked my own off-key efforts. I didn't care anyway; I just let myself be, saying and singing what I felt like.

Things got wilder until we ended up outside, practicing Sumo in the snow. My technique was nothing to behold, an impromptu fusion of football and wrestling moves, but it served me well. I wrestled them all in succession, winning more than I lost, then retired exhausted.

Feeling warm, drunk, and full of adrenaline, it seemed to me a natural thing to leap off an embankment into a huge snowy drift. At first, they all thought I was crazy, but when Tom dove, then Igarashi, it soon became a free for all. We jumped and jumped, each leap longer and more imaginative, each effort received with laughter and encouragement.

When we were all thoroughly frozen, we headed back into the kitchen for hot saké. Even Hiro laughed and talked eagerly now. The young instructors—Naomi, Miya, Yoko, Yasu—they smiled more in those few hours than they had all winter. Seeing this, I had to fight back a tear. I felt kinship finally, even if it was alcohol induced. It seemed strange, but again, it was the Japanese way.

twenty-nine

As the days grew longer and warmer, we shed our heavy jackets and traded our goggles for sunglasses. The snow changed rapidly during the course of the day. Mornings were hard and icy, especially in the shadows, forcing us to stay light footed and alert. For a magical period at midday, we slid sweetly on moist corn snow, reveling in the texture. Slush developed slowly as the sun beat down, making turns feel like they were carved in honey. Finally, as shadows came over the mountain and the temperature dropped again, we skied warily and listened for the sound of ice.

I was skiing well now. Not only were these conditions familiar to me, my knee had healed and my thighs were like bands of steel. I had kept up with the morning stretching and afternoon running, and each evening in the lounge I did my T'ai Chi forms. My skis were in ideal condition, thanks to the techniques I learned from Miura's father, and I could now sense, feel, almost visualize them responding appropriately. Most importantly, I stayed clear in my mind, free of overthink.

I approached the group with the same sensitivity, listening for subtle changes, relaxing, not pressing, to get things done. Things were still delicate, and at times confusing, but as I relaxed, I sensed others relaxing around me. At any rate, I was being myself finally. Now that we understood the hierarchy better, Tom and I began sharing kitchen chores with the young instructors, an act that placed us as *Kohai* among the group. Although still guests of Miura technically, we both felt better playing a "junior" role.

The English lessons had been forgotten but everyone spoke far more fluidly anyway. My Japanese was improving as well, giving me further insight and enabling me to blend more easily with the others. The one thing I did less frequently was to write in my journal. After filling countless pages in the initial months, mostly with anxious speculations, I had written little since my evening with Takao and Nancy. I felt like skiing and living now, not thinking all the time.

As the weeks passed, and I drew closer to Takao, the more impressed I became. Perhaps appreciative was more accurate. Or admiring. Takao was daring and effervescent, yet totally simple. Give him a cliff to jump or a hundred feet of unbroken powder and he was happy. Fear seemed unknown. The steepest, the deepest, the narrowest—his reaction never varied: "Let's try that." His cheerfulness overcame me. I found myself laughing more, thinking less, and skiing with his youthful abandon.

Just when things finally seemed pleasant, however, the winter was almost over. Everyone had obligations and destinations looming. Miura had planned an expedition to New Zealand, while Hiro, Makoto, and Saito were slated to take the highest-level instructor's test at a Honshu resort. Daichiro and Emiko were perhaps the busiest, heading to Tokyo to make final preparations for their wedding. Yasu and Naomi both had summer jobs waiting, while Miya, Hide, and Yoko would attend spring classes at university. Igarashi was leaving to defend his national mogul title, and Takao, typically, was following him to enter unseeded into the All-Japan mogul championships. Tom was returning to teach at an English school in Tokyo, and he offered to put me up and get me enough work to afford a ticket home.

The critical date was the final instructor's session when Miura would evaluate our progress. Everyone felt the pressure, especially since Miura's new ski area needed instructors and their performance would affect his decisions. It was particularly acute for the senior three, Hiro, Makoto, and Saito, who were still jockeying for the top position on the new mountain. As for Takao, Tom, and me, we would ski simply for the respect of Miura and the group.

One morning I received an unexpected blessing. It began when I was delayed in the lodge and came out to find everyone already gone up the mountain. I didn't mind. In fact, I would enjoy skiing alone for once, especially with a sun-filled blue sky and a fresh dusting of snow.

I slid through the lift line and directly onto the chair, poking the lift operator playfully as I passed. "*Ohayo gozaimasu*," I said.

"*Ohayo*, Rick-san," he said, smiling as he loaded me on the chairlift.

I rose with exhilaration above the sparkling mountain. Seldom had I felt so ready to ski, my body in mid-season form, my mind full of perfect skiing images. Only one thing made my zest bittersweet: the end was looming near.

Next week the winter will be over, I thought. *I'll be gone. Have I learned what I came to learn?*

Delighted whoops caught my attention. I had come over the rise above Kitakabe and spotted Takao taking a treacherous path through the trees. Tom was behind him on slightly more sane ground, hooting madly. I saw their smiles and Takao's bright eyes and felt love for them both. Takao was a Master in his own right, indeed a "purifying force in the Universe." By remaining natural and unaffected, he helped me clean up, scrub down, and wash myself of overthink. Tom was there for me also—to talk to, to share things with, to bridge the aloneness I had so often felt. As outsiders, we were a group of three on Mt. Teine.

They disappeared below as the upper station came into view. I would catch them later. I slid down the ramp and gathered speed. The snow was moist underfoot. My skis felt like a paintbrush upon an oily canvas, touching down in bold strokes and soft flourishes. My hands were in front, my weight forward; I was precisely aware of my balance shifting as I carved gentle arcs on the white surface. The snow was so yielding and malleable, and my legs so strong, I felt I could create and explore new shapes, new feelings, new textures.

The sun cast my shadow out ahead of me. The silhouette was fascinating to watch, like an instant video. With a trained eye, I recognized the aggressiveness and the racer's profile. Changing direction, I lost the view, but still I felt the wind and sun and that surging, rhythmic motion. I cruised off the intermediate run and onto the deep moguls of the Ladies' Giant Slalom, softening where the sun poured down but still like frozen blue marbles in the shade. I started swiveling, bumping, and bobbing. It felt good. Little turns, like small jokes, just happened, as if of their own will. There was time, so much time, to adjust and react. The seconds were opening up now, letting me inside.

Entering the icy shadow, I tightened into a flurry of light-footed turns. My mind was as slow and certain as before; I simply turned more often to control my speed. Where patches were shaved sheer, causing my skis to rasp, I held my edges softly until I crossed into snow. Other times I turned deliberately on the boilerplate, allowing an extra margin for the slide. Although tricky at first, it grew easier as I experimented with the causes and effects.

When I got to the bottom, I heard my name called. Walking up the hill, skis in one hand and poles in the other, was Yuichiro Miura. His black hair accented his tanned face and white smile. He wore an orange jacket that glowed in the sunlight, and blue pants that revealed the muscular contours of his legs. We chatted casually while he put on his skis and I kept expecting someone else to appear. Surprisingly, no one did.

So we set off alone, sliding quickly through the short line and onto our respective chairs. A few skiers noticed Miura and began speaking rapidly and pointing upwards. He gave a friendly wave but otherwise sat still, his skis and poles dangling in space. In the rapt gazes below, I saw the respect an individual can earn in Japan. Their spontaneous awe, and the love and loyalty of his instructors, was vivid evidence of Miura's role in Japan. Whether connected by proximity or by association to Miura, he was to them all a hero, an adventurer, a leader in a land of followers.

As Miura began to maneuver and hold his skis in different positions, I studied him against the backdrop of the mountain. He had lived all his life there, honing skills he used around the world. What propelled him down Fuji, Kilimanjaro, or Everest? Was it his heritage, urging him on? His fascination with the ultimate challenge? Whatever his motive, he had parlayed his deeds and himself into national prominence. He was his own best pupil when he said: "If life is a dream, let's dream a great dream."

Disembarking at the top, I slid behind Miura toward the Ladies' Giant Slalom. He paused to let me catch up and then we skied onto the run together. It was strange to ski without waiting but there were only the two of us, descending beneath that beautiful blue sky. The bumps were soft but firm enough to initiate turns. I played with the motion as if dancing, in various moments, to different tunes. Off to my right and slightly ahead, I could see Miura swiveling smoothly. He stopped finally, looking down over the next stretch of moguls, and I slid up to join him. Neither of us spoke. There was nothing to say.

We skied down easily, naturally, then rode up the Men's Slalom chairlift. Again I watched Miura manipulate his skis on the chair ahead. By maneuvering through them slowly, he seemed to reinforce his muscle memory so that his body would recognize each position as it occurred. These poses were like a kinesthetic alphabet that he linked together while skiing. I imitated his motion, feeling with fascination the difference that the slightest shift made.

We disembarked and came around under the lift to the throat of a deeply mogulled gully. We stood quiet for a moment, and then Miura pushed off. He dropped through the bumps as surely as he would descending stairs. There was no rush, no recovery, just simple, perfect skiing. As he disappeared, I looked around me; I was alone. Earlier in the winter, I had stood in that same spot, terrified to ski down toward Miura's watching eyes. Now I felt a delicious emptiness.

Pointing my skis toward the first mound below, I leaned forward. The light, white coldness exploded up over me, moistening my face and clinging to the folds of my suit. I had blown through the top of it, disintegrated what seemed solid, and was dropping fast to the next. I collapsed my legs, lessened my speed, and glanced off two small bumps before blasting a third. Again came the icy maelstrom, the swiveling drop, the compression and pivot. I sensed Miura's presence, but only as a component of the scene and situation. There was no fear of injury or failure, no sense of time, no thought of where or how to turn—just the single, utter intention to ski, to harmonize with the gravitational rhythm.

Suddenly I understood Miura's chairlift positions as never before. I felt them, one after another, as I compressed and extended and adjusted my way through the moguls. Just like Miura, I was connecting kinesthetic dots, creating a spatial picture. By imitating his motions beforehand, I had shown my body what to look for, like signs or landmarks on a neural pathway. Miura was creating ideal forms, like those of T'ai Chi, knowing that our bodies would recognize them and link them together smoothly.

Miura's calmness was the secret. Only while studying and performing in the right frame of mind, that is, with total focus, can one access this enhanced method of integrated learning. I understood this instantly.

It's so simple. Relaxed attention allows you to slow things down, to perceive accurately what is happening. I can ski a thousand runs in terror and learn nothing, or just once calmly and understand the patterns. Only with pure attention can I discern which action causes which reaction.

I kept skiing, unraveling a silky spool that brought me down to the lodge. Miura invited me for lunch, then went into the ski school to invite a few others. I waited, bathing in the sunshine and watching the recreational skiers on the sundeck. They were relaxed and smiling now, but by the next morning they would again be rushing tight-lipped down the streets of Sapporo or Tokyo, much like their harried counterparts in New York or London or other cities around the world where millions daily wear masks of concern.

What is it that we fear? I wondered.

But the answer came too easily: We fear everything, at one time or another: Fear of injury or pain, fear of embarrassment, rejection, or loneliness, fear of sameness or newness, fear of failure or success, fear of death, fear of life, fear that nothing really matters in the end. We even have fear of fear.

I thought back to painful moments earlier in the winter, moments when I had wrestled though turns or struggled to understand my Japanese hosts. I worried so much then that I could barely function. That desperation was so different than the crystalline clarity, the luxurious sense of time, I had enjoyed in the moguls a few minutes earlier.

Fear is the prime distraction, I realized. *Like gravity upon the lightness of our being.*

Miura emerged with Takao, Tom, Daichiro, and Igarashi and we tramped together through the snow to his house. The room appeared as it had my first day, Miura's wife at the stove and his father hunched at the table over his handheld power grinder. They looked up as we entered, Tomoko calling out the traditional welcome: "*Okaerinasai.*"

Miura invited me to sit with him at the end of the table. I looked around. The group seemed to approve of the privilege he showed me. A little late in coming, but I finally felt a sense of belonging.

Tomoko counted heads, put down cups of steaming tea, and minutes later served soup, fish, rice, and vegetables. Everyone set to eating, with easy talk and laughter over lunch.

Toward the end of the meal, I tried to thank Miura quietly for having me as his guest that winter. The words, hard to select and utter, seemed insufficient. Perhaps he saw something more in my eyes, for when I finished, he said softly, "You are a good person."

Our gaze met, and I saw within his eyes the compassion that had so often fascinated me while traveling in Asia. It was completely unguarded, trusting. There seemed to be a gentle telepathy between us, his attitude as kind and gentle as his gracious words. I bowed my head finally, out of thanks and respect.

Conversation continued around the table. I shifted my gaze to Miura's father, ski grinder at his side, and recalled the evening he had shown us his ski tuning techniques. Like Miura's chairlift positions, he taught nonverbally, as the Japanese have for centuries. Miura and his father, Yumi and her father, Mrs. Morita and her tea ceremony, the man in black at the driving range, Brian's *aikido* master, the Roshi at the monastery—they possessed another common attribute. They all served as living examples, not just of proper technique, but of proper awareness.

I looked down into the clear broth of my soup, watching as the spoon stirred the miso into a languid swirl of divination. At any given moment, we are somewhere on the spectrum between total distraction and total attention. At one end, we are so bombarded by thoughts, fears, and images that we are overwhelmed and unable to access our most basic abilities. At the other, we are so focused as to feel completely in control, almost clairvoyant, as time slows down and we function with precise skill and exquisite judgment.

Seldom, and only briefly, do we dwell at these far extremes of the attention spectrum. Instead, we move up and down during the course of the day, being more or less focused, more or less effective, more or less in touch with the people and activities around us, and with our physical, intellectual and social skills. Rationally, of course, we always want complete concentration, improved performance, and heightened awareness, but therein lies the spiritual rub. Knowing about this optimized state is not enough and, ironically, seeking it consciously is yet another distraction.

I shifted my gaze back to Yuichiro Miura. Alone with him finally that day, and in the proper frame of mind/body myself, my learned familiarity had decoded his examples and used them to guide me. Doing this also helped me understand even more deeply the importance of watching and doing, of direct learning the Oriental way. In a leapfrogging process of self-betterment, as the difference shrank between what I visualized and what I actually did, I could then better detect the subtler techniques.

We must accept also that learning is a slow road, paved with disappointment. Why? Because the inherent gap in the process—between envisionment and enactment, between dreams and reality—is marginal failure. This is a crucial truth. Even if you watch the Master carefully and emulate as best you can, you will seldom do the technique perfectly. If you get it eighty percent correct, that means you are also twenty percent wrong. Everything depends on your reaction. If you chastise yourself for the marginal failure, you'll be stuck at that level. If you calmly accept the result however, and go back and study the ideal form of the Master, you might now detect a more subtle detail that will assist you. Even if you again do it eighty percent right, you are now studying a slightly more advanced technique. Persevering over time with right attitude takes you through countless cycles on the spiral of learning until the margin of failure is miniscule, masterful. The failing is not in falling, but in not getting up again with the right attitude. Only when we accept the process of evolving can we home in on our continually enhanced image of the ideal.

As Miura and his ancestors knew, these lessons have to be learned directly—physically, emotionally, spiritually—for in the realm of thought, of intellectuality, it is difficult to overcome doubt, distraction, and fear. So we learn best by doing, by experience. With faith and discipline, we learn to trust ourselves regardless of the consequences, to perform as surely while in danger as we would while at ease. We must be pure enough in intention that nothing ripples the calm mind that reflects our imagined ideal. For when the image held within is undistorted, it guides our motions in ways beyond our ability to comprehend, let alone regulate consciously. Call them what you wish—dreams, hopes, plans, prayers, goals, wishes, objectives, or visualizations—these are blueprints for the soul, the road maps of destiny.

thirty

The final day came. I gathered my things in the morning so I could leave directly after skiing to catch the overnight train to Tokyo. It felt strange to be packing, preparing to leave what now seemed so familiar. The bedroom, the lounge, the kitchen, they all felt comfortable, almost homey. The Japanese had also begun laying out their bags, removing posters from the walls, gathering and bundling gear. I felt the pangs of separation sadness, so familiar after dozens of ended seasons and disbanded teams. After spending months together in such a wonderfully difficult cloister, who knew if I would ever see any of these friends again? Each had a place in my heart now, even Hiro. I would meet up with Tom in Tokyo, and perhaps visit Takao and Nancy in Seattle, but the others would likely remain only in memory.

Besides the looming separation, the instructors were nervous about the ski-off, scheduled for late afternoon. It was a personal test, enormously important for them all in their placement and ranking the next year. We would all ski twice in front of Miura and the group, with absolutely zero room for errors or excuses. There was little conversation while packing, or later during breakfast.

Within a half-hour I was in front of the lodge, savoring the scene, anticipating the excitement and poignancy of that last day. I heard my name called and squinted to see Takao and Tom calling me from the lift line. "Come on, Rick," Takao yelled. "Let's ski."

Joy welled up within me. *Sure, Takao*, I thought. *Let's ski.*

I snapped into my skis, slid toward the chairlift, and we rode up the mountain—one, two, three—just as we had all winter.

We debated our options at the top. We hadn't had fresh snow in ten days, so Takao and Tom, the inveterate powder hounds, had already sniffed out their favorite spots. Then I remembered the gully that Hiro had taken me to, the scene of his challenge in the early days. It was well shielded from the sun and wind, and I saw no tracks heading toward it.

I held up my hand. "I know just the place."

Minutes later, we were looking down on perfection, a tiny chute in pristine condition. Neither the bordering rocks nor the seamless snow caused me fear. Now that I understood it, the powder was no longer intimidating. Barely able to control my voice, I said, as seriously as I could, "I'll just check to make sure it's all right."

With that and a laugh, I was off the edge and dropping fast into the silky white. The softness was delicious and welcoming, like a warm bed on a cold morning. I bounced up and swiveled gently, letting gravity do the work. Snow rose like a wraith, ethereal, over my chest and chin, forcing itself into my mouth. I choked and sputtered as I skied, almost out of breath, but the raw beauty and excitement made me wildly happy. Gliding, sliding, dancing in depth, I bobbed through three turns then curved through the narrow, rocky exit.

I stopped to wait, my chest pounding. The sky seemed tangible, the wind's voice discernible. Time bubbled up large and lucid. Takao dropped first out of the chute, then Tom, and the two of them wove with wide smiles toward me. It was beautiful. I wanted to transport others that I loved to that instant. But I couldn't. Takao's mastery, Tom's game spirit, these were for my eyes only.

By late afternoon, after a dozen or more runs, the sun porch and parking lots had begun to empty. The day was winding down; the season was nearly over. I stood in front of the lodge, waiting with the others for Miura and Daichiro. Finally, they came outside. Time for the ski-off, the final challenge.

Miura went first up the mountain then, one after another, in order of rank, we followed. Below us, long lines of school children streamed like ants up the mountain, girls in pink and boys in blue, skiing and climbing a short stretch over and over, each student in turn mimicking the teacher. A hundred yards over, a platoon of Japanese soldiers in white camouflage clothing and ancient equipment imitated their sergeant. In small groups scattered over the mountain, the last few skiers taught each other the same time-honored way: watching and emulating.

I reached the top. The chair left me on the ramp and clanged around to begin its descent. I joined Miura and the instructors near the start of the Ladies' Giant Slalom, and then followed them down onto the run. When we were all stopped in a line facing him, positioned according to seniority, Miura spoke briefly in Japanese and gave a two-turn demonstration of a swivel technique. He climbed back up and looked around for questions. There were none.

Off he went, skiing like a Master. He flowed with the mountain, accepting the speed it gave him, absorbing its challenges and using them to his advantage. There was fluidity and power in his movements, aggressiveness, and passiveness in balance. There was tradition too; you could see it in Miura's manner and the keen attention of the instructors. Miura was teaching as he was taught, as Japanese for centuries have conveyed their arts.

The technique he displayed was his trademark "Dolphin Kick." Critical yet simple, it was a last-second pressure on the turning ski that enhanced the rise to weightlessness and eased the transfer of weight. Good skiers, especially racers, do it unconsciously, and Miura had isolated this as the subtle, yet integral, teaching point for his final session. He had exaggerated the motion a few times and then displayed it perfectly for us during his run. Now it was our turn.

The preliminary stretch was not difficult; it was really a warm-up to the long, steep section ahead. Upon it, one after another with Miura looking up, we would try to integrate his technique into a graceful run. Daichiro set off and skied beautifully, showing the grace and confidence of leadership. Hiro, Makoto, and Saito followed him in turn, each skiing with poise and confidence. As my turn approached, I drew myself into focus. I listened to my breath, coming into my lungs and then steadily out again, propelled by the muscles of my lower diaphragm. I felt excitement in my stomach, tingling in my fingertips, dryness in my mouth. I wanted to start.

Igarashi took off, then Ogata and Yasu. Now it was a tossup between Naomi, Sasaki, and myself. I shuffled forward to indicate my readiness. When Yasu reached the group below, their faces turned upward.

I leaned forward and wove gently into the first sequence, but my mind wouldn't quiet down. My balance was good, my legs and arms moved well, but there was no flow or certainty in my motion. As I rejoined the group, Miura looked straight at me. His eyes touched mine, bridging the gap between us. They were supportive, kind, fathomless—perhaps carved out by the yawning crevasse of Everest as he slid helplessly toward it. My thanks could never be expressed to this man. I had to prove myself worthy.

We stood now above the testing site, the wide, steep, deeply mogulled section of the Ladies' Giant Slalom. When Miya, who came last, skied into the group, Miura began to speak and demonstrate again. He now wanted the same technique used on all surfaces of the moguls. If we were receptive enough, our skis would retain relatively constant contact with the snow and allow us to turn at any instant. He demonstrated again, swiveling and double-pumping his way down the mountain.

Daichiro and the senior three stepped up. Even they were nervous, their faces drawn. At Miura's signal, Daichiro set off. He again skied smoothly, keeping a close contour on the moguls, turning frequently with quick and decisive movements. Hiro stepped up next, exercising his familial privilege. He, too, started well, skiing powerfully through the initial section, but suddenly, he caught an edge and twisted awkwardly. Although he recovered and skied on, the damage was done. At this level, even slight mistakes were glaring.

Makoto went next, then Saito. Both were flawless. I watched the routes they chose, but deliberately didn't select my own path beforehand. I preferred to trust my spontaneity from the beginning. Despite my uninspired start, I felt a soothing tranquility. I was ready to ski, to perform my last act on this Japanese stage.

Time to go.

A voice behind me called out, "*Gambatte*, Rick-san." *Go for it.*

With an even, forceful exhalation, I pushed off. I rose up over the first mogul, using my downhill ski as Miura showed us to initiate a reverse pump. The next bump came slowly, sweetly, huge but friendly, and I turned easily, then again and again in quick succession. I was molding, extending, carving—changing speed and direction at will—savoring the sensation of control, of regulated speed, of gravity's checked rush. My balance was exquisite and there was a delicious calmness to my perception. It felt like a slow motion movie in which I was at once seeing the ski run and the Japanese below, the cosmic merge of ocean and sky beyond, and the parade of my life leading to that moment.

This is a dream. It's all a great dream.

This surreal notion entered my perception like something into a vacuum, like a gaseous cloud suddenly crystallizing. Before that instant there had been no thought, or rather, a sole thought—a pure intention: to ski well, to do my best.

I felt an urge to cling to the instant, but I knew it to be a rare thing, an essence, not something induced or retained with mere effort. Instead I returned my focus to the next mogul, rose gently over the crest, and suddenly it was perfect again. I made delicious, caressing turns, relishing every instant. I was back in the warp of time, collating the input of my senses and moving in precise accordance. My intentions and actions merged, leaving no gap between what I visualized and what I actually did. I was an entity, a sum total, coordinated in motion and united in purpose. I was Skiing Zen.

I stopped in front of Miura. Our eyes met again for the briefest of moments, yet it seemed to last forever. Just before he turned uphill to the next skier, I saw a slight nod and the faint flicker of a smile.

When everyone had skied into the group, Miura made a few last announcements. Our last dinner would be held early so that everyone could make his or her travel connections. He, in fact, would already be on his way to New Zealand. He thanked everyone for their work that winter and said that the decisions for the following season would be announced soon.

Miura wished Igarashi and Takao luck in the Japanese Mogul Championship, and urged Makoto, Saito, and Hiro to do well in their senior level qualifications. Lastly, Miura thanked Tom and me for sharing the winter with them, the group joining in heartily to wish us well. Then it was over. The instructors bowed deeply to Miura and then went streaming down the mountain like kids let out of school for summer.

I slid quietly toward the lodge, numb with clarity. A great weight was gone and the lightness was intoxicating. I could have laughed or just as easily cried. When I reached the bottom and found myself unable to go inside with the others, I turned instead and caught the day's last chairlift up the sunny side of the mountain.

My skis hung in space below me. As if the thought to move them was the movement itself, they tilted upward in unison. I maneuvered them, one at a time and then together. It seemed so easy. I played with the water drops on one ski, moving them up and down and from side to side. I was enormously aware of the feel of my ski in such slow, controlled motion, sensing which action caused which reaction, and the nearness of my actual movement to what I had intended.

The day was done for the upper lift attendant. He was preparing to ride down as I disembarked. I thanked him for his hard work, as I had each day all winter, then slid down and around under the lift. Traversing the bowl to an untracked, sunny opening in the trees, I took off my skis and fashioned a seat for myself. The birch trees around me glowed yellow in the long, golden light. Beyond them, I could see the plains of Hokkaido and the panoramic coastline of the Sea of Japan.

The wind was whispering. I felt exquisitely conscious yet unconcerned, just as I had during my last run. Call it lucid detachment, primal awareness, ego-lessness, or the Japanese term: *No-mind*, but what the Samurai experienced with swords, what Miura attains on skis, is what all skiers, all athletes, feel in our finest moments. This precious reward occurs when you focus effortlessly past your fears and allow yourself to perform reflexively. This, the ultimate faith, opens the ever-present portal to spirituality, the omniscient vantage point of Zen.

Staring out over the Sea of Japan, I understood ever more deeply that Zen was not uniquely Japanese. It is a name only, a label, a reference point for a concept that helps us see all activities, including sports, as forms of meditation capable of producing sublime insight. Most athletes don't see it this way. Not yet. Like me at first, they have moments of clarity but don't recognize them as trail markers on the spiritual path.

Yet if we understand this, we can each integrate our lessons from skiing and sports into our other activities and enjoy a more balanced and compassionate existence. The essence of Mastery is not to be the best calligrapher, painter, poet, swordsman, or skier, but the best human being. As such, you help people both by your actions and your example. Each one of us can become, like Takao and Miura, a purifying force in the Universe.

If sport is our *way*, we need to recognize that. Sport is more than mere competition in the modern world. Physiologically, it is a means to develop and maintain agility, strength, and stamina. Psychologically, it is a level proving ground where the challenges, risks, and rules are defined, where people encounter fear, experience winning, and suffer losing, all without tragedy. Aesthetically, it is manifest passion and creativity in motion. Socially, it is a cauldron of camaraderie, an acceptable coping mechanism for stress. Intrinsically, it is a classroom of morals, a forge of habits, a litmus test of character. Philosophically, it is a re-integration of body and mind, a union of physical and meta-physical. Spiritually, ultimately, sport is moving meditation, an act of love.

The more we love, and pour our attention into people and activities, the more alive we feel. Why? Because to love is to be totally focused, to be meditative, to allow the variously named greater power to flow through us. Because love, when it is pure, creates a melding, a mystic warp, between oneself and the universe. You become what you love.

This truth is cloaked in the most wonderful mystery. To sense it is to crave it. To seek it is to lose it. To forget it is to allow it. To feel it is to know it.

My mind refocused on my surroundings. The sun was dipping below the crest of the mountain, casting a rising shadow toward me. Time to go. Moving slowly in the deep snow, I readied my skis and stepped into the bindings. I shuffled my legs to warm them, then slipped on my gloves and pulled my goggles down. I swung my downhill ski around until it pointed toward the setting sun, then dug the heel into the snow up to my boot. The second ski followed and I was ready.

A gust of wind touched the mountain lightly, and in the ensuing silence I heard a melody, a tinkling like a chandelier. *Was I imagining it?*

I listened more closely. It was distinct and seemingly all around me. Then something caught my eye and I immediately understood. The wind was dislodging the icy glaze from the branches and the shards were bouncing and sliding down the frozen snow to create a natural symphony. A crystalline chorus.

Yielding to an urge, I leaned and grabbed a handful of snow. As I compressed a snowball with my hands, I took aim on a small space between two forking branches on a nearby tree. When the ball was firm and round, I envisioned it passing cleanly through the center space into the blue void beyond.

I knew that my body could enact what I foresaw. I knew that faith with snowballs was the same as any other faith. I knew that success was contingent upon purity of intent. I knew, finally, that purity was beyond even the notion of "doing my best," since that entailed the very idea of "doing." Purity was intention without conscious thought, total immersion.

I emptied my mind with a long breath and then threw without pause. The snowball had good direction and a perfect trajectory. Ghostly white, like the full moon on a blue-sky day, it seemed to pause for my approval in the targeted area, then sail cleanly through.

With that, I pushed off. I turned first where the sun still shone warm on the mountainside, and then swooped down into the shadow. I adjusted to the colder snow and sharper pitch, curving and swerving down the flank until I slid onto the main run. It was wide, steep, and empty, and the lights of the lodge looked warm at the bottom. I skied steadily toward them, aware only of my skis on the white snow.

acknowledgements

I would like to thank the many people who have offered their gracious assistance over the years. I apologize to any I might have forgotten.

Mary Aarons

Rueben Aaronsen

Shana Alexander

Larry Booi

Yumi Harai

Robert Kent

Tiko Kerr

Kerry Knoll

Charlie LeBaron

Norman Margolus

Grace Mercereau

Rudy Miick

Yuichiro Miura

Kuniko Okubo

Lynette Palmer

Kathy Pasternak

Lee Phipps

James Pickett

Jim Ragan

Jill Shinefeld

Doug Stumpf

Nancy Tereda

Takao Tereda

Ted Thomas

Jessica Wolf

Tom Wright

If these ideas touched you,
please pass this book along.
There are many others searching
for the spirituality of sport.

about the author

Rick Phipps is a writer, speaker, and entrepreneur. He has developed and written numerous films and articles for such clients as National Geographic Television, Daytona Speedway, *Snow Country*, and *Skiing Magazine*. Through his company, Brainstorm, he has helped to plan and build several complex media and retail projects. He has delivered speeches and workshops on business creativity and sports psychology throughout North America. He currently works as a contractor managing strategic planning and project management for private and public clients.

Lightning Source UK Ltd.
Milton Keynes UK
UKOW04f0942040116

265729UK00001B/234/P